BUILDER'S GUIDE TO BOLT-TOGETHER STREET RODS

A Complete Guide to Planning, Buying, Assembling, and Enjoying Your Street Rod

BRUCE CALDWELL

S-A DESIGN

CarTech®
Auto Books & Manuals

Edited By:
Steve Hendrickson

ISBN 1-884089-61-5

Order No. SA72

Printed in China

CarTech®, Inc.,
39966 Grand Avenue
North Branch, MN 55056
Telephone (651) 277-1200 • (800) 551-4754 • Fax: (651) 277-1203
www.cartechbooks.com

OVERSEAS DISTRIBUTION BY:

Brooklands Books Ltd.
P.O. BOX 146, Cobham, Surrey, KT11 1LG, England
Telephone 01932 865051 • Fax 01932 868803
www.brooklands-books.com

Brooklands Books Ltd.
1/81 Darley Street, P.O. Box 199, Mona Vale, NSW 2103, Australia
Telephone 2 9997 8428 • Fax 2 9997 5799

Front Cover Photo: *Photographer Robert Genat is a good example of the new breed of street rod builders – he wanted a car that he could build by himself, in his own garage. To get the job done, he ordered a Total Cost Involved Stage III chassis, and a fiberglass '32 Ford five-window body from Gibbon. Power comes from a Chevy 327 small-block and a 4-speed manual. (Robert Genat)*

Top Back Cover Photo: *The '32 Ford highboy roadster is by far our number one pick for a bolt-together street rod. These cars can't be beat for popularity, parts availability, and ease of reselling. John Carmody's brilliant red highboy features a Gibbon fiberglass body mounted on a Rod Factory chassis.*

Inset Back Cover Photo: *Bolt-together street rods can be nostalgic, too, as evidenced by this '32 highboy. Black paint with flames, a simple red interior, red steelies with big 'n' little wide whites, and you have a perfect '50s flavored cruiser.*

Left Back Cover Photo: *Swinging an engine is one of the milestone events in building a bolt-together street rod. Most of the construction will just require basic hand tools, but engine hoists are cheap to buy or easy to rent. The adjustable engine tilter makes it easy to install an engine in a finished car.*

Title Page Photo: *While all '32 Ford highboy roadsters have many elements in common (some even deride them as a "belly button" car, at least until they have the chance to own one), the truth is it's easy to build one that's distinct from all the others. Wheels, tires, stance, trim, paint, and engine choices all have a profound impact on a Deuce highboy's look. You can build one that suits your tastes exactly.*

TABLE OF CONTENTS

ABOUT THE AUTHOR

Bruce Caldwell is an automotive journalist and photographer who has been a bona fide car nut since age five when he got his first set of wheels, a Garton Kidillac pedal car. While friends perused comic books, Bruce devoured car magazines and built countless model cars. He had a subscription to *Hot Rod* while he was still in grade school. He fully expected to get a '40 Ford coupe for his eleventh birthday and was very disappointed to get a deluxe bicycle (that cost more than the car) instead. He later fulfilled his childhood dreams when he became a Feature Editor at *Hot Rod* magazine and purchased the first of several '40 Ford street rods. He has served as editor of many high performance and special interest automotive magazines and has written numerous automotive how-to books.

Bruce has owned more than 100 cars, trucks, and motorcycles, many of them street rods. The cars have ranged from total trash to magazine cover cars. He owned seven cars in college when he had a single car garage, and his total hasn't dropped below that number in 30 years. His current home on the outskirts of Seattle has more shop space than living quarters — the house came with a six-car garage and Bruce soon added a 3,000-square-foot barn, which is filled with cars and equipment downstairs and old magazines and spare parts upstairs.

When not photographing, writing about, or working on cars, Bruce enjoys hiking and bicycling with his family.

An experienced hot rodder and journalist, Bruce Caldwell is just as comfortable with a word processor as he is with a wrench, although he usually uses something with a little more finesse than what's shown here.

Street rodders like to look at other street rods almost as much as they like to build and drive their own cars. Talking about cars or "bench racing" is always the topic of the day.

PROCRASTINATION PAYS

Life can get in the way of dreams. Serious pursuits like getting an education, starting and nurturing a family, establishing a career, maintaining a home, and doing your part to keep television networks, sports franchises, breweries, and snack food manufacturers solvent can suck time and dreams right out of your life. The procrastinator's perpetual mantra, "I'll get around to it someday," can tarnish years of once-bright dreams.

Well, before you resign yourself to a semi-comatose life in front of the TV, there's good news for procrastinators. If one of your dreams was to build a hot rod (the politically correct term these days is street rod), there has never been a better time. If, like most people, your desires exceed your mechanical skills, state-of-the-art street rods are now so refined that almost anyone can build one. All the difficult work—like welding and fabricating—has been done by professionals, so you can essentially build yourself a very large model car kit.

Cruising down a country road (or just showing off in front of your friends, family and neighbors) on a sunny day behind the wheel of a '32 Ford highboy roadster with the top off and the wind rushing through your hair is one of those uniquely American experiences. It's democracy on wheels; very few restrictions and lots of freedom expressed in an outrageously impractical vehicle that justifies its existence purely by the amount of enjoyment it provides.

It's a visceral rush: you hear and feel the power of the unbridled V-8 as you quickly launch from a stop sign; you see the uncovered tires spinning; you can barely hear the stereo; conversation is little more than gestures; other motorists smile, crane their necks and flash their "thumbs up" approval; pedestrians and kids on bikes point and wave; and you're grinning like a kid on the best Christmas of his life as you leave your worries in the dust.

Yes, it's escapism. No, it's not particularly grownup behavior. It's not practical, economical, politically correct, or even easy to justify. All a street rod is good for is fun. It's fun to own, fun to drive, and fun to build. There's a tremendous sense of satisfaction knowing that you built this rolling fun factory. Forget about the knotty pine bookcase that your neighbor built, you built an honest-to-God hot rod. You can't top that with a thousand bookcases.

Well, that dreamy little scenario might appear to be right up there with losing weight while you sleep and developing six-pack abs in just three minutes a day. The problem with no-effort weight loss and instant fitness is that you can't get someone else to do the work for you. The great news about building a bolt-together street rod is that you *can* get experts to do the most difficult work. And, because of the economies of scale and mass production, that specialized work doesn't cost anywhere near as much as having a one-off street rod built.

With enough money, you could buy a turnkey street rod and even pay someone to do the laborious task of turning the ignition key. The purpose of this book is to show you how to find a happy compromise between building your car from a pile of ore and buying it with a pile of cash. By doing your own assembly work, you can save money and have a lot of fun at the same time.

Building a street rod used to be a complex, time-consuming proposition. You needed lots of fabrication skills, especially the ability to do first-class

Street rods have a tremendous "smile-per-mile" factor. Cruising around in a '32 Ford highboy roadster on a sunny day is a guaranteed mood elevator.

welding. Other skills like bodywork, painting, engine building, and upholstery were necessary. It was also a good idea to be a talented machinist and to own a shop full of expensive equipment like a lathe and a mill.

It's always nice to learn new skills, so maybe you thought you'd take a few night classes at a vo-tech school. Maybe you could take a correspondence course while you watched TV. Then again, maybe you've been too busy to learn new skills.

Whether you were seriously occupied or just spinning your wheels, this is one of those times where procrastinating paid off. The street rod industry has made incredible strides in the last twenty years, and has gone from mostly backyard businesses to a full-fledged industry, complete with its own trade organizations.

All those years of hard work and tremendous progress means almost anyone can build a bolt-together street rod, regardless of their prior mechanical experience. If you can follow directions, have a minimal amount of common sense, and a smattering of patience, you can build your own street rod. Street rod parts manufacturers and mail-order parts companies have so refined the process that it's more like assembling a full scale model car than fabricating a car from a pile of old metal.

At first glance, building an entire car from the ground up can seem like an overwhelming task. One look under the hood of your current car could make you wonder how skilled engineers could even build such complicated machinery. The good news about street rods is that they're as simple as modern cars are complex. Street rods are basic. They're not luxurious or sophisticated, they're transportation stripped of all but the most vital components. That's why they're easy to build. No frills; no fuss.

Going fast on a budget was the goal of early hot rodders, and the idea of a raw, no-nonsense car has always been the essence of street rods. That goal could be reached by either increasing horsepower or shedding weight. Since removing weight was the easiest and least expensive of the two choices, items like fenders, running boards, and hoods were frequently discarded. Most early hot rodders stripped their cars and added engine upgrades as their budgets permitted.

Building a modern street rod is pretty much the reverse of how old time hot rods were built. These days, builders start with the frame and add the components necessary to create their ideal street rod. Performance isn't much of a concern, because virtually any modern V-8 engine will provide exceptional acceleration in a lightweight street rod.

Modern street rods rely on uncomplicated systems of pre-assembled components. You can increase the amount of complexity, but those street rods aren't the focus of this book. A neat thing about the modular nature of bolt-together street rods is that you can do as little or as much of the work as you please. Using the component approach to street rod building provides a maximum of flexibility with a minimum of complexity.

There are as many ways to build a street rod, as there are individual street rods. The approach of this book is a little arbitrary, but that's because we want to make building your first street rod an enjoyable experience. Toward that goal, we intend to show you strategies that offer maximum satisfaction with a minimal amount of construction or financial problems.

Three key elements of this book are: popularity, modularity, and flexibility. Those concepts will be explained in detail in the following chapters. There's also a lot of overlap among concepts.

Popularity means building a street rod that's universally popular. A car's popularity is closely tied to its ease of construction and financial considerations. For example, it will be much easier to build a '32 Ford roadster than it will be to build a '35 Nash coupe. Why? A '32 Ford is and always has been more popular, so more parts and services are available for it.

Modularity refers to the use of pre-fitted, thoroughly tested subassemblies in the construction of a bolt-together street rod. The whole process will seem easier when approached as a series of small modular assemblies rather than one big overwhelming project.

Flexibility allows the builder to change components and/or the style of the car as it is being assembled. There's little doubt that you will change your mind about various components during construction. The flexibility of our plan makes changes easier to accommodate without incurring large financial setbacks.

Building your first bolt-together street rod will provide a wonderful sense of accomplishment. This book explains how to divide the project into as assortment of easily handled smaller tasks. You build on your successes as the car approaches completion. There's something uniquely satisfying about building something with your own hands. Not many people can point to a car surrounded by a group of admirers and say, "I built it myself." This book is the first step in being able to make that statement. So stop procrastinating and get building.

A fair amount of time is spent cleaning and polishing cars at street rod events. When you own something as neat as a '32 highboy, you just want to keep it in top condition.

STREET ROD BASICS

The term street rod encompasses many vehicles and building styles. It's easy for someone new to the hobby to be a little confused or overwhelmed by all the choices. The goal of this book is to help you narrow your focus. You can always expand your hot rod horizons as you gain experience, but in order to make your first experience a positive one, you need to concentrate on a few of the most popular, easiest to build, and easiest to resell cars. By limiting choices, it's easier to stay on track and build a successful first street rod.

Street rods aren't for people who view cars as mere appliances. You need a certain exuberance and joy of driving just for the sake of driving in order to fully appreciate a street rod. Always remember that the underlying concept is fun, not practical transportation. If you want practicality, buy a bus pass.

THE BEAUTY OF GENERIC STREET RODS

Street rods can represent infinite variations on a few basic themes. Yet, there are a handful of cars that are icons of the hobby. Those are the cars that you want to build for your first street rod. The idea isn't to build the most unique

We refer to the '32 Ford highboy roadster as a generic car, but that's a positive term. The Deuce roadster is the quintessential hot rod. It's universally accepted as a hot rod icon. Even though a '32 highboy may be generic, there are countless variations on the theme.

rod around. What you want is essentially a generic street rod. If you were to poll a majority of street rod enthusiasts, industry professionals, and journalists, the elements that they list to describe " a street rod" are the things you want on your first rod.

"Generic street rod" can have a negative connotation. It brings to mind the differences between products like Tide detergent and a plain white box labeled "SOAP." They both get the job done, but many people feel better about using brand name products, whether or not the product's performance justifies the price differential.

We're not suggesting anything as bland as generic grocery store products, but we do advocate spending your street rod dollars wisely. Buy quality components, especially the core items like the

chassis and body, but hold off on the flashy accessories until you're sure you want to continue with the hobby.

You should know going in that you might encounter a certain amount of negative comments when you build a generic street rod. The world is full of critics (mostly people who either don't have a finished street rod or people who are insecure about their own cars), but the only person you really have to please is yourself. Always consider the source of the criticism. When you do, most criticism loses its sting.

Derogatory terms for a generic street rod include belly button car, kit car, 1-800 car, catalog car, or credit card car. Don't be influenced by negative comments. There are a lot more positive terms related to street rod ownership than the negative ones. Concentrate on

The '32 Ford is the universal street rod and the small-block Chevy V-8 is the default engine. Lift the hood of any street rod and chances are excellent that you'll find a Chevy engine.

the positive aspects. Have your fun and let the critics pound sand.

Very few people build (or have someone build for them) the small group of cars that seem to get most of the magazine coverage and win most of the awards. The majority of street rod builders just want to enjoy their cars. Almost anyone you might encounter that isn't into street rods will just think you've got a great old car. If your goal is to win lots of big trophies, then this book isn't for you.

It can be difficult not to fall prey to peer group pressure. I know because I've been there, automotively and sartorially. At least the goofy clothing was easier to change than the motorized miscues.

Peer group pressure can be more in your head than any real negativity expressed by other street rodders. Being in the business of photographing and writing about street rods means I get to see some incredible cars, both home-built and pro-built. All that exposure to excellence made me insecure about some of my own cars. I had a Model A roadster that I worked on for years because I wanted it to be close to the caliber of the cars I photographed.

As a result of trying to keep up with people whose skills and incomes far surpassed mine, I almost didn't finish the car. At the same time, my brother bought a really rough Model A roadster pickup. It was an old, old rod that had been built many years before and had

deteriorated considerably. There wasn't an expensive part on the truck. Not much matched or fit very well, but it ran strong and it was a street rod.

My brother bought the whole truck for about what I had invested in my roadster's chromed, independent Jaguar suspension. Both suspension systems kept the wheels on the ground and did all the things a suspension system is supposed to do. Mine looked neater if you were lying on the ground, but rolling down the highway, it was tough to tell the difference.

We had a lot more fun in my brother's basic street rod than my expensive one. We went places in his rod and had a great time. We actively enjoyed the car. My car ended up being a garage queen. I was tense every time my kids got near the expensive mohair upholstery. My brother didn't care if they jumped all over the basic vinyl seat in his roadster pickup.

I sold my Model A roadster shortly after I finished it. I sold it at a loss, because even though people appreciated all the expensive parts, they didn't want to pay a premium for them. The blue-printed, dyno-tested, highly-detailed 350 small-block Chevy engine in my car was a beautiful engine, but the junkyard 283 small-block in my brother's roadster pickup did the same basic job of getting the car from point A to point B. My brother's engine cost less than what I paid to have the intake manifold polished on my show engine.

Many people spend incredible amounts of money on trick engines; yet a basic small-block Chevy in even tired condition will provide ample power for a lightweight street rod. It's nice to have a little better engine than the oil-covered veteran in my brother's rod, but you don't need to spend a fortune to have a reliable, attractive street rod engine.

A much more basic '32 Ford phaeton followed the A roadster in my garage. It cost much less to build than the pseudo show car. It was still a bright red, open-air street rod that received incredible amounts of positive attention. My whole family got a lot more enjoyment out of the '32 phaeton than the Model A roadster. It also did a much better job of holding its resale value.

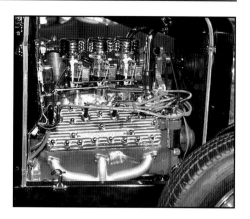

Flathead Ford V-8 engines made their debut in the 1932 models, so they're a natural when building a traditional style street rod. The later versions of the engine are used almost exclusively. There's lots of neat vintage speed equipment still being manufactured.

The point of these examples is that a basic street rod is usually more fun than an expensive show rod. Building a basic street rod means much quicker gratification. You can be out having fun while the trophy seeker is still slaving away on expensive details that may or may not bring the attention he's seeking. There will always be people with fancier street rods than yours. This year's show winner is next year's also-ran and by the year after that, it's old news. A basic, generic street rod will maintain its fun value for many, many years. Certain street rods never seem to go out of style. That's the type of car you should build for your first street rod.

WHAT IS A STREET ROD?

By broad definition, a street rod is a modified car or truck (or a reproduction of one) that was manufactured prior to 1949. The 1948/1949 dividing line is used by the National Street Rod Association (NSRA). It's generally followed by the major street rod publications, although many non-NSRA events have much later cut-off dates for participating vehicles. The general public frequently misuses the term "street rod," much like they've severely diluted the term "classic car."

Why 1948? Most post-World War II cars and trucks were essentially carry-over models from before the war. Demand was so high after the war that manufacturers could sell anything that moved. Cars were rushed into production as automakers hurriedly phased out building military equipment. The postwar sales boom gave the auto manufacturers time to catch up on the development work that had been curtailed during the war.

Most Ford, General Motors, and Chrysler Corporation cars were totally restyled for 1949. The redesigned cars were much more modern with sleeker styling. Fenders were much better integrated with the body, especially the rear fenders. Instead of the old style rear fenders that could be removed as separate components, the new cars had quarter panels that were welded to the body. Up front, fenders were still separate units, but the whole front clips were much more cohesive. Hoods were flatter and not pointed like the '48 and earlier ones.

Ford came out with a new coil spring front suspension instead of the old single I-beam axle and transverse leaf spring arrangement. The old Ford "buggy springs" were an essential part of early hot rods. When the National Street Rod Association was formed, old Fords made up the majority of street rods. So, the major changes between 1948 and 1949 Fords, both in terms of styling and suspension, made for an obvious cut-off point. Styling differences between 1948 and 1949 Chevys were also very pronounced.

STREET ROD STYLES

Two principle factors determine whether or not a vehicle is a street rod: the year of manufacture and how the vehicle is modified. A dead stock, totally original '40 Ford coupe isn't a street rod. If it looks like a stocker, but has a modern V-8 engine and an automatic transmission, it's a street rod. A '40 coupe that has been lowered, custom painted, and fitted with newer wheels and tires, but still has all the original 1940 running gear is a street rod, but maybe not as much so as the stock-bodied version with the modified running gear.

To further confuse the issue, some people might call the coupe with the stock running gear and modified exterior a custom rod, a kustom kemp, a lead sled, or just a custom. Others might call the above car a street rod with the sub-classification, custom rod. There are many other subsets that are explained in the photo glossary. Most street rods have drivetrain, chassis, and body modifications.

Two subset styles that will be discussed in this book are highboy (also known as hi-boy) and full-fendered street rods. Highboy is another way of saying fenderless. A highboy's body is mounted in its stock position on top of the frame rails and the frame is exposed. If a fenderless body is dropped over the frame rails (the process is known as channeling), that's what's called a lowboy. A highboy with some type of abbreviated cycle fenders is still a highboy, but not in the most accepted sense of the term.

Fender laws used to be a big concern with hot rodders. Many areas had laws that required fenderless vehicles to weigh 1500 pounds or less. Lots of rodders claimed their cars made the weight break, but most of them weren't within a couple hundred pounds. It doesn't take a lot of parts to weigh more than 1500 pounds.

Nowadays, many states have statutes like "fair weather laws" which permit the driving of fenderless cars when it's not raining. There's less to splash on to other cars when the pavement is dry. Even if there are old fender laws on the books, most law enforcement officers pay more attention to how you're driving rather than what you're driving. If you drive like a responsible, law-abiding citizen, they'll leave you alone. If you drive like a juvenile delinquent in a fifties' "B" movie, they'll write you up.

Running sans fenders is a sure way to classify a car as a hot rod or street rod. All modern cars have fenders. Fenders are civilized. A person would have to be a rebel to ignore the sanctions of polite

The Deuce coupe is a close second in popularity to the roadster. Coupes were available in 3-window and 5-window body styles. Both bodies are reproduced in fiberglass. The 3-window coupes look very slick when chopped a couple inches. They have a slight popularity edge over the 5-window coupes.

There basically wasn't an ugly model in the '32 Ford passenger car lineup. One of the most stylish models was the Victoria, or Vicky. It's a pleasing cross between a Tudor sedan and a 5-window coupe. Notice how well the smoothly flowing fenders work with the street rod rake.

motorized society and not use fenders. Early hot rodders were rebels. Modern street rodders may be as conservative as the next 9-to-5 worker bee, but in their free time they like to at least think they have some of that old rebel spirit.

Highboys make a lot of sense for a bolt-together street rod. There's no question that the vehicle is a street rod. Not having to deal with fenders, running boards, and splash aprons makes construction a lot easier. Not having to buy and paint those extra parts saves money. If you discover that open wheel motoring isn't quite what you had in mind, you can always add fenders later.

HORSEPOWER

Engine choices frequently have more to do with designating a vehicle as a street rod than any exterior modifications. That sentiment dates back to early hot rods. In those days, the emphasis was on "hot." Hot rods were do-it-yourself performance cars. Removing an anemic four-cylinder engine and replacing it with a far more powerful V-8 produced an instant hot rod.

The vast majority of street rods are V-8 powered. There are some V-6 (and occasional inline sixes) and four-cylin-der street rods around, but they're definitely a minority faction. Some free-thinkers will occasionally drop an imported power plant in a street rod, but domestic engines are the rule. Domestic and V-8 engines are the best way to go for your first bolt-together street rod.

Early hot rods increased their speed potential by shedding as much weight as possible. Along with fenders and running boards, hoods often landed in the trash bin. Having an exposed engine that wasn't "hot" seemed rather pointless, so most early rods either had aftermarket speed equipment on their original four-cylinder engines, or they installed a V-8. The swapped V-8 engines usually had aftermarket cylinder heads, intake manifolds, and exhaust systems.

Two engines have dominated street rodding: the original hot rod engine was the revolutionary mass-produced Ford flathead V-8, which made its debut in the stunning 1932 Ford lineup. After decades of stubbornly clinging to the four-cylinder engine, Henry Ford leap-frogged his competition by introducing a smooth running V-8 engine in a car the common man could afford.

Flathead Ford engines were produced in various iterations from 1932 through 1953. The name comes from the flat cylinder heads. The intake and exhaust valves are located in the block, unlike modern overhead-valve engines that have their valves in the cylinder heads. Flatheads have the spark plugs threaded through the outer surfaces of the heads. Inside the heads are the relieved pockets that form the combustion chambers.

Flathead Ford engines helped establish the speed equipment industry. Hot rodders cast finned, high compression, aluminum heads and multiple carburetor aluminum intake manifolds for these engines. Industry leaders like the Edelbrock company started out manufacturing speed equipment for flatheads.

There are still street rodders who run flatheads. Most of these cars are either restored old rods or new ones built as nostalgia rods. You can still buy new speed equipment and there are companies that have greatly improved flathead technology. Flatheads look neat, but they're not an engine a first-time builder should use – parts are expensive, harder to find, and it's tough to find an engine builder who is willing and able to put one together anymore. The few that do are expensive specialists.

It was almost twenty years before General Motors and Chrysler got into mass-producing V-8 engines. It was more than twenty years before Chevrolet introduced the V-8 that revolutionized street rodding (and the rest of the high performance universe).But once that happened, the flathead's demise was swift. Even though Ford beat Chevy to market with an OHV (overhead valve) V-8 in 1954, the Ford OHV engines never caught on with street rodders. Those same rodders were quick to realize the performance potential of the small-block Chevy though, and it immediately became the engine of choice for hot rodders. It wasn't until much later that V-8 Ford engines like the 289/302 small-blocks and 390/428/460 big-blocks made some inroads against the small-block Chevy monopoly. Some diehards believe Ford street rods should be Ford-powered, but most rodders prefer Chevy engines in their Ford street rods. As you'd expect, Chevy street rods are virtually never seen with Ford engines.

Full fendered '32 roadsters don't have quite as much "hot" going for them as the high-boys, but they're still icon street rods. Some builders choose to leave the exterior features very close to stock, but use modern drivetrain components.

Today, the phrase "small-block Chevy" is almost synonymous with the word engine when it comes to street rods. If someone asked you what type of engine was in a particular street rod and you answered "small-block Chevy," you'd be right more often than not, even if you never looked at the engine. The small-block Chevrolet V-8 was introduced in 1955 and its descendants are still produced and used today.

Small-block Chevy engines have been produced in a number of displacements over the years. The general progression was 265-283-327-350. Small-blocks reached 400 cubic inches at one time and there have been other iterations including 262, 267, 302, 305, and 307 cubic inches. The 283 and 327 were rodding mainstays until the 350 was introduced in 1967, and it wasn't long before the 350 Chevy small-block was the most popular engine in street rodding.

The 350 cubic inch Chevy small-block V-8 is *the* engine to use as far as this book is concerned. Using any other engine drives up building costs and difficulty, and makes a vehicle harder to sell. You can't beat the 350 for availability, affordability, dependability, and overall performance. The 350 small-block is the default engine for all street rod chassis and aftermarket performance equipment.

OTHER DRIVELINE COMPONENTS

In the early days of street rodding, automatic transmissions were unheard of. Toward the end of the flathead's run, you could buy a new Ford equipped with an automatic transmission, but they never caught on with owners of flathead powered street rods. The most common early transmission was a manual 3-speed. The '39 Ford unit was particularly popular, especially if it was fitted with Lincoln Zephyr gears.

Manual transmissions (usually 3-speeds) were commonplace even with the new small-block Chevy V-8. Most street rod builders disdained the early 2-speed Chevy Powerglide automatic transmissions. Some '50s and '60s hot rodders used Olds or Buick Hydra-Matic transmissions with some success,

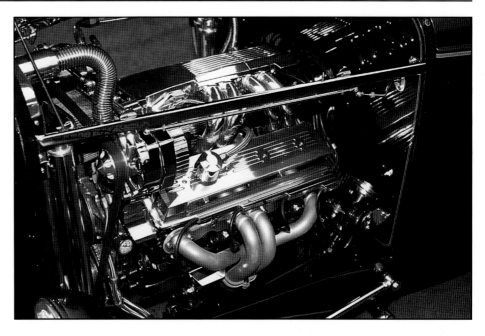

The popularity of the flathead V-8 was quickly surpassed by the small-block Chevy V-8 which was introduced in 1955. Carbureted versions are still popular and affordable, but there has been a tremendous upsurge in the use of modern fuel injected models. The economy, performance, and reliability of a modern TPI system are tough to beat.

but it wasn't until the GM Turbo 350 arrived in the sixties that automatic transmissions found more acceptance in street rods.

The Turbo 350 quickly became the transmission of choice to mate to a 350 small-block. The popular combination was and still is known as a 350/350. The stronger (and larger) Turbo 400 automatic is also pretty popular in street rods, especially those with big-block Chevy engines.

When modern automatic overdrive transmissions became the favored gear changers in new cars, the use of those transmissions in street rods followed. There are several variations of the GM overdrive automatic, but the 700R-4 is most commonly used one. Street rods with Ford engines do well with Ford's AOD (automatic overdrive) transmission.

Some rodders feel that a high performance engine should be backed by a 4-speed manual transmission. Running through the gears with a smooth 4-speed is fun, but cruising around in heavy traffic (like the kind often found at street rod events) with a killer clutch can quickly get tiring. Also, manual transmissions involve more linkage than an automatic

transmission. For a bolt-together street rod, a GM automatic overdrive transmission is the best way to go.

General Motors seems to have a lock on street rod driveline components, but that domination doesn't extend past the transmission. The universal street rod rearend is the 9-inch Ford unit. There are some smaller variations like the 8-inch Ford that work fine with all but the most powerful engines. Ford no longer puts the 9-inch in passenger cars, but there are companies that build new street rod versions of the 9-inch rearend. Plus, the supply of used 9-inch rearends is still good.

Other solid axle rearends like the GM 12-bolt and GM 10-bolt units can be used, but you can't beat the 9-inch Ford for durability, affordability, and availability. The 9-inch Ford rearend is the default rearend for street rod chassis builders.

CHOOSING AN ICON CAR

Earlier, we said that certain street rods seem to maintain their popularity, no matter what the current hot trend might be. We call those cars icon rods. They're cars that are universally admired and have been pillars of the

A chopped '32 5-window coupe with an exposed Chevy V-8 topped with multiple carburetors is an image many people associate with the automotive star of the classic movie "American Graffiti."

hobby for decades. An icon car is a perfect choice for a first time street rod builder. You can't go too far wrong with an icon rod.

Our number one choice for icon status is the '32 Ford. The '32, or Deuce, is universally recognized as a hot rod. Within the '32 Ford family, there tends to be a sliding scale of body style popularity. Roadsters top the list followed closely by coupes (both 3-window and 5-window models). After coupes it's a toss-up between 2-door sedans and phaetons. At various periods in street

rodding history, the open-air phaetons were very popular, but, today, we'd give the advantage to the sedans.

Deuce sedan deliveries are kind of a subset of sedans. Like the phaeton, this body style has had its popularity ups and downs. Real, factory-built sedan deliveries are extremely rare (the rarest of '32 Fords, in fact), but there are kits to convert sedans into deliveries, and some fiberglass manufacturers make deuce sedan delivery bodies also.

A subset of the roadster is the Cabriolet, which has a soft top and

roll-up windows, unlike the roadster, which doesn't have side windows. Cabriolet bodies seem to offer the best of both open and closed cars, but they're not very popular as street rods. With open-air street rods, the trend seems to be all or nothing. It's either all wind or get a closed car.

A subset of the 2-door sedan (Ford calls them Tudor sedans) is the Victoria or Vicky. Vickies are like Tudors, but with shorter rooflines. They are one of the more handsome early Ford bodies and they're popular as street rods.

Other Deuce body styles include 4-door sedans (Ford calls them Fordor sedans), station wagons (woodies), the B-400 convertible sedan, roadster pick-ups, closed cab pickups, and panel deliveries. The B-400 is a very rare and desirable body style that's a cross between a Victoria and a Cabriolet. The pickup, roadster pickup (real ones are incredibly rare), and panel delivery are based on '32 Ford trucks. They're not as handsome as the passenger cars.

With so many Deuce body styles to choose from (a large number of them are available in fiberglass), there are only three that we would recommend for a bolt-together street rod. Far and away the best choice is the '32 roadster. This is a car that always will be thought of as a street rod. Second and third choices are actually a tie. Either coupe model (3- or 5-window) would be a good choice if you must have a closed car.

The 3-window coupe is generally considered the sleeker looking of the two coupes, but the 5-window coupe has a very strong recognition factor due to its starring role in the movie, *American Graffiti*. Deuce coupes also owe their high recognition factor to the Beach Boys' classic ode to car culture, "Little Deuce Coupe." Ironically, the blue deuce coupe that graced the famous Beach Boys' album cover had a customized grille instead of the icon '32 shell. That car has achieved its own cult status, but it's not a style that is (or ever was) widely copied.

It's a little odd that the '32 Ford should be so popular, as it was a one-year model. Back then, Ford had a tendency to make series of cars that were

The '32 Tudor sedan is both handsome and practical. Sedans have great back seat room that also allows flexibility in where the front seats are mounted. This Tudor has a great stance.

quite similar. For example, the Model T had few changes over its long life span. The Model A Ford had a four-year run from 1928 to 1931, with the first two years and last two years being slightly different from each other. After the Deuce came the '33/'34 Fords, '35/'36 Fords, '37/'38 models, and '39/'40 models. Nineteen forty-one Fords are kind of alone style-wise, but mechanically they are related to the '42-'48 models.

Our second choice for an icon car would be the Model A Ford. Our first choice for a Model A street rod is actually a combination car, a Model A road-

body styles are available, but there doesn't seem to be as much popularity latitude as there is with '32 body styles.

The main benefit of building a Model A instead of a '32 Ford is a modest cost differential. Model A bodies and chassis don't cost quite as much as a similar Deuce. Virtually every other aspect of building an "A" street rod is the same as building a '32. The best reason for choosing a Model A as a bolt-together street rod would be a strong desire to own one. If a Model A roadster is your all-time favorite street rod, go ahead and build one.

Fords keeps their prices elevated and makes them easier (and quicker) to sell.

Lack of interior space is very evident in our third choice icon car. Hot rod Model T Fords are pretty close to '32 Fords as far as being readily identified as street rods. The fenderless, open-engine, roadster pickup with big rear tires and very small front ones is commonly referred to as a T-Bucket. The most famous T-Bucket of all time was Norm Grabowski's flamed hot rod that was featured on the late fifties TV show, *77 Sunset Strip*. Edd Byrnes played the hip parking lot attendant, Kookie, who

Another variation on the '32 theme is the Sedan Delivery. They have the added convenience of a rear door, although the solid side panels hamper visibility. You can get fiberglass sedan deliveries with windows for the best of both worlds. Dan Petersen built this perfectly proportioned highboy sedan delivery.

The '29 Model A roadster on a '32 chassis is one of the original hot rod combinations. It was an easy way to get V-8 power in a light car. This classic highboy was built in the seventies by Magoo's Street Rods, but it would still fit in at a contemporary street rod event.

ster body on a '32 Ford chassis. An "A" on Deuce rails was an early hot rod combo. People could get the '32's V-8 power and save weight by using the smaller, cheaper, and more common "A" body. The traditional combination is a '28/'29 "A" roadster body on a Deuce frame, although the '30/'31 body can also be used.

A Model A highboy on a Model A chassis is also acceptable, but we would suggest going the full fendered route when using the "A" frame, because the Model A frame was not integrated into the car's body styling, like the '32. The roadster and roadster pickup are the two prime body choices for building an icon car, and both are available in reproduction steel or fiberglass. Other fiberglass

There are two main negative points about choosing a Model A. All twenties and early thirties Ford bodies are snug compared to later cars. Deuces have noticeably more legroom than Model A's. I had the seat modified three times in my Model A roadster in an attempt to gain more legroom, and I moved the gas pedal so far over that it made more sense for the passenger to operate it. After all those alterations, I still wasn't very comfortable (I'm 6'2" when I stand up straight and I can make the scale read 200 pounds if I stand on one leg).

Besides space, the other main con on A's is their lower resale value. No matter how nice a Model A may be, it won't bring as much money as a similar Deuce. The extreme popularity of '32

drove the flashy T-Bucket. That car did a great deal to popularize T-Buckets in the sixties and early seventies.

T-Buckets are almost always based on fiberglass replicas of a 1923 Model T roadster pickup. The pickup bed is traditionally shortened to such a minimal length that it can barely accommodate a small gas tank and the battery. Some people use the alternate roadster trunk (which isn't much bigger than the shortened pickup beds), but the icon version is the roadster pickup.

Even with near-vertical steering columns and small steering wheels, interior space is very limited in T-Buckets. We would only recommend a T-Bucket to people who are below average in stature. Two people are a cozy combina-

Full fendered '33/'34 three-window coupes are very sleek looking. The handsome grille has a slight slant that accentuates the whole front-end styling. These cars are both popular and practical.

tion in a T-Bucket. Deuce roadsters are also two-passenger cars, but they do have optional rumble seats that will accommodate two extra passengers.

Substantially lower costs are the best thing about building a T-Bucket. Bodies and frames are much less expensive than '32 Ford or Model A parts. Paint and upholstery costs are also less because there's so much less to cover.

Low initial costs and the simplicity of their design are favorable points for T-Buckets. The financial downside is that T-Buckets have poor resale value. Check out the prices of T-Buckets that are for sale at a big street rod event and you'll see how low resale values are.

A cousin to the T-Bucket is the Track T. These Model T street rods are usually based on the slightly larger '27 Model T roadster (Track T's are always roadsters, not roadster pickups) Ford. We would classify the Track T as a near-icon street rod. The style of Track T's is based on circle track racecars that were popular in the forties and fifties.

Track T's aren't quite as affordable as T-Buckets, but compared to Model As and Deuces, they're very reasonable. We would rate the Track-T as being superior to the T-Bucket in interior space, popularity, and resale value.

The pluses of a Track-T aren't anywhere near those of a Deuce, but a Track-T can make a reasonable bolt-together street rod if the investment is kept as low as possible.

There are other icon street rods like the '33/'34 Ford coupe (another TV star, *The California Kid*, a '34 3-window coupe did a lot to elevate the recognition factor of these cars) and roadster and the '40 Ford coupe. Building a '33/'34 Ford highboy is a little more expensive than building a similar Deuce, and building a '40 coupe is even more expensive and complex. These icon street rods would be better suited to someone building their second or third street rod.

GET THE REAL ICONS

All the icon cars that we've discussed are reproductions. You can still find original real steel versions (usually at very unreal prices), but this book is about reproduction bodies and frames. Even though we're dealing with reproductions, there are some bodies that are closer to the mark than others.

Some differences are good; others can be problematic when you decide to sell the car. The good differences are where body dimensions have been slight-

ly stretched to provide more room for members of our predominantly XL society. Other changes can include things like eliminating a factory feature that's rarely used, such as the trim tack strip around the rear of a roadster cockpit.

The problem changes involve fiberglass bodies that aren't accurate. There are some bodies that are "off" just enough to be annoying, but close enough that a novice might not recognize those very important differences. A very noticeable area is the nose of a car. The grille, hood and front fenders are a focal point, so if they're not right, people are sure to notice. In an effort to economize some manufacturers end up with noses that just aren't right. To an experienced street rodder, those problems stick out like a sore nose.

The best way to avoid styling problems is to use a body that relies on factory original-style reproduction grilles and fenders. These are products that could be used on a 100% correct restoration as well as a street rod. The "close, but no '33 coupe" parts could never be used on a stock Ford (in fact, they're so far off they won't fit at all). A correct repro body should be able to use accessory body parts from a variety of manufacturers, not just the company that built the body.

There are also fiberglass bodies that are very obviously not modeled after stock cars. These high tech bodies are so extensively modified that it's clear that was the intent. No one would ever mistake one of these swoopy shells for a stock Deuce, so there's little chance of a novice inadvertently buying one. Some of these bodies are clones of famous show cars and others are modern interpretations of classic Fords. These cars can be very popular, but they're just not the same as a stock-bodied icon car. These wild rides are best for experienced builders.

As with any hobby, the longer you participate, the more you'll learn. Don't let all the complexities and subtle nuances of street rod building and culture put you off. Concentrate on the basics as outlined in this book and you'll be fine. You'll have a great car that you can drive as you learn more about the hobby.

DOLLARS AND SENSE

Let's cut to the chase—what's it gonna cost to build a bolt-together street rod? The answer: somewhere in the neighborhood of $20,000 to $30,000 for an up-and-running street rod. The exact price depends on whether or not you use all-new parts, the quality of paint and bodywork, the amount of performance desired, the level of detail, the body and construction style you choose, and your shopping skills.

Twenty-to-thirty big ones might seem like a pretty expensive neighborhood, until you consider what types of bland new cars inhabit the lower end of that zip code. Building a bolt-together street rod isn't a pocket change operation, but compared to mass-produced transportation modules, it's a lot of excitement for the money. A well-built street rod has a much slower depreciation rate than a new car, too.

It's nice to dream, but it's even nicer to see those dreams come true. We know how much fun it is to fire up a new street rod for the first time and take it for a spin around the block. Just driving a street rod is fun, but that enjoyment is multiplied when you build it yourself. It's a shame when financial misgivings taint the fun or prevent you from realizing your dreams.

When you have a realistic picture of the project's total cost (plus a contingency factor for the inevitable cost overruns), you keep the fun factor high. I've built cars that thousand-dollared me to death. By not planning and by making impulsive changes, I spent far too much money duplicating previous efforts. As a

result, the financial fiascoes overshadowed the fun.

When I've planned a street rod buildup and kept within my budget, I was able to leave financial worries out of the equation. Having things work out financially is a big plus. Anyone can build a street rod if you throw enough money at it. Staying on budget is a sign of a successful builder. It's also good for domestic tranquility.

Prices were hinted at in the discussion on icon street rods. Actual costs can and should be a major concern when building a bolt-together street rod. If you're realistic about costs going in,

you'll be much less likely to be shocked or unhappy later.

Relative to any number of leisure time activities, building a street rod can be a veritable bargain. We're talking about hobbies that involve specialized equipment or expensive animals. Lots of other hobbies are far less expensive than street rodding, but you don't end up with a complete car. A street rod is a valuable asset; so much of the costs can be recouped if you get tired of the hobby or need money for something else.

Street rod parts aren't inexpensive. You can't find them at major discount retailers. The two biggest expenses are

Dazzle costs dollars and the price of perfection isn't cheap. It's not hard to have a six-figure street rod when you demand the kind of innovation and perfection that professional street rod shops are capable of producing.

the body and the chassis. These are areas where you shouldn't try to save pennies. The body and chassis are the car's foundation. A high quality foundation provides a solid starting point for any future upgrades.

You can't buy a new car a piece at a time; they're a take-it-or-leave-it proposition. Since street rods are essentially component vehicles, you can buy them in smaller increments. Buying parts as you need them or as you can afford them means you have the ability to avoid the heavy interest charges associated with a new car purchase. Street rod parts manufacturers and retailers do make package deals more attractive than piece-meal purchases, but at least you have lots of options.

KEEPING IT REAL

Building a bolt-together street rod involves a certain amount of mental discipline. There are so many choices and emotions involved in building your dream car that it's easy to go astray. It's a challenge to build the neatest car possible at a sensible price. There's no way to beat the cubic money crowd, but you can be a winner by building a nice car on a practical budget.

Monte Shelton built this screaming yellow 1930 Model A roadster on a very tight budget. He updated a previously built car, but his many years of car building experience allowed him to do most of the work in his workshop. As far as we could tell, he was having as much fun as the owner of the megabuck Deuce.

We're discussing costs early in the book to help keep the dream as real as possible. There's a tendency in magazines (whether automotive, home improvement, fitness, or whatever) to underplay costs, time, and effort involved with a particular project. Cover blurb stories about super low dollar projects sell magazines, as do blurbs about completing impressive projects in incredibly short amounts of time.

Accompanying photographs often depict beautiful people gleefully turning wrenches on shiny new components in a spotless workshop. Home improvement magazines and TV shows show smiling couples working in complete harmony (obviously fiction) as they add a second story to their house in an afternoon. Fitness magazines feature people who are already so fit that they don't need any advice offered in the article. The only fat in their diets is the cooking oil they rub on their fake tans.

We realize it would be difficult to sell many magazines if the covers depicted a couple of sweaty guys working on a battered hulk in a muddy driveway. Fitness magazines would go broke if their cover models looked like their average readers. Magazines want to inspire readers by presenting attractive covers and articles. It's nice to think of a street rod project in the best possible terms, but be aware of the fantasy factor. Temper any overly optimistic magazine cost claims by doing your own research.

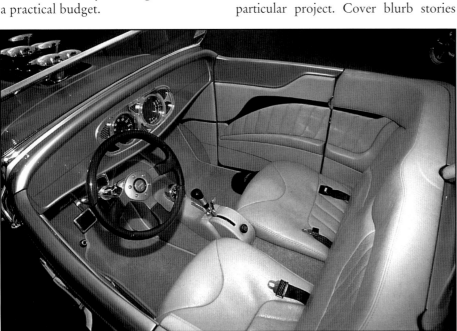

It's possible to spend as much on just the interior of a high dollar car as the total cost of a budget street rod. Only the finest materials were used on this beautifully designed and executed Deuce interior.

IT'S THE LITTLE THINGS ... THAT ADD UP!

Estimating costs of major components like the chassis and body is pretty easy. It's all the little things that can add up to some surprising numbers. If you ignore the small parts, fasteners, and supplies, your wallet will be in for a rude reality check.

Magazine articles frequently omit items in their price lists. Sometimes costs are kept low by using parts they just happened to have "laying around the garage." You can save a lot of money if you have a few extra sets of aluminum cylinder heads, a blown big-block, and a race-prepped transmission cluttering up the corners of your shop. It's also nice when you have incredibly generous friends (who just happen to own performance-related businesses) who will trade you state-of-the-art parts for a handful of magic beans.

Another cost saving technique for magazines is when they do things like blurb "Paint It Yourself" and then have a professional do it for them. Some of their favorite rationalizations are: we had to shoot the photos, we wanted to show you the correct way to do it (a valid reason, but one that eliminates the do-it-yourself factor), and Joe Generous (owner of Joe's Altruistic Auto Body) just happened by our shop and volunteered to help.

A sneaky trick that really irritates us (we won't be casting the first honing stone; we've done our share of "Low Buck" stories) is when a story sticks pretty close to its budget premise and then adds a few things "just for the photos." When a budget car project uses steel wheels and used tires to keep costs down and then shows the final project with a couple thousand dollars worth of billet wheels and Z-rated tires, that leaves a false impression of how the car would look if you built it and tried to stick to the budget.

AIM HIGH AND BE HAPPY

We mentioned the importance of including a cost overrun contingency in your budget. Cost overruns are part of life. They're going to happen whether it's because prices went up, you damaged a part and had to get a replacement, or you saw a more expensive part that you wanted instead of the one in the original plan.

Cost overruns in street rods are like house remodeling projects. Contractors usually advise adding an extra 10-20 percent to the estimate to cover unexpected costs. That's a good idea for any bolt-together street rod project, too.

In terms of estimating costs, we like the psychological advantage of aiming high and then being happy when you

Instead of a beautifully milled billet dashboard, the budget roadster uses a flat aluminum panel with some holes cut in it for some aftermarket gauges. The seat was covered with free-range vinyl.

bring the project in under budget. If you can live with a budget that's purposely high, you have a much greater chance of being happy with the final tally.

We call our budgetary theory "Reverse Optimism." It's a tricky way of being a little pessimistic. We hope we can spend less, but by aiming high, we leave room to feel good about ourselves. If we aimed for a lower total and then didn't make it, we wouldn't be as happy as if the higher total was our original target. If this psychobabble makes us sound like we've inhaled a few too many nitromethane fumes, please bear with us. There's a reason for the mental gymnastics, which are discussed in the next chapter on keeping the dream alive.

MONEY SAVING STRATEGIES

Costs of building a street rod can range from a couple thousand dollars to a couple hundred thousand dollars. With such a wide range, you need to pay careful attention if you want to keep costs in line. While we're not trying to show you how to build the least expensive car possible, we do want to point out areas where considerable sums can be saved without greatly compromising the finished product.

There's a tremendous amount of latitude between cars built out of rusty, bullet hole-riddled hulks found in Death Valley and one-off, mega-buck cars chiseled from an incredibly expensive billet of Unobtanium. A wisely built bolt-together street rod will have a lot more in common with expensive cars than any roadside refuse rod.

Using our example of a '32 Ford highboy roadster, you can see the benefits of careful shopping. We don't care

This stunning '32 five-window coupe is an example of a car we wouldn't recommend for a first-time street rod builder. It's loaded with slick features including a blown engine, high tech wheels and tires, and a brilliant red paint job. The problem is that it's a '32 Chevy, not a '32 Ford. It's a great car, but it's not mainstream as far as parts availability and popularity are concerned.

how great of a scrounger you are; you're not going to find good Deuce parts in drainage ditches. So, if you want an ultra low-buck rod to look like a '32 Ford, you're going to need to buy a reproduction roadster body. You could mount the body on some hacked-up, late model chassis, but you need '32 frame rails if you want it to look like an authentic Deuce Highboy. By the time you purchase the repro body and frame rails, you're well on your way to building the kind of car this book advocates.

On the expensive side of the equation, a mega-buck, hand-crafted Deuce highboy has to look similar to a reproduction body and frame if the builder wants it to be recognized as a '32 Ford clone. The coach-built car will definitely have exquisite attention to details. The body will be stretched, pinched, nipped, and tucked to enhance the original Ford styling. Fit, finish, and precision construction will be awe-inspiring, but from a distance, the car will still look like a '32 Ford highboy.

When you build an icon car like a '32 Ford roadster, the fact that it's a '32

roadster defines so much of the car. It's possible to screw up a Deuce, but you'd have to work at it. If you stick with a stock, reproduction roadster body and repro frame rails, all you have to do is get the stance right and pick an acceptable wheel/tire combo and you're home free. A close inspection will show where money was saved, but the car will still be a very popular street rod.

BIG BUCKS BODIES

Information about choosing a body will be covered in greater detail later, but the bottom line on bodies is: don't scrimp. A quality, reproduction fiberglass or steel body is the second most important component, next to the chassis. The biggest way to save money is by building a highboy instead of a full-fendered car. Eliminating the fenders knocks off about a grand for starters. That savings is multiplied by not having to prep and paint fenders. You also avoid dealing with running boards and any fender-related bracketry.

Roadster bodies are less expensive

to buy and build than closed body styles. The only glass you need is the windshield. You can either forego a top or wait until later to add one. You can run a highboy without a hood or add one later.

There are some price differences between the various brands of reproduction bodies. There isn't any one universally praised body manufacturer. Professional street rod builders have their personal favorites. What one builder might cite as a negative aspect of a certain company, another builder will praise.

Deciding on which manufacturer to choose is a personal matter. It's a good idea to look at raw bodies in person. Check the fit and finish. Look into how the body is reinforced and how thick the fiberglass is. Most of the well-known body manufacturers have been in business for many, many years. Talk to their customers to learn about their satisfaction with the product and the company.

Often, the choice of a body manufacturer will come down to availability instead of price. Manufacturers of major street rod components don't tend to maintain large inventories. Since there are various body options, bodies are commonly built to order. That means waiting times of a couple weeks to several months.

One relatively new twist to the reproduction body price equation is the availability of steel bodies. Excellent steel reproduction bodies of popular models like Deuce and Model A roadsters are now being made by a couple companies. Steel bodies are more expensive than fiberglass, but some people like the idea of having a metal body. When original bodies were still relatively available (and fiberglass reproductions weren't as prevalent) there was some "Steel is Real" snob appeal. That isn't a very popular sentiment anymore, but steel bodies do have a certain cachet.

The bottom line on bodies is: comparison shop for the best price and availability, but don't skimp on quality. A poorly constructed body can end up costing as much or more than a quality body if you have to spend extra money to reinforce it or if it takes a lot of work to make the body straight enough for paint.

CUTTING CORNERS ON CHASSIS

A good chassis is the very foundation of a street rod. You can save lots of money on details and options, but don't cut corners on the basic chassis. Top quality frame rails and crossmembers are a must if you want all the components that attach to the chassis to fit and work correctly. Using top quality chassis and suspension parts is vital to building a safe street rod. You don't want anything to do with flimsy parts or shoddy welding techniques when you need to make a panic stop or perform some defensive driving maneuver.

You can save money by buying the frame rails and crossmembers in unassembled form and then doing your own welding. That type of construction is beyond the scope of a bolt-together street rod book. Unless you're a welder with access to a frame jig, you want a chassis that is pre-welded. Chassis builders that use precision jigs and certified welders build quality frames. If you could match their quality, you wouldn't be reading this book.

Where you can save money on a chassis is by avoiding the extra cost chrome and/or stainless steel options. Don't arbitrarily pass on the shiny stuff without comparing costs, though. Sometimes the deluxe parts don't cost too much more when you buy them with your initial chassis order. You can save by sticking with basic, traditional suspension components instead of the more elaborate independent suspension systems. Cost differences between solid axle suspension and independent suspension are easy to see.

ENGINE ECONOMICS

Engines and, to a much lesser extent, transmissions, are where huge economies can be realized. Too many people get carried away with the hot rod aspect of street rods. They think that they need 600 horsepower to assert their masculinity. Most rodders appreciate the mechanical muscle of a race-prepped engine, but they're just as nice to look at in someone else's car as they are to own and drive.

Too many street rod builders tend to grossly overestimate the amount of horsepower they need. The light weight of street rods (especially highboys) means that it doesn't take a great deal of power to provide a serious kick-in-the-pants blast of acceleration. When you add in the rushing wind and extra noise associated with an open car, it seems like you're going faster than you are.

An old racing adage says: "Speed costs money, how fast do you want to go?" Not only does speed cost money, those costs tend to rise exponentially above a certain level. It's like in drag racing where huge initial gains can be made with improved induction and exhaust systems, minor transmission modifications, simple traction aids, steeper rear axle ratios, and stickier tires. Several seconds can be knocked off elapsed times relatively easily and affordably, but after a certain elapsed time, each additional tenth of a second improvement gets exceedingly more expensive.

A neat engine is certainly a big part of a neat street rod, but it's one of those items that can be improved gradually. The primary function of the engine is to propel the car from Point A to Point B. A decent running, couple hundred dollar, wrecking yard 350 Chevy will handle that job as well as a blown, fuel-injected, all-aluminum, blueprinted 350 that might cost $10,000 or more. The trick engine will run circles around the wrecking yard engine in a status contest, but with the hoods closed, or when you're crawling along in congested traffic, it's hard to tell the difference. Actually, in the kind of congested traffic that often surrounds street rod events, the milder engine might run smoother than the temperamental thoroughbred.

In-between wrecking yard engines and Pro Stock power plants are a lot of excellent engines. For approximately $2,000 to $3,000 you can get a brand new small-block GM replacement engine. You can also find high performance engine kits in the same general price range. We'll get deeper into engine possibilities in the chapter on engines.

PAINT AND BODYWORK

Paint and bodywork is an area that's littered with financial land mines. When

There are vehicles that should be considered "overpriced at free" like this badly rusted Ford truck. As a novice street rodder there's no way you could come out financially on a basket case like this. Rust isn't for the faint of heart.

you listen to car enthusiasts complaining about high prices, paint and bodywork are usually at (or very near) the top of the list. Problems tend to fall into two main categories: severe cost over-runs or poor quality workmanship.

It's hard to get a definitive estimate when you're dealing with custom paint and bodywork. The shop owner doesn't always know what problems might arise. There isn't a flat rate shop guide to ease estimating like there is for production body shops. Many custom painters end up charging for time and materials. Perfection takes a lot of time and materials.

Material costs keep rising. The old days of buying all the supplies to paint a full size car for $100 are long gone. Depending on the type of paint and the colors (reds are among the more expensive colors), material costs alone can easily exceed $1,000. As Environmental Protection Agency regulations keep getting stricter and as multi-stage paints keep getting more expensive, the cost of painting a street rod has no place to go but up.

You wouldn't think that a car with as little surface area as a '32 highboy would cost much to paint, but you'd be wrong. For starters, most regular body shops don't care to work on street rods. They can make much more money churning out insurance-paid collision jobs. That means you need to find a custom painter. Throw the word custom in front of painter and prices go up. Roadster bodies are less expensive to paint than coupes or sedans, but "less" is a relative term in custom painting circles.

You might also think that since the bodies are brand new, fresh-from-the-mold, fiberglass reproductions that they'd be ready for paint as delivered. Again, you'd be wrong. Fiberglass bodies are far less expensive to prep than old metal bodies. You don't have to deal with rust or dents, but glass bodies still need lots of blocking and sanding to get them ready for paint. It's also common to spend time adjusting door gaps. If you're building a full-fendered car, expect to spend quite a lot of time adjusting the fenders and running boards. Hoods and grilles take a fair amount of adjustment regardless of whether or not the car has fenders.

It's possible to save money by doing your own prep work. Block sanding and filling minor imperfections doesn't require a lot of expensive equipment. Body prep is labor intensive and it can be done at home. The problem is that you can also do a lot of expensive damage if you don't know what you're doing. Beginners tend to get overly zealous with power sanding tools.

Body prep is an area where you can save a lot of $50-$60 an hour shop time (twenty hours will blow right through a thousand dollar bill). You can read all about body prep techniques, but only experience will give you confidence and the ability to "feel" imperfections. Professional bodymen use their very sensitive hands to find high and low spots. A body panel might look perfectly smooth and straight to a beginner, but it's a lunar surface to an experienced bodyman. We're reluctant to recommend doing your own body prep on your first street rod, but it is an area where lots of money can be saved if you have the experience.

Our best money saving paint tip is to have a body shop simply scuff the body and apply a couple thin coats of primer. Primered street rods have always been acceptable to hot rodders, and there has been a certain amount of backlash to high dollar cars in recent years, which has made primered rods all the more popular. The primer can be used as a base for future blocking and painting, but it still looks cool while you're saving up for a custom paint job.

Primered is actually a misnomer. Although primer can be applied and left on a body, it isn't made to act as a topcoat. Builders who plan on retaining the unfinished look for a long time usually use a catalyzed primer/surfacer or apply flat or semi-flat black paint instead of primer.

INTERIOR INVESTMENTS

Beautiful leather interiors are another area that can easily boost the cost of building a street rod. Like the body, you'd think that since there is so little surface area to cover that upholstery would be cheap. It's not, because, once again, it's specialized, custom

All you really need to drive a street rod is something to sit on and a steering wheel. A speedometer would be nice, but maybe you're a good judge of speed. There are upholstery kits for popular street rods. A kit can lower costs substantially over those of a custom upholstery job.

work. Top-notch upholsterers are often booked up a year in advance.

The good news about interiors is that there are relatively inexpensive alternatives that will get you by until you decide if you want to step up to a custom upholstery job. It's no shame to have an unfinished interior. Many rodders put their cars on the road to sort out any problems. Then, after the bugs are worked out they take the car apart again and have it painted. After reassembly, they finally get around to the upholstery. The upholstery job is usually the last thing done to a street rod.

Alternatives to expensive upholstery include upholstery kits, used bucket seats, and the always-popular colorful blankets. You can get pre-sewn vinyl upholstery kits for popular cars like Deuce roadsters. Seat springs are available in stock and custom configurations. A do-it-yourself upholstery kit can look a little pedestrian, but it will get the job done.

Used bucket seats (usually from smaller, import cars) are a good way to get affordable seating. Pick a popular color like black, gray, or tan. Those colors go OK with most body colors and they're much easier to resell when you upgrade your interior. There are also aftermarket seat companies that specialize in street rod seats. These seats can be purchased bare for custom upholstery or already upholstered. Aftermarket bucket seats are a good way to get a sharp interior at a reasonable price.

Bright colored blankets (variously known as Mexican or Indian blankets) have always been popular, but with the increased popularity of primered and low-dollar cars, blankets have almost become status symbols. The trick with blanket upholstery is to use it over foam-covered seat springs. You don't have to sew the blankets, but you should fold them around the edges of the cushions and secure them with hog rings.

Carpet kits are inexpensive, or you can cut your own. Highboy roadster interiors have very little area to carpet and most of it's pretty flat. More important than carpet is the underlying insulation material. This is an area where is pays to buy top quality materials.

American Racing's Torq-Thrust II wheel is an icon wheel that's very affordable if you stick to the 14- and 15-inch sizes. The polished finish takes more upkeep than the chrome finish, but there is a noticeable price differential.

Sufficient heat and noise insulation will make your street rod much more enjoyable to drive. You can always upgrade the carpets later.

As mentioned before when discussing body style, omitting the convertible top on a roadster is one way to save. Most roadster tops don't fold, so you need to make a decision before you leave home. If the weather is bad enough to need a top, chances are you'll stay home anyway. There are also removable fiberglass tops. Either style of top can be added later.

WHEEL DEALS

Wheels and tires can make or break a street rod. Picking a good combination is critical to the overall look of the car. Wheel style says a lot about the flavor of the car, be it traditional, high performance, or high tech. Tire and wheel sizes have a lot to do with stance which is another critical element of building a successful street rod.

Given the importance of wheels and tires, you need to choose wisely. Money can be saved if you stick with more conventional wheels instead of the latest, high tech offerings. Some very popular wheels are actually ones that are very affordable. A prime example is the classic American Racing Torq-Thrust five-spoke mag wheel. This wheel has been

around since the early sixties in various forms and finishes. There are differences between spoke styles (very minor differences), finishes (natural, polished, and chrome), and type of construction (one piece or two piece).

The way to save money is to buy polished Torq-Thrust II wheels that are very affordable, but are still universally recognized. Polished wheels cost less than chromed ones and with a nominal amount of upkeep, they'll stay bright and shiny. Torq Thrust wheels are now available in diameters up to 20-inches, and while the big diameter wheels are popular, they cost considerably more than the 15-inch and 14-inch ones. A combination of 15's in back and 14's in front is a classic highboy choice. Some people like to use tall 16-inch tires on highboys. The 16-inch Torq-Thrust wheels are pretty reasonable, at least compared to the big 17-20 inch ones.

Painted steel wheels with stainless trim rings and small hubcaps are a popular, but inexpensive combination for traditionally styled highboys. Brightly painted (usually red or orange) steel wheels add color to a primered highboy. Tires that match the traditional looking wheels don't need to be high speed Z-rated ones. Authentic old-time highboys usually ran tall, bias-ply tires. We don't recommend them. There are new tires that have a nostalgic look (including

Here's another '32 coupe built on a budget. The primered body represents a huge savings over a perfect, finished paint job, but you can bet the owner still enjoys the car. The point is, you don't have to spend a lot to have fun.

items are rampant under the hood. Besides the previously discussed cost extremes related to the basic engine, accessory items have great price ranges. Street rodders love trick brackets and engine dress-up items, but the plain, original part functions just as well as the custom machined, aluminum part. A nicely painted factory alternator bracket gets the job done just as well as the billet aluminum bracket.

Cast iron exhaust manifolds can be cleaned and protected with heat resistant paint. They don't look as slick as chromed exhaust headers and they don't provide the same level of performance, but they do accomplish the same basic function: removing exhaust gases from the engine. Any of these bolt-on engine accessories can be easily upgraded at a later date.

Save Now, Spend Later

Engine accessories are a prime example of the benefits of the "save now, spend later" school of street rod building. By focusing on the most important aspects of the car, you can get it on the road quicker and at a lower cost. Since the focus of this bolt-together book is largely first-time street rod builders, we expect that other street rod projects will follow in your garage.

So much is learned the first time someone builds a street rod that the second one is much easier. The odds of someone building the perfect car the first time out and keeping that car forever are remote. Knowing that at the start of a project makes it easier to hold back on the flashy, expensive items.

Building a car with a strong possibility of reselling it is a good reason for financial frugality. Used street rods rarely sell for their total investment (labor costs should be included for a truly accurate total even if it was your own labor). Unless some very famous professional builder was involved, the extra money spent on premium-priced components and accessories rarely returns as much of the investment as more generic parts. Building a street rod with resale in mind will be covered more in a later chapter.

wide whitewalls, if desired) but use modern, radial construction. This is the way to get "the look" without sacrificing handling and performance.

Wheels and tires are the easiest items to change on a street rod; yet, a different wheel/tire combination can greatly alter the personality of the car. Used wheels and tires never sell for anything close to what they cost new. Remember that if you're tempted to buy an expensive 4-pack of billet aluminum.

You can sometimes use the lower prices of used wheels and tires to your advantage. People who want something different for their street rods often take the old wheels and tires to a swap meet. You can get good deals at swap meets, but you can also make some costly mistakes.

A big problem with swap meet wheels is getting the correct offset for your car. Offset determines where the wheel/tire combination is relative to the body and suspension components. The wrong offset can position the tires either too close, causing interference problems, or too far away, leading to an overly wide track and a goofy look.

If you're contemplating doing some swap meet wheel shopping, take along your own measuring tools. There are inexpensive bolt pattern measuring devices. Bring a straight edge and a tape measure to determine wheel width and offset. Don't rely on the seller's word. A favorite ploy of swap meet sellers is to answer the question, "What's it fit?" with the evasive, "What do you have?" Returning swap meet merchandise is somewhere south of impossible.

Detail Dollars

Little details can run up big bills. We complained about magazine articles that "conveniently" omit lots of miscellaneous items from project car costs. Not accounting for the "little things" can destroy your budget. Two things should be considered in relation to detail items. First, account for everything, down to fasteners and chemical supplies if you really want to know the true cost of a bolt-together street rod. If your financial situation allows a lot of latitude, you might want to ignore the small items that together can add up to thousands of dollars.

The second and most important point is that considerable sums can be saved if you're prudent about which detail items you purchase. We don't advocate cutting corners on the quality of essential parts, but we do suggest careful consideration of the "eye candy" items.

Examples of style over substance

KEEPING THE DREAM ALIVE

One of the best street rod building skills you can possess is enthusiasm. You have the greatest chance of successfully completing a street rod if you can maintain a high level of enthusiasm throughout the project. Building a street rod is one of those daydream type ventures. You don't *need* a street rod, but it's fine to want one.

There's a considerable gap between a big pile of parts on the garage floor and the beautiful street rods you see in magazines and at car shows. If you can keep each segment of the project fun, it will be much easier to build the car. A street rod project that holds your attention is like a great book; you hate to put it down because you're so anxious to find out what happens in the next chapter.

If you had a magic Garage-Cam that could peek into all the garages in the country and gather data about their contents, we think you'd be amazed by the number of unfinished projects serving as dust depositories. Whether these projects were abandoned for lack of time, money, or skill, a lack of enthusiasm was most likely a common denominator. With enough enthusiasm, you will eventually conquer any problems or setbacks.

Enthusiasm is what keeps bringing you back to the garage instead of spending evenings in front of the TV. You can't will yourself to be enthusiastic, but you can do things to bolster your enthu-

siasm. You need to structure the project to best keep the dream alive.

DIVIDE AND CONQUER

One of the best ways to maintain enthusiasm is to break the buildup into a series of smaller projects. Then take those subsets and further reduce them to smaller sub-assemblies. By breaking up the tasks, you can focus on each successfully completed section, rather than looking so far down the road to the finished car.

Here are some examples of how you might divide the buildup. Start with the

planning and gathering information. Then, make your parts purchases. You can buy most of the components at one time or buy a few parts at a time depending on your budget.

Start with the chassis. The short-term goal would be a rolling chassis. That's a major step in building a street rod. A rolling chassis is very tangible. It's easily identifiable as a key part of the street rod instead of a pile of parts. The sub-assemblies for the chassis would include the front suspension, rear suspension, steering, brake system, and fuel system.

You need to formulate a solid building plan and stick to it. Otherwise, you might not know if you're coming or going.

When the frame and chassis components arrive, it's nice to lay out all the parts to be sure everything is there. Taking photos of each major step is nice for future reference and the memories of the project.

Put wheels and tires on the chassis as soon as possible. The wheels and tires make the chassis easier to move around and they also maintain enthusiasm because the chassis looks more complete. You may choose to use some old "rollers" or you may want to install the new wheels and tires that are slated for the finished car. Installing a set of custom wheels and "big 'n' little" tires does a lot to make the rolling chassis look like a real street rod. Scabby wheels detract from the project and can dampen your dreams.

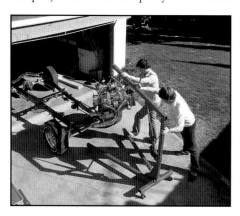

It's always nice to have help, especially when doing heavy tasks like installing an engine. Building a street rod with a friend or family member makes the whole experience more fun. This is obviously a vintage photo because both the author (right) and his brother have an abundance of brown hair.

The only possible problem about mounting custom wheels and tires is that you need to be sure that they're the right combination for the car. Choosing the right set of wheels and tires is critical to the overall "look" and "stance" of a street rod. We'll cover those all-important elements in a later chapter. If you do your research well, you can determine your ideal wheel and tire combination in advance. We're strong advocates of getting the chassis up on the trick wheels and tires as soon as possible.

Admiring a rolling chassis (especially if it has the engine installed) is a great morale booster. We paint the engine block either to match the final color of the frame rails or in a contrasting color. We try to have the custom wheels and new tires available so they can be mounted. We so enjoy looking at a beautiful street rod chassis, that it seems like a shame to cover it with the body.

After the chassis, we suggest working on the engine and transmission. How the drivetrain is handled depends on whether you buy a complete engine, build an engine kit, rebuild a used engine, or simply steam clean a used motor and drop it in the chassis. The transmission purchase closely follows the various engine possibilities. When the engine and transmission are in place, the chassis really starts to look like something.

Installing the exhaust and cooling systems means you have a chassis that's practically ready to drive. You might choose to hook up a battery and run the engine. Milestones like running the engine can do a lot to make completion seem closer.

Some builders skip the drivetrain until after they've finished dealing with the body. We're partial to admiring the finished chassis complete with the engine, but it's easier to work on the body without the engine in place. As long as it's not wired and plumbed, taking an engine in and out of a highboy roadster is a matter of a few bolts. When you install the engine, the extra weight helps settle the front suspension. That gives you a better idea of how low the finished car will be.

Bodies should be trial-fitted and adjusted before any paintwork is performed. How the body sits on the frame, how the fenders and running boards fit (if used), and the uniformity of door and trunk gaps are important aspects of building a quality street rod. Those adjustments take time and frequently, a fair amount of trial and error.

One of our primary cost-cutting suggestions is to not have the body painted until after the car has been assembled and driven for a while. It's always a very good idea to assemble the car and work out any bugs before it gets painted. That way you can take care of the inevitable problems without worrying about damaging the new paint.

We suggest going beyond the shakedown phase and leaving the body unpainted except for priming it. We advocate driving the car for a substantial period of time (or miles) before you decide if you even want to get it painted. Since paint is so expensive, you should plan on keeping the car a couple years. If you think you might want to sell the car, you'll be a long ways ahead financially by not investing in an expensive paint job.

Wiring is usually done with the body in place, although some people do subassemblies like the dashboard and gauges out of the car. Street rod wiring kits are one of the best products around. They took the tedious, confusing task of wiring a car and turned it into a color-coded, pre-cut, easy to follow kit. Some kits even have plug-in modules so the body can be easily separated from the chassis without disturbing the wiring.

The interior is one of the last things to do on a street rod. When you tackle it and how thoroughly depends on when and if your car will be painted. It also depends on the type of upholstery you're using. Custom upholsterers usually wait until the car is painted. If you're using an upholstery kit, you may want to do the seat, insulation, and carpet first and wait for items like door panels. Whatever type of interior you use, it needs to be removed before the car is painted.

FAMILY AND FRIENDS

Like the phone company ads say, reach out and touch someone. Enlisting the help of family members or friends is a great way to keep enthusiasm alive. It's

Getting a chassis up on wheels and tires makes it look a lot closer to finished than when it's just sitting on jack stands. Reaching goals like this help keep the enthusiasm alive. (So-Cal Speed Shop)

fine to build a car as a solitary, get-your-mind-off-work undertaking, but it's much more fun with other people.

Involving others helps keep the momentum going. When one person starts to get tired or discouraged, the other person can get them back on track. It's tougher to put off a friend or family member than it is to rationalize laziness to yourself. An extra person is great for helping lift heavy components or position parts while you bolt them in place.

Letting one or more of your children participate can be both very rewarding and potentially frustrating. Building a street rod isn't an activity for young children, but kids around ten or older are big enough to actually help. Building a street rod is a great way for fathers to interact with their children in a non-competitive environment. The child will learn about cars and how they work. They can learn how to safely use tools. Using tools gives them confidence that they can fix things instead of having to rely on outside help. Their sense of accomplishment and pride in the finished project is a terrific self-esteem booster.

Our suggestion regarding children is to not pressure them. Offer to let them participate, but don't put any guilt on them if they're not interested. When participation is mandatory, the project becomes work instead of fun. We found that our daughter was much more interested in street rod projects than her brothers. They all liked riding in the finished cars, but our daughter was sincerely interested in how things worked.

VIRTUAL STREET RODS

Progress photos of a street rod project have always been a fun way to document your new car. Nowadays, it's easier than ever to keep a video journal or digital diary. Besides keeping a record for you and your immediate family, you can post photos on your computer and share them with friends and relatives.

You might go as far as to create a website about your street rod project, www.billbuildsastreetrod.com, so you can share your progress with the world. If you have friends who are car enthusiasts, using the Internet makes it easy to keep them informed. By committing to such a public display of your progress, you put more pressure on yourself to keep the car going.

The Internet is an increasingly fertile source of information about street rods. Lots of street rod companies have web sites where you can learn about their products and place orders. You can find sites for almost anything special interest, auto-related group.

Depending on your computer skills, you could even help plan your street rod digitally. You can do things like scan in photos of finished cars you like. You can mix and match features to see how they might look on your car. Budget programs and spreadsheets can be used to keep track of expenses, parts numbers, specifications, and status of mail order parts.

DO YOUR HOMEWORK

Turn lots of pages before you ever turn a wrench. If you're interested in building a street rod, you're probably reading the major street rod magazines, *Street Rodder* and *Rod & Custom*. Those

Tasks like mounting the body require the help of several strong friends. Most fiberglass bodies are light enough to do without a hoist, but metal bodies usually require some mechanical assistance. A hoist allows a slow and careful alignment of the mounting points.

two publications are the big dogs, but there are other smaller street rod publications that can also be sources of good ideas, like *Street Rod Builder, American Rodder,* and so on. Besides getting ideas about the type of street rod you want to build, the big magazines are loaded with advertisements from mail-order companies and manufacturers.

It's well worth the money to order catalogs from lots of street rod businesses. Magazines frequently run special sections where you can order a large number of catalogs on a single form. Study the catalogs carefully. Look past the pretty photos and compare features and construction techniques.

Checking out products in person is even better than looking at catalogs. There are many large-scale street rod events that feature extensive manufacturers' displays. Two organizations, the National Street Rod Association (NSRA) and the Goodguys Rod and Custom Association produce the most major events. There are lots of big regional, independent street rod events that rival the NSRA and Goodguys shows. A good place to learn about the independent regional events is in the event calendars of the big street rod magazines. Also, the biggest events are usually covered in the magazines.

Joining the NSRA and Goodguys is a good idea. Annual membership costs are similar to a magazine subscription. Both organizations publish excellent monthly magazines, NSRA's *StreetScene* and the Goodguys *Goodguys' Goodtimes Gazette.* Both publications have lots of photo coverage of their own events. Goodguys sticks strictly to events they produce, but the NSRA also includes smaller, local events put on by NSRA affiliated car clubs.

Extensive want ads are a big benefit of both publications. The ads are a good source of both reasonable and unreasonable street rods. Interspersed with the deals are the dreamers. Just because someone has (or claims to have) a small fortune invested in a car, that doesn't mean it's worth that much. Use the ads to gauge average prices. Remember a key axiom of buying and selling street rods: it's negotiable.

There are always lots of street rods for sale at major car shows. Some people seriously want to sell their cars and price them accordingly, but too many people are looking for low-flying pigeons. A sure sign of a high priced car is one that has "for sale" painted on the windows. Another Fantasy Island tip-off is when they use "K" instead of a dollar sign. What's the exchange rate on K's? I'm all out of K's, would you take some J's and L's instead? Some egomaniacs place unrealistically high prices on their cars never seriously intending to sell them. The high prices are just a way of inflating their egos.

The best thing to do at big (or small) street rod events is look at the cars and manufacturers' displays. Street rodders are a friendly group and it doesn't take much to get a rodder talking about his or her car. They're pretty frank about parts they like and parts that were disappointing. A video camera is an excellent tool to take to a street rod show. If you see cars you admire, take lots of footage of them. Make audio notes of things like tire sizes.

ADDITIONAL TIPS

You probably know what motivates you best, but the following are a few enthusiasm boosters that you may not have considered.

- **Build a model of your car.** When you build a popular street rod like a '32 Ford, it's easy to find plastic model car kits with similar equipment to your real project. You can build more than one model to try out different paint schemes or to see if you prefer a full fendered car to a highboy. A finished model of your street rod project is a nice thing to keep in a prominent place (either at home or at work) to remind yourself what you're trying to achieve.

- **Get it outside.** Roll the chassis outside as soon as it's up on wheels. Working in a garage usually puts you in close proximity to the car. It's neat to roll the chassis outside where you can stand back and better take in the whole thing. Rolling the chassis out into your driveway is also a way to visualize the finished car sitting in the driveway.

- **Turn the wheels.** Mount a steering wheel as soon as the body is put on the chassis.

The people in magazines seem to live better than the rest of us. Keep in mind that photos like this scene of a happy couple working in harmony on their street rod project are staged. There's a difference between what sells magazines and real life.

This is something you might want to do in private, but when you put the body on the chassis, try to at least temporarily mock up the steering column. Installing a steering wheel makes it much easier to steer the car around the garage, but what builds enthusiasm is being able to pretend you're driving. Put a milk crate or some type of seat in the car so you can sit in it. This is the adult version of pretending to drive the family car when you were a child.

Placing the body on the chassis is a major step toward making the car look complete, so sitting in it makes it easy to imagine how you'll feel when the car is finished. On the practical side, you can get an idea of how you'll fit and determine if the steering column needs to be repositioned. Playing Beach Boys music is optional.

- **Set time goals.** Some people naturally work better under deadline pressure (e.g. writers). If a schedule helps you stay focused, divide the various tasks and subassemblies into weekly and/or monthly performance goals. Having a big checklist and seeing it diminish can help some people stay on track and increase their sense of accomplishment. If you don't like deadlines, at least keep a big "to do" list on the garage wall, and cross off items when they're done. It's a good way to measure your progress.

Enthusiasm is free, but it's a critical component of a successful street rod building project.

BLUEPRINTS FOR SUCCESS

A good game plan is the backbone of a successful bolt-together street rod. Without careful planning, you're looking at an expensive bad time. Sticking with a plan requires some discipline, but we're confident that you'll be pleased with the results if you stay the course.

Wasted time and money are common consequences of poor planning, regardless of the endeavor. While building a street rod is fun, completing it and driving it is even more fun. Therefore, the less time and money you waste, the quicker you'll be behind the wheel. You want to be driving down the highway, not some metaphorical dead end.

Street rods can be an infinite variation on a basic theme. Since there are so many vehicles that qualify as street rods and there are many styles of street rods, it's easy to go astray. Our blueprint for success depends on a very narrowly defined type of street rod. That definition includes a small number of very popular twenties and thirties Fords in a few select body styles.

These blueprints for success rely heavily on the previously discussed icon cars. Always remember that the focus of building your first street rod should be fun. If it's not fun, why do it? By following these blueprints for success, you'll minimize the opportunities for trouble, both in terms of construction and finances.

Following an arbitrary blueprint in a hobby that's supposed to be all about individual expression may seem contradictory, but it's not. With the suggested cars, the uniqueness is in just building a

street rod. A blueprint street rod won't be unique within the realm of street rods, but in the general transportation world, any street rod is extremely unique. You may see dozens of similar '32 Ford highboy roadsters at a street rod event, but when is the last time you saw one in your neighborhood or at the local shopping center?

After you complete your first street rod, you'll have a much clearer picture about whether or not you want to build another one. You'll have a better idea of things you'd like to change. You'll know if an open car really isn't for you or if you'd like a car that can carry more people. You'll have an insider's perspective instead of the often-distorted view of an outsider looking in.

Your second street rod can be much more unique. Since your first one was a generic street rod, the odds of selling it quickly, easily, and for a good price are very high. It's doubtful that you'll make a profit, but with a well-built generic street rod, you should recoup the majority of your investment.

Most people need to sell their previous rod in order to finance the next one. A car that's too unusual can be a slow seller. Taking a year or two to sell a one-of-a-kind street rod can be both frustrating and demoralizing. It's hard not to take it personally when potential buyers criticize the unique features or make insulting offers because they figure they'll have to redo much of your work.

The '32 Ford highboy roadster is by far our number one pick for a bolt-together street rod. These cars can't be beat for overall popularity, availability of parts, and ease of reselling. John Carmody's brilliant red highboy features a Gibbons fiberglass body mounted on a Rod Factory chassis.

The fact that big rod runs draw so many Deuce roadsters makes it easy to study them. Bring a still or video camera to every event so you can take comparison shots.

A slow, protracted sale can take a lot of fun out of the project.

If you ask the owners of the wildest rods at an event about their first street rod, most of them will tell you that it was far less impressive than their present masterpiece. Unless a newcomer is strictly an open checkbook builder, their first car was probably much more modest. It's natural to get caught up in the fantasy of building a Top Ten street rod, but don't lose sight of the fact that driving a finished generic street rod is immeasurably better than staring at an unfinished dream car in your garage.

BLUEPRINT ONE: 1932 FORD HIGHBOY ROADSTER

A 1932 Ford highboy roadster is far and away our number one choice for a first time, bolt-together street rod. It's such a popular icon car and so many manufacturers make Deuce parts. A '32 roadster isn't the cheapest car, nor is it the most expensive, but it is a car that has a very high resale value. You would have to work hard at screwing up a '32 roadster to severely affect its value. If you follow our suggestions, you'll end up with a car that's a safe choice, both financially and popularity-wise. Here's the shopping list:

Body
- 1932 Ford roadster fiberglass reproduction body.
- Hidden or stock door hinges.
- Reverse-hinged trunk lid for possible rumble seat.

- Remote deck lid latch.
- Stock style windshield posts, chopped 2 inches.
- Stock or recessed firewall.
- Insert-style dashboard (Auburn).
- Three-piece metal hood, solid side panels.
- Fiberglass, filled grille shell.
- Stock style stainless steel (or painted) grille insert.
- Stock style gas tank.
- Reproduction '39 Ford or '50 Pontiac tail-lights.
- King Bee headlights or stock '32 Ford style headlights.
- Hot rod primer, semi-gloss black, bright red, or gloss black paint.

Chassis
- 1932 Ford reproduction boxed steel frame rails.
- Lowered front crossmember.
- Rectangular or round tube center cross-members and braces.
- Dropped I-beam or tubular front axle.
- Transverse front spring
- Power boosted front disc brakes.
- Parallel 4-link front suspension.
- Tube front shocks.
- Ford 9-inch rearend, 3.00:1 to 3.50:1 axle ratio.
- Rear drum brakes.
- Parallel 4-link rear suspension.
- Coil-over rear shock absorbers.
- Panhard bars, front and rear.
- Vega-type steering box

Engine/Transmission
- Small-block Chevrolet, 350 cubic inch displacement.
- Single four-barrel carburetor or fuel injection system.
- Hydraulic, RV grind camshaft.
- Small diameter tubular exhaust headers.
- Four-speed automatic overdrive transmission.
- Heavy-duty radiator with built-in trans cooler.
- Electric fan with shroud.

Wheels and Tires
- Tall rear tires and short front tires, black-wall radials, with a relatively high aspect ratio.
- 15x8-inch rear rims.
- 15x6-inch front rims.
- American Racing Torq-Thrust II polished mags or steel wheels (bright color, like red

or orange) with small center caps and trim rings.

Interior
- Bench seat.
- Reproduction vinyl upholstery kit in black or tan.
- Seat belts.
- Ample insulation and sound deadening material.
- Analog gauges: speedometer, tachometer, oil pressure, water, temperature, fuel gauge, voltmeter.
- GM style tilt steering column with column mounted transmission shifter and shift indicator.
- Leather rimmed steering wheel.
- Custom wiring kit.
- Hidden FM radio and CD changer with remote control.

Option A: '32 3-Window Coupe Highboy
- Same components as above but with '32 3-window coupe fiberglass body.
- Chopped top 2-1/2-inches.
- Filled roof panel.

Option B: Full Fendered '32 Roadster or Coupe
- Same components as '32 highboy but full-fendered.
- Either roadster or 3-window coupe.
- Smooth running boards.

Body Notes
Hidden hinges, a filled cowl vent, smooth hood side panels, no outside door handles, a remote rear deck lid release, and a filled grille shell all make

The simple, '39 Ford teardrop style tail-lights and stock style gas tank are winning elements. The small horizontal bar isn't a minimal bumper; it's the rear frame spreader bar.

the car look smoother and make paint prep easier. A functional cowl vent is nice for airflow around your legs and feet on a hot day, but it's no substitute for modern air conditioning. Some builders even install compact air conditioners in roadsters. A functional cowl vent makes more sense in a '32 coupe than a roadster, but air conditioning is the best choice.

By omitting the outside door handles and the rear deck lid handle, a few bucks are saved on handles, but more importantly, the body looks smoother. Solid hood side panels go along with the smooth look and they're much easier to prep for paint than louvered hood panels. Louvered hood panels are available in either the long factory-style louvers or multiple rows of short, hot rod louvers.

Louvered hood side panels will keep the engine compartment cooler than solid panels, but if you ever want to flame the car, louvers greatly complicate a flame paint job. Hood side panels are an easy item to change if you decide you want a different style at a later date.

We advocate a reverse-hinged rear deck lid because it gives you the option of converting it to a rumble seat. Without the seat cushions, the area functions as a trunk. It's a little harder to access, but not much.

The basic windshield configuration choices are stock height windshield posts, chopped stock style posts, and a custom Duvall-style windshield. The slightly chopped windshield fits the whole cut-down, smoother look of a hot rod. Stock style windshield posts are less expensive than a split Duvall windshield or custom billet windshield posts.

The laid back, swoopy, art deco-style Duvall windshield is quite popular on highboy Deuce roadsters. Who knows if they will stay popular since their popularity has come and gone before? The stock style windshield posts are the classic, traditional choice, so there's very little chance of them going out of style. Stock style windshield posts are hinged at the top, so the bottom edge can be opened a little to allow the wind to cool you.

There are several dashboard choices, including a stock '32 dash, a totally

flat panel, the Auburn style, and a cut-down '40 Ford version. The Auburn style has a larger central rectangle than the oval of the stock dash. The larger space makes it easier to mount six gauges. It's a very acceptable dashboard.

Using reproduction stock stainless steel grille bars is much less expensive than the trendy custom grille bars. Custom grille bars can be quite expensive, but from any distance, it's hard to tell if the grille bars are stock or custom. This is a good example of where the added expense doesn't yield a very impressive return.

There are several options for front and rear lighting, but it's tough to go wrong with classic choices like the aftermarket King Bee headlights or the larger, reproduction '32 Ford headlights. The King Bee lights are less expensive and changing headlights (either by you or a subsequent buyer) isn't difficult. The '39 Ford "teardrop" taillight is a street rod standard and it looks fine on a '32 highboy. The simple, round, convex '50 Pontiac taillight is another street rod classic that looks good on the flat panel below the deck lid.

You can save money by not using a hood. That simplifies the body fitting process, but it puts more emphasis on having an attractive engine. This builder got around the sticky issue of front license plates by leaning it back so far that it almost looks like a mini spoiler.

Paint can be a "make or break" item on a street rod. It was critical enough back when paint jobs were inexpensive, but given the ever-escalating custom paint costs, picking the wrong color can be a financial disaster. The goal with a generic street rod is to pick a color that transcends fads and time periods. The less dated a car

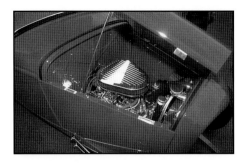

Three-piece hoods are very popular, but they can take a while to properly fit. By having the side panels fixed (they can be unbolted) engine access is a little difficult. The ubiquitous small-block 350 Chevy V-8 is the best engine choice for a blueprint street rod.

is, the easier it will be to sell and the longer it will appear contemporary.

There are two street rod colors that never seem to go out of style: red and black. Red is sometimes derided as "resale red" but that's a good thing for your first street rod. Black is kind of a challenging color to many street rod builders. It takes a super straight body and outstanding prep work to make a black paint job work the way it should.

Since a bolt-together street rod has a large affordability component, a black paint job shouldn't be your first choice. You won't go too far wrong in the popularity department with black, but in order to get a great black paint job, you'll have to spend lots of time and/or money. Black paint is notorious for showing any flaws in the body.

Red paint should be very, very bright red. There are many shades of red, but most street rodders prefer the absolute brightest hues. Sports car colors like Porsche, Viper, and Acura NSX reds are all very bold and very popular. Many builders use fleet colors and toners to achieve maximum red. They also boost the impact with light colored undercoats.

Primered street rods have been up and down on the popularity charts. Currently, they're pretty popular. The best thing about a primered '32 highboy is it's very acceptable and much more affordable than a finished paint job. A body needs to be in primer before the topcoats can be sprayed, so a primered body can be used as is and then painted later.

Most primered cars are just primer as it comes out of the can. They usually have some clear mixed in to help it last longer. Primer is designed as an under-coat, not a topcoat, so it needs some help if it is to remain out in the elements for long. A way to get the primer look, but take it slightly upscale, is to use semi-gloss black paint.

The sleek DuVall style windshield is a popular option on Deuce roadsters, but it costs more than a stock style wind-shield. An item like this can set the tone of the car, so you need to decide if it's an area where you want to spend the extra money.

You will see some cars in red oxide primer, light gray primer, and the odd yellow of DP-40 primer/surfacer, but the most acceptable shade for extended use is dark gray. It's just one of those arbitrary street rod "rules."

A body doesn't have to be perfect to be painted with primer. It's nice to have the bodywork done, but you can always go back and do more bodywork before any actual color coats are applied. Putting a street rod together in primer is good for the shakedown period. It doesn't matter if a primered body gets scratched while components are being adjusted. If you finish paint the body before the primary assembly process, there's a good chance of causing some damage.

Black primer works well as a base for flames. It doesn't make a great deal of sense to paint flames on a primered car and then sand them off for the real color, but flames over primer often look great enough to keep as the final combination. A flame job will add a lot of impact to an otherwise plain car. If you don't like the

flames, they can removed much easier than if they were on a painted car.

Chassis Notes

A first class chassis is the foundation of a good street rod. The goal here is to pick top quality, time-tested parts without spending unnecessary money on extras. For example, you can get many suspension components in bare metal, chromed, or stainless steel. They all do the same job, but chrome and stainless cost more. Nicely painted steel parts look fine and you can also get them powder coated at reasonable prices.

Frame rails are the two outside steel beams that run from the very front of the chassis to the back of it. Original '32 Ford frame rails were "C" shaped with the open part of the channel facing the center of the chassis. Reproduction street rod frame rails are boxed (that is, the open side of the channel is filled with metal plate, so the cross-section is box-shaped) to better handle the weight and torsional forces of a modern V-8 drivetrain.

You can find some '32 chassis that are totally tubular, but those only work on a full fendered car. Even on a full fend-ered Deuce you could run into some resistance to the tubular frame when it comes time to sell the car. Your best bet is to use the authentic looking '32 frame rails. Authentic looking rails have all the original beads stamped into them.

A popular chassis trick is to use a Model A style front crossmember in a '32 frame. This lowers the front end an inch. Quality reproduction frames make sure the front crossmember is designed to provide the correct front-end geometry.

A dropped axle is another traditional means of getting the front of a street rod nice and low. We specified an I-beam axle, but a tube axle is equally acceptable. Items like the transverse front spring, tube shocks, and 4-link locator bars are part of the package needed to run a dropped front axle. Some builders use the more traditional hairpin radius rods in place of the 4-link bars, but the 4-link setup is more universal.

A 4-link system can also be used to locate the rearend. With a 4-link, coil-over shock absorbers take the place of conventional springs, and they can be

adjusted to modulate the firmness of the ride. A Panhard bar should be used to control lateral movement of the rearend. Basically, a Panhard bar attaches to the rearend housing on one side of the car, and the chassis on the other side. The rearend is free to move up and down, but not side-to-side. Generally, the longer the Panhard bar is, the better it works. If it's too short, the bar will actu-ally induce limited side-to-side move-ment as it swings through its arc of trav-el. A Panhard bar is also a good idea for the front suspension.

There are other rearend setups like a transverse rear spring with ladder bars to locate the rear axle housing; it's a very simple arrangement, but it's a little primitive and a little limited. The tried-and-true 4-link setup is our choice for a bolt-together street rod, because it's simple, very adjustable, and it offers the most clearance and flexibility for rout-ing exhaust.

Ford's ubiquitous 9-inch rearend is the default rearend for street rods, street machines, and racecars. The 9-inch Ford is to rearends what the small-block Chevy V-8 is to engines. Even diehard Chevy builders are apt to put a 9-inch Ford under their cars. There are other

There's a lot to be said for buying as many of your parts in one place, espe-cially when it comes to having the body factory fitted to the chassis. Harwood Street Rods offers basic bodies and com-plete rollers like this '32 highboy. (Harwood Street Rods)

variants of the popular Ford rearend, like the smaller 8-inch version. Unless you have a mega-horsepower engine, the 8-inch is probably fine. Still, we sug-gest sticking with the 9-inch because it is so universally accepted. People expect to find a Ford 9-inch in cars that don't have independent rear suspension.

A wide array of axle ratios can be used in the 9-inch rearend. Something in the low to mid-threes (3.00:1 to 3.50:1) is a good compromise between performance and economy. In a lightweight car like a Deuce highboy, you don't need 4.11:1 gears to launch it. Some people like gear ratios in the upper twos because they provide nice, quiet, low-rpm cruising at highway speeds and they give good fuel economy.

Part of the thrill of driving a street rod is its performance. Quickly leaving a stop light is what most people enjoy, not high speed, top end blasts. The lower the gear ratio (higher numerically), the quicker a car will leave the starting line. The problem with gears that are too low is that the engine runs at higher rpms. Extra steep gears can be noisy, which, depending on your viewpoint, is either annoying or the sound of a quick car. Lower rpms are easier on the engine and make for more comfortable cruising. That's why a gear ratio in the low to mid-threes is a good compromise.

Tire diameter affects the final gear ratio. Since street rods in general and highboys in particular favor rear tires that are considerably taller than the tires that came with the rearend, this factor must be considered. Extra tall tires have the effect of numerically lowering the final gear ratio (lower numerically); so a little number crunching needs to be done to obtain a gear ratio that's in the low to mid-threes.

Good brakes are important on any car, but even more so on a street rod. Street rod bumpers are marginal (if the car even has any) so you want to stop long before encountering any obstacle. Four-wheel disc brakes are great, but the standard front disc/rear drum combination works very well on a lightweight street rod. This combination is much more affordable than rear disc brakes. A dual master cylinder and a power brake booster are also good ideas.

Engine and Transmission Notes

Small-block Chevy V-8—that's almost all you need to know about selecting a street rod engine, at least the first time around. There are more desir-able and less desirable versions of this icon engine, but the small-block Chevy (most commonly the 5.7-liter, 350 cubic inch displacement model) is the default street rod engine. The small-block Chevy V-8 is like the Ford 9-inch rearend in its overwhelming popularity and availability.

People can talk until they're hoarse about their Chrysler Hemi engines, big-block Chevys, flathead Fords, Buick V-6's, and small-block Ford V-8's, but you can't get around the unparalleled popularity of the 350 Chevy. It's great to see unique street rod engines, but remember that unique usually means more difficult and expensive to build and maintain. Look all you want, but we'd recommend putting a 350 Chevy in your bolt-together street rod.

Everything about the aftermarket speed equipment industry is based around the small-block Chevy. If a particular part is made for anything, it's most likely the small-block Chevy. The ubiquity of the Chevy 350 extends far beyond the realm of street rods. Millions of cars and trucks were built with the 350. That's why if you're on a trip in your street rod and something breaks, your odds of finding replacement parts in the most out-of-the-way location are best with a Chevy 350. Besides parts availability, the engines are very reliable, easy to work on, affordable, and they fit well in street rods.

Modified small-block Chevys are common in street rods, but a good running stock version will provide ample

A first class chassis is a key element of any successful street rod. TCI Engineering is one of the giants of the street rod industry with over 25 years of chassis building experience. They offer everything from small components to complete chassis. (TCI)

When it comes to building near perfect highboys, it's hard to beat the multi-talented crew at So-Cal Speed Shop. As avid students of hot rod history, their parts reflect the best of classic styling and modern technology. This overhead shot shows their beautiful So-Cal windshield, which combines the flowing posts of a DuVall windshield and a single piece of glass. (So-Cal)

power for a '32 highboy roadster. The real world usable difference between a $1,000 Chevy 350 and a $10,000 one is so negligible that it doesn't make financial sense to spend the extra money on a first-time, bolt-together street rod. This Blueprint Deuce is a closed hood model anyway, so some exhaust headers and high performance mufflers will provide plenty of cruising level power. If you want a loping idle, install a more aggressive camshaft.

A closed hood street rod that sounds good provides the perception of power and in non-competitive situations like rod runs; perception is a big part of reality. If you're used to driving a standard-issue daily transportation module, a modest Chevy 350 in a '32 highboy will make you smile. A truly awesome engine can be frightening if you're not used to that kind of raw performance.

Along the lines of solid, reliable performance, our blueprint calls for a hydraulic lifter camshaft with a mild, RV type camshaft. The noisier solid lifter camshafts and the more radical grinds sound nasty with their ragged lope, but they can get old quickly when you're stuck in a long line waiting to get into a street rod event. An RV style camshaft provides a good combination of low-end torque and reasonable fuel economy.

A '32 Ford 3-window coupe is our first choice for a closed cab blueprint street rod. It combines the great hot rod style of the roadster and weather protection. This is a Harwood Street Rods '32 coupe roller package. (Harwood Street Rods)

Speaking of long lines and slow traffic, a street rod engine should be built to handle those conditions. Street rod events usually involve a fair amount of cruising, and with so many street rods (and even more spectators) at an event, lines are inevitable. Most street rod events are held in the warmer months, so a car that doesn't idle smoothly and won't stay cool isn't much fun.

A top quality street rod radiator is a must. Buy the most efficient radiator you can find. Some type of mechanical or electrical (or both, if possible) fan is important. Depending on how the motor mounts are set up, you may or may not have enough clearance to run a regular fan. A well-engineered fan shroud is a good idea. You want to get the most air where it's needed.

Some traditionalists insist on a manual transmission. To them, banging off shifts in a four-speed manual transmission is part of the whole hot rod mystique. The trouble with a 4-speed is the added linkage in an already snug chassis – it can be done, but it adds cost and complexity. An automatic transmission is a more realistic way to go in a bolt-together street rod. A good automatic transmission should be an install-it-and-forget-it proposition.

Another drawback to a manual transmission is the endless clutch action in heavy traffic and long lines. Creeping along in a parade of street rods can wear out your left leg.

It's easy to improve the performance of a modern automatic transmission. A simple shift kit will give quick, crisp shifts in a lightweight street rod. You can get the snap of a manual transmission if you want, or can soft-pedal it for easy shifts. A modern automatic overdrive transmission (with an appropriately geared rearend) can return excellent fuel economy along with brisk performance.

Several GM automatic transmissions will work well with a small-block Chevy. The old standby is the Turbo 350 3-speed automatic. The combination of this transmission with a small-block V-8 is known as a 350/350. The automatic transmission that's rapidly replacing the Turbo 350 is the GM 700-R4. It's an automatic overdrive transmission so you can run lower (higher numerically) gears for good off-the-line performance and cruise comfortably in overdrive.

Wheel and Tire Notes
Wheels and tires can make or break a street rod, and the importance of picking a good combination cannot be over-

looked. A beautiful car with goofy wheels and odd-sized tires will be ridiculed. Conversely, a rough rod with ideal wheels and tires will be much more venerated than its construction quality should warrant.

Wheel and tire selection affects the stance of a street rod. Stance is how the car sits, the relationship of the rear of the car to the front of it. Stance is one of the key ingredients of a successful street rod. The right stance on an affordable car will trump many, much more expensive modifications.

The right wheel and tire combination doesn't have to be expensive. Solid steel wheels are very acceptable if they are the right size and offset and mounted on the ideal tires. We prefer alloy wheels because they add sparkle to a vehicle that has very little bright work. Another great thing about polished alloy wheels is how visible they are since the wheels and tires are completely exposed on a highboy.

Wheels are a matter of personal taste, but if you want to build an instantly acceptable icon rod, certain wheels are much safer bets than others. An affordable custom wheel that has been around since the late fifties in various incarnations is the American Racing Torq-Thrust five spoke mag wheel. The wheel has always been popular, but it has enjoyed a tremendous upswing the last several years.

It's possible to spend a lot of money on certain Torq-Thrust wheels, but the entry level Torq-Thrust II wheels look great and they're very reasonably priced. Custom wheel experts may argue about the particular spoke design, but to most people, a Torq-Thrust wheel is a Torq-Thrust wheel. This is another example of where careful shopping can give you a product that accomplishes 95% of what the most expensive version does, but at a fraction of the cost.

Highboy rear tires tend to be rather tall because they need to be proportioned correctly to the rear wheel radius shape on the side of the body. Even full fendered deuces need tall rear tires so they fill the fender. Many street rodders are incorporating high-tech, ultra low-profile tires with huge diameter wheels (like twenty inches) on their cars. The super low sidewall aspect ratios make these tires look like rubber bands wrapped around massive billet wheels.

High tech, big diameter wheels and tires aren't right for a bolt-together highboy. Besides being contrary to the traditional styling of highboys, they're very expensive. They could turn out to be an expensive fad, but traditional "big 'n' little" wheels and tires will always be a street rod standard.

Highboy front tires need to have aspect ratios similar to the rear tires so their appearance is consistent. Front tires are noticeably shorter and narrower than the rear ones. Just how far one takes the small front tire is a matter of taste. We suggest sticking with a tire that's on the upper end of the acceptable range. Slightly larger front tires have the advantage of more road contact and better braking than skinny little tires.

Interior Notes

The interior of a '32 Ford highboy is one place that you can save money, at least initially. A beautiful leather interior is always appreciated and admired, but rodders tend to be much more forgiving about interiors than the rest of the car. There's even a little bit of reverse snobbery about having an obviously unfinished interior. A Mexican blanket draped over a simple bench seat says you were more anxious to get out and drive than you were to build a trailer queen.

The proliferation of small Moon tanks mounted in front of the grille is a tribute to the days when Deuces were raced at the drag strip. These small fuel tanks are usually empty nowadays. The front of this highboy illustrates several other features including a drilled I-beam axle (another competition styling element), small King Bee headlights, and a working cowl vent.

Street rods aren't nearly as comfortable as modern passenger cars or trucks, so maybe an unfinished interior isn't what you want. The key to an affordable, comfortable interior that's peer group acceptable is to keep it simple. There are excellent aftermarket seat frames designed to provide maximum legroom and comfort. Some seats are available already upholstered. A simple bench seat provides the maximum seating area and it's easy to get in and out. Door panels should match the seats. Again, a simple fabric or a basic roll and pleat pattern is a safe way to go.

Ample insulation will make a car cooler and quieter. You're in close proximity to the engine, transmission, and highway. All of these things can generate lots of heat. Don't skimp on installing first class insulation materials on every possible surface. Heat and noise are rather insidious; they tend to find their way through the smallest openings.

Seat belts are a must. People don't tend to put a lot of miles on their street rods and they usually drive them during nice weather, so you don't hear of many street rod accidents. Still, you're quite

exposed in a roadster so don't omit seat belts. Street rod owners tend to be extra careful when they're driving their cars, but you have to watch out for "civilians" that tend to drift into you as they gawk at your car. The body may be fiberglass, but you'd think it was a giant magnet the way a street rod attracts other vehicles.

As an example of the latitude in building supposedly "cookie cutter" cars, consider these two 3-window Deuce coupes. A chopped top, hidden hinges, smooth running boards, a filled grille shell, no bumpers, and white wall tires with baby moon hubcaps makes a slick combination on example number one.

Deuce coupe number two has a stock height roof, chrome windshield frame, exposed hinges, rubber running board covers, a stock grille shell with the Ford oval emblem, cowl lights, bumpers, and polished Torq-Thrust mag wheels. Both cars are similar, but distinctive.

It's also possible to build a '29 highboy on Deuce rails with a modern flavor. Larger diameter wheels and low profile tires go a long ways toward changing the car's character.

A tilt steering column should be considered mandatory. It will allow you to vary your driving position. Some street rods are a snug fit and a tilt steering column makes it easier to get in and out. Some people still use tilt columns out of wrecked cars, but it's easier to get one of the new aftermarket columns that were designed especially for street rods. The inner parts are all new, which is so much better than dealing with a 200,000-mile wrecking yard column. These columns are available in paintable steel, chrome, and aluminum. They're available with or without a column shifter.

Regarding shifters, our suggestion is to put it on the steering column. That will give you the most available floor space. Floor mount shifters that look like vintage manual transmission shifters

Mounting a '28/'29 Model A roadster body on a '32 chassis is a classic highboy combination that can cost less, because Model A bodies cost less. This A V-8 has a Model A grille, which gives a whole different flavor to the combination. The flathead engine and Kelsey-Hayes wire wheels are other vintage touches.

are very popular for automatic transmissions, but they take up more space than column shifters. Whatever style of shifter you use, it must include a neutral safety switch.

A relatively small, but not too small, diameter leather trimmed steering wheel will make driving the car more pleasant. You need a small enough steering wheel for easy ingress and egress, but you don't want one that's so small that you don't have much steering leverage. Power steering is rare on highboy street rods.

Simple is great when it comes to the dashboard. Analog gauges are widely accepted, traditional, easy to install, and easy to read. The six gauges to use are speedometer, tachometer, oil pressure, water temperature, fuel level, and voltmeter. A dashboard with a dozen obscure gauges looks like an airplane cockpit and it's a waste of money. Digital gauges aren't always the easiest ones to read in the kind of bright sunlight encountered in an open car.

Clean and simple applies to the sound system as well as the dashboard. There's nothing wrong with putting the stereo control unit in the dash, but it looks cleaner if it's under the dash or totally hidden and controlled with a remote. Some clever rodders make a stereo unit that drops down from behind the dash and then retracts to maintain the smooth look. Other people build them into the seat riser.

There are also units that have the CD disc slot in the dashboard with all the guts hidden behind the dash. A stereo or CD player of some kind is a must, because cruising and classic rock-and-roll music are meant for each other. A very nice feature for open cars is where the stereo volume rises and lowers with the surrounding noise. This great feature is found on many late model GM cars like Corvettes and Camaros. That way you can hear the music on the freeway and not hurt your ears when you slow down.

Option A Notes

Following the above blueprint, but substituting a '32 coupe body is a fine idea if you don't like to be so exposed to the elements. A coupe will be warmer

(and definitely drier) if the weather should suddenly change, but it will also be warmer in hot weather unless you install air conditioning.

Air conditioning is a good reason to build a closed car. Americans have become so accustomed to air-conditioned cars, that they almost take it for granted. If you're one of these weather lightweights, don't be ashamed to install A/C.

In its basic form, a reproduction fiberglass coupe body will cost a little more than a roadster, but if you add a top to the roadster, costs will be closer. Coupes have more glass and the mechanisms to make the side windows work, whereas roadsters have only a windshield. There is the added cost of a headliner in a coupe when it comes time to upholster the car.

If you were inclined to build a deuce coupe, we'd give the popularity edge to the 3-window version over the 5-window model. Both are fine, but the 3-window is a little sleeker. The 5-window coupe has the strong "American Graffiti" tie-in. With either coupe, a modest top chop helps give that hot rod look.

Option B Notes

Deuce highboys are our first pick because they're less involved and less expensive than full fendered cars, but there's nothing wrong with build a bolt-together street rod with fenders. There are many practical reasons to use fenders and in some areas, fenders are a legal requirement.

Deuce fenders are very handsome with a great flow from the front to the running boards. Fenders will enhance the low look of a properly set up deuce. They keep debris off the body for easier maintenance.

Fenders raise the cost and complexity of a project. Besides the additional costs of the fenders, running boards, and related braces, there's more surface area to prep and paint. Fitting the fenders and running boards to the body is much more involved because there are many parts that have to be adjusted. The more components you have, the more involved it is to adjust body seams and gaps. Every time you adjust one part, it changes the

A key element of building a '29 on '32 rails is the right set of rails. The So-Cal speed shop's A-V8 highboy chassis is specially contoured to match the narrow Model A cowl. The rear of the frame rails are also narrowed slightly for a proper body fit. (So-Cal Speed Shop)

relationship between several more parts.

There's nothing wrong with a full-fendered street rod. For your first street rod consider building it as a highboy first and adding fenders later if you still want them. Adding fenders at a later date will significantly change the personality of the car. That's an easy way to change the car without much work or a large investment.

BLUEPRINT TWO: THE '29 MODEL A ROADSTER ON DEUCE RAILS

Our second blueprint for success is a variation on our first choice. With the exception of the body, everything else is virtually the same as a deuce highboy roadster. Model A Fords were built in far greater quantities than '32 Fords since they had a four year run. The combination of the smaller, lighter, more plentiful '28-'29 Model A roadster body on the factory V-8 chassis of the '32 Ford was known as an A-V8. That term is still used along with Model A highboy and an A on Deuce rails.

The primary reason for someone to pick the model A highboy over a similar deuce is styling. Some people just prefer the classic hot rod look of this combina-

tion. Model A parts are slightly less expensive than '32 parts, but that difference could easily wash out when it comes time to sell the A.

A big thing to remember about an A-V8 is the noticeably smaller Model A cockpit. The first series Model A's, 1928-29, have more of a pinched cowl than the second series, 1930-31. The narrow cowl seems to be an extension of the 1927 Model T's styling. Before you start buying Model A parts, you should try to sit in several Model A and '32 roadsters. See if the difference matters to you.

Body

All the body suggestions listed for the deuce highboy apply to the Model A. The firewall needs to be recessed to clear a small-block distributor. When fiberglass manufacturers build an A body for use on a '32 chassis they usually modify the floor pan to fit the '32 frame.

Unless the stock cowl gas tank location is used, the cowl should be filled. We've never liked the idea of having ten gallons of gas right above our legs, but if you don't use the stock location on a highboy, you have to sacrifice some trunk space to the gas tank. Even though a '32 chassis is used, the stock rear-

mounted deuce gas tank isn't usually installed on a '29 A-V8.

Special hoods are available to mate the model A cowl to the deuce grille shell. Using a '32 Ford grille shell is part of the A-V8 look. How the hood, grille, and cowl line up are critical visual elements of an A-V8. The goal is a smoother than stock look for the Model A.

Chassis

In order to get the correct look when a Model A roadster body is mounted on a '32 frame, the frame rails need to be narrowed at the cowl. The '29 Model A cowl is noticeably narrower than the '32 cowl. The rear of the deuce frame is also wider than the A body, so the chassis should be narrowed the appropriate amount. Getting a chassis that's designed for an A-V8 is one of those seemingly minor things that make a big difference in the finished car. Paying attention to these details is what separates the "almost there" car from one that's right on.

Some street rod companies seem to really understand what it takes to make the ideal chassis for an A-V8. The So-Cal Speed Shop is one of those companies. When you're building a hybrid

Probably one of the best known street rods ever is this '34 Ford 3-window coupe built by Pete Chapouris (current president of So-Cal Speed Shop), which starred in the made-for-TV movie, "The California Kid." The chopped top and bold flames are classic hot rod touches.

car, little style and fit details make the difference between a so-so car and a great one.

Engine/Transmission, Rearend, Wheels, Tires

The suggested parts for the deuce highboy engine, transmission, wheels, tires, and interior apply to the A-V8. The smaller interior makes picking the right seat profile even more important than it is in a '32 roadster. Things are a little tighter for anyone desiring a manual transmission, although that was the only transmission used in the original A-V8 hot rods.

Option A: Full-Fendered Model A

The best way to save over the cost of a Deuce is to build a Model A with a Model A chassis. It's best to build a full-fendered car because the exposed A frame rails don't have the good looks of the '32 rails. Highboys have been built on Model A frames, but they're not a mainstream car. That might seem like a nit-picky point, but that's the kind of thing that make one car an icon and the other just another street rod.

The savings realized by building a full fendered Model A over a similar '32 could amount to a couple thousand dol-

Five window coupes trail the three window models in the popularity race, but that doesn't mean they don't make neat hot rods. This wild '33 coupe has a blown big-block Chevy for power and rolls on a set of classic big 'n' little Halibrand Sprint wheels.

lars. Generally speaking, the '32 will return that difference when it gets sold, but if your budget is really tight, a carefully configured A roadster could make the difference between being on the road or still stuck in the garage.

An open car is your best Model A bet. There are fiberglass A coupes, but they're quite a ways down on the popularity charts. The '29 Model A roadster pickup is as popular (if not more so) than the regular '29 roadster body. There are '30-'31 Model A roadster pickups, but they don't have the same following as the first series A's.

A unique Model A body style that looks good as either an A-V8 highboy or a full fendered car is the '30-'31 two-door phaeton or touring. These cars look particularly good with a '32 hood and grille.

BLUEPRINT THREE: THE '33-'34 FORD HIGHBOY

The 1933 and 1934 Fords are very handsome cars. Their grilles are more streamlined than the upright grilles of Model A's and '32 Fords. The gracefully slanted grilles start a theme that continues through the hood and cowl. The front fenders have pronounced splash aprons that give a much different look than the more open '32 fenders.

Both '33-'34 roadsters and coupes are very popular street rods. We've split the billing on this blueprint because the coupes are just as popular as the roadsters. A case could easily be made that the coupes are more popular than the roadsters. A chopped 3-window coupe has that rebellious hot rod image, helped in part by the media attention garnered by the flamed '34 coupe in the movie, "The California Kid."

The '33/'34 series cars are a little larger and slightly more expensive than the '32 Fords. Their popularity and acceptability is top notch. They're definitely icon street rods.

Our first blueprint suggestion is a '33/'34 highboy roadster or coupe simply because of the lower costs and lesser complexity than full fendered cars. If it wasn't for the added costs, we'd pick the full fendered '33/'34 over the highboy versions. The fenders go well with the slick styling of these cars.

Body

- 1933/34 Ford reproduction fiberglass roadster or coupe body.
- Chopped top on coupe.
- Hidden hinges.
- Reverse hinged rumble seat deck lid on roadster
- Conventional trunk opening for coupe.
- Remote deck lid latch.
- Shaved door handles, remote door solenoids for coupes.
- Stock style roadster windshield posts.

The smooth look works very well with '33/'34 Ford 3-window coupes. A chopped top, smooth hood panels, smooth running boards and lack of bumpers all contribute to the car's slick styling.

TCI makes '33/'34 Ford chassis with dropped front axles or independent front suspension. The IFS works great with full-fendered cars, but it is more expensive. The rear suspension on this chassis consists of equal length trailing arms, coil-over shocks, a 9-inch Ford rearend, and a Panhard bar. (TCI)

- Solid hood panels, 3-piece metal hood.
- Reproduction '34 grille shell and grille bars.
- Stock location gas tank.
- No bumpers.
- Stock style headlights.
- Paint: primer, semi-gloss black (with or without flames), bright red or yellow.

Chassis

- 1934 Ford reproduction steel frame with boxing plates.
- Full length frame horns.
- Tubular crossmembers.
- Dropped front axle, I-beam or tubular.
- Transverse front spring with reversed eyes.
- Parallel 4-link suspension, front and back.
- Power front disc brakes.
- Rear drum brakes.
- Brake proportioning valve.
- Front tube shocks.
- Rear coil over shocks.
- Panhard bars.
- Ford 9-inch rearend with 3.00:1 to 3.70:1 axle ratio.
- GM steering box.

Engine and Transmission

- 350 cubic inch small-block Chevy V-8.
- Fuel injected or single four-barrel carb on performance intake.
- Conservative, RV-style, hydraulic lifter camshaft.
- Compact, gear reduction starter.

- Exhaust headers with small diameter primary pipes.
- GM 700R4 automatic overdrive transmission.
- Shift improver kit.
- Transmission cooler.
- Heavy-duty radiator with A/C condenser provisions.
- Fan shroud.

Wheels and Tires

- Oversized rear tires, tall and relatively wide blackwall radials.
- Shorter, narrower front tires with high aspect ratio.
- Rear wheels 15x8, 15x10, 16x8, or 16x10.
- Front wheels 15x6 or 14x6.
- Five spoke Torq-Thrust style mags or slotted, Halibrand style mag wheels.

Interior

- Bench seat for roadster, bench or bucket seats for coupe.
- Vinyl or tweed upholstery in black, gray, or tan.
- Seats belts. Three point shoulder harnesses in coupe.
- Analog gauges: speedometer, tachometer, oil pressure, water temperature, fuel gauge, voltmeter.
- New, GM style tilt steering column.
- Leather rimmed steering wheel.
- Custom wiring kit.
- Hidden or remote control sound system.

Option A: full-fendered

- Same components as highboy roadster or coupe, but with full fenders and running boards.

Option B: Cabriolet or 5-window coupes

- Cabriolet or 5-window coupe bodies on either highboy chassis or full-fendered version. Cabriolet should be full-fendered.

Body Notes

The 3-window coupe body has a considerable edge over a 5-window coupe. Chopped tops can be had in either a straight windshield post style or a slanted post style. Straight chops are usually 2 to 2 1/2 inches. Slant chops are usually 3 inches. There are many variations on 3-window coupe top chops including ones that rework the rear corners of the roof. For a bolt-together street rod, stick with the chop that comes with the fiberglass body.

Hidden hinges are suggested, but stock style hinges and door handles are quite acceptable on coupes. All '33-'34 coupe and roadster bodies have suicide doors, so some sort of safety lock, such as a dead-bolt, is necessary for the doors. The rumble style rear deck lid is great for roadsters because it allows a rumble seat to be added later. Rumble seats on coupes aren't as common as they are on roadsters so a conventionally hinged deck lid is suggested.

The stock style gas tank isn't as traditional on '33/'34 highboys as it is on '32 highboys. Many builders like to place the gas tank in the trunk or install one behind a rolled rear pan. This makes for a smoother, cleaner rear view. This option exposes the rear axle housing, which is good if there is something trick to see, and not as good if the rearend is strictly functional.

The grilles and hoods are slightly different between the two years. The 1933 grille bars have a curved profile and a more slender rim, and the hood sides have curved louvers. The 1934 grill bars have a straight profile, and the hood louvers are straight. It's a matter of personal preference. Before the advent of

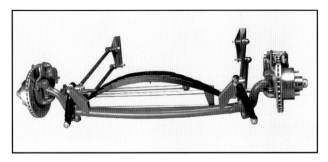

Chrome and polished stainless steel parts are nice, but there's nothing wrong with a painted dropped tube front axle with a 4-link setup. Using quality suspension parts is more important than using flashy parts. (TCI)

reproduction grilles, nice, undamaged '33 grilles seemed to be harder to find than '34 grilles. Solid hood panels are suggested because of their paint prep ease, but hoods with hot rod louvers are very acceptable. The louvers work especially well with chopped coupes that have a drag racing flavor.

The big, stock style headlights work well with the larger features of the '33/'34 bodies. Smaller aftermarket headlights are also fine. Taillight choices include '39 Ford teardrop style, rectangular '41-'48 Chevy units, or recessed LED lights in the panel beneath the deck lid. Even stock style taillights and brackets are OK.

Bright red paint is always a winner, but bright yellow is quite popular on these cars. Primer or semi-gloss black fits very well on chopped coupes because it ties in with that rough, hot rod image. Flames are always good. The "California Kid" did a lot to popularize bold flames on '33/'34 Ford coupes.

Chassis Notes

Highboy chassis for '33/'34 Fords are very similar to those used on '32 highboys. There are varying schools of thought regarding the frame horns. The rear frame horns are mandatory when the stock style gas tank is used, but they're generally cut off when the gas tank is mounted in the trunk.

A slightly lower rear axle ratio was listed because these cars tend to be a little heavier than deuces and Model A's. The heavier a car is, the more power it takes for a quick launch. Lower gears (higher numerically, like 4.11:1 instead of 3.50:1) help give you that quick kick feeling.

Engine and Transmission Notes

Small-block Chevys rule in '33/'34 Fords, just like every other street rod,

but big-block Chevys tend to be a little more prevalent in these cars. A big-block 454 built along the same lines as the small-block suggestions would provide extra torque for those hot rod starts. A higher (lower numerically) rear axle ratio could be used because the big-block's extra torque compensates for the less aggressive gears.

Wheel and Tire Notes

All highboys favor big, tall rear tires and this is particularly true on '33/34 Fords. As with the '32 Fords, the rear tires need to work with the fender styling bead in the rear quarter panels. Given the large area there is to work with, 16-inch diameter wheels work well on these cars.

Torq-Thrust mags are always an excellent wheel choice, but so are several versions of the slotted mag. Real Halibrand wheels can be a little expensive, but there are several wheels from other manufacturers that approximate that classic hot rod look. A wheel that's popular on 3-window coupe highboys is the deep, big window (or slot) ET III mag wheel. These wheels tie in with the drag racing theme favored by many 3-window coupes. When these wheels are used in back, some builders use a smaller version in front while others use the ten spoke wheel that's also made by ET.

Wider rear tires work better on these cars than deuces and Model A's. Some builders recess the wheel wells to accommodate super wide rubber, but this needs to be done judiciously in order to avoid the "wall of rubber" Pro/Street look.

Interior Notes

The same concepts of simplicity, comfort, and ample insulation that were

stated for deuces also apply to the '33/'34 Fords. A bench seat is always fine, but we're a little more inclined to recommend bucket seats in the coupes. Air conditioning is almost mandatory in the rather close confines of a chopped three-window coupe.

Option A Notes

There's something about the full fendered '33/'34 Fords that many rodders find extremely appealing. The fenders are very graceful and smooth flowing. The front fenders in particular work very well with an "in-the-weeds" stance. The splash apron part of the fender puts the fender closer to the ground, which accentuates a good rake. On a full fendered car, the stock gas tank location should be used.

Full fendered cars can't use as wide or as tall of a rear tire as the highboy versions. The tires need to adequately fill the fenders, but not overly so.

Option B Notes

Reproduction 5-window '33/'34 coupe bodies aren't as available as the more popular 3-window bodies. There is a larger popularity gap between the 3-window and 5-window '33/'34 coupes than with the '32 coupes. There's nothing wrong with a 5-window coupe, but they just don't seem as sleek as a chopped 3-window coupe.

A better choice than a 5-window coupe might be a '33/'34 Cabriolet. These cars are an excellent compromise between an open car and a closed one. Cabriolets have fixed windshields, roll-up side windows, and a convertible top. They are much more like modern convertibles than basic roadsters. The added complexity of the roll-up windows and the convertible top make the cabriolets significantly more expensive than roadsters, though. Cabriolets trail roadsters in popularity and ease of reselling, and they have more of a resto-rod look than the hot rod look of a roadster or a 3-window coupe.

We think any of the above mentioned blueprint cars would make an excellent first street rod. By looking at the popularity of these cars, it's apparent that many street rodders agree.

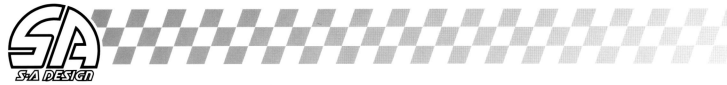

RESALE REALITIES

It might seem odd to be talking about selling a car before it's even built, but if you plan wisely with reselling in mind, the whole experience will be much more enjoyable. When it comes to cars, street rodders are a bunch of philandering, lust-crazed, Neanderthals with very short attention spans. They have no qualms about drooling over some tarted-up, topless roadster with big headlights and loud pipes right in front of their first street rod, the one they swore they'd be true to forever.

People who stick with one car for decades are rare. Even those who do keep a favorite for years aren't ashamed to add one or more mistresses to their garage. Many street rodders enjoy the planning, acquisition, and building as much as the owning and driving of a car. That's why it's common to see recently completed street rods for sale. The challenge of building the last car is over and it's time to move on to a new project. Street rods encompass such a tremendous variety of vehicles, that there's no reason to ever be bored.

Understanding this resale mentality before you start on your first bolt-together street rod will save a lot of emotional and financial heartaches later on. Street rods are as much about attitude as they are about transportation. When you go into a project with your eyes wide open, you're less likely to run into problems. As we keep reiterating, street rodding should be fun and problems aren't fun. Minimize the problems and you'll maximize the fun.

BUILDING FOR RESALE

If you plan your first street rod with resale in mind, you'll be ahead even if you keep the car for a long time. Just because resale factors are part of the plan, that doesn't mean you'll sell the car as soon as it's finished. By having several contingencies, you're not locked into a particular plan. When you have escape plans, it's easier to relax and enjoy the project.

Take a look around at any street rod gathering and count the number of cars that are for sale. There aren't that many bad cars or owners who want out of street rodding. There are just a lot of people who want to build something different and they need to sell their current car, either to finance the next one or to make room in their garage.

In addition to all the cars that are obviously for sale, the vast majority of the others can be had "for the right price." Street rodders love to engage in hypothetical conversations like, "Have you ever considered selling your car? What would it take to talk you out of this beauty? If you ever decide to sell, call me first." Given this Baghdad

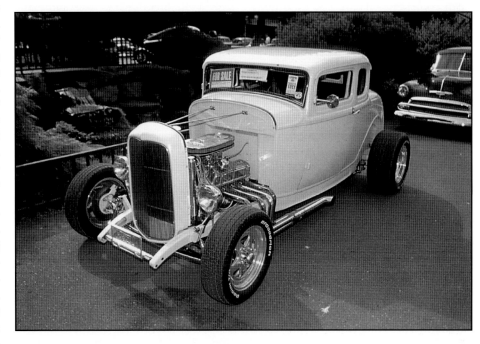

Within the '32 Ford spectrum, there is a popularity hierarchy. Roadsters and 3-window coupes top the list, but 5-window coupes are also popular. This coupe was done in the style of the American Graffiti coupe, but it has a small-block Ford engine.

Popularity is street rod equivalent to location in real estate. Make your first street rod a popular one like a '32 Ford roadster and if you decide to sell, your chances of a sale are greatly improved.

Bazaar atmosphere at street rod events, buying and selling cars is only natural. Your goal is to be in a favorable position should you decide to sell your car.

The notion that you'll keep a particular car forever is a myth or, at least a way to rationalize spending too much. Times change, family situations change, you take up camel racing, you get transferred to Iceland, or whatever. The point is, don't go into a street rod project with the idea that you'll keep the car forever. Even if it's the car you've been dreaming about for 30 years, don't plan on long-term ownership. If you end up driving to your funeral in the car, great, just don't make that assumption up front.

POPULARITY, POPULARITY, POPULARITY

In real estate, the three most important factors for buying or selling a home are location, location, location. In street rodding, the three most important factors for excellent resale potential are popularity, popularity, popularity. If affordability can be added in either situation, you've got an instant winner.

Build a popular car without spending too much money and you'll have a street rod that's as liquid as any car of this nature can be. Popularity and affordability are two key concepts that run throughout this book. We can't stress them enough if you want to make this experience as financially painless as possible.

Popularity alone won't guarantee resale potential. There are plenty of mega-buck street rods that almost any-

one would love to own, but very few can actually afford them. As with almost any product, the larger your potential audience, the easier it is to sell the item. The bigger the pool of potential buyers is, the quicker a car should sell. A big group of potential buyers promotes quick sales because of the real or perceived competition from other buyers.

Popularity is a very pervasive concept in building a street rod with excellent resale potential. It's not enough to pick a popular year, make, and model. The major components of the car also have to adhere to pretty arbitrary popularity precepts. That's why the blueprints for success suggestions are so rigid. There are a lot of unwritten rules in street rodding that can have a big affect on a car's salability.

A deuce roadster with army camouflage paint, studded snow tires, a diesel engine, and a splintered wood "bench" seat is obviously going to be difficult to sell for much more than salvage value. Yet, it doesn't take anything nearly that ridiculous to hamper a sale. A red '32 Ford roadster with a 2.8-liter Chevy V-6, automatic transmission, and white bucket seats will be a much more difficult car to sell than an essentially identical vehicle with a 5.7-liter Chevy V-8, automatic transmission, and black bucket seats.

How can such seemingly insignificant differences affect the car's sales

This chopped 5-window coupe looks very similar to the coupe on the previous page, but it would be more difficult to sell because it's a '31 Model A on a Model A chassis. It probably wasn't much less expensive to build than the '32, but those savings could easily be lost when it comes time to sell.

potential? It's a matter of popularity and perception. People expect to find a small-block Chevy V-8 in a '32 Ford. It doesn't matter that the builder chose the little V-6 because of its superior fuel economy. The vast majority of street rodders value performance over fuel economy. Decent mileage is always a plus, but it's the performance of a small-block Chevy that they expect. The V-6 powered street rod is perceived as a much less desirable car than the same vehicle with a V-8.

This '32 Ford has a lot going for it except that it's a 4-door sedan. It's probably a fine family street rod, but it's not a winner in the financial department. It can easily cost as much (or more) to build a Fordor as a roadster, and the market for 4-door sedans is limited.

Installing a small-block Chevy V-8 in the first place would have cost about the same. Even though removing the V-6 and replacing it with a V-8 is relatively simple, most potential buyers will seek a car with a V-8 already installed. If they buy the car as is, they'll expect a substantial discount for making the swap themselves.

White upholstery is far less popular than black, gray, or tan. It wouldn't be difficult to replace the white bucket seats with some black ones or even have the white ones dyed black. Still, the perception of the car is less positive because of the less popular upholstery color.

If the only thing that will stabilize the orbit of your little world is a 2.8-liter V-6, white bucket seats, and tiger-striped carpeting, go ahead and build a car that way. Just remember to accept the consequences of your unique choices if the car should prove difficult to sell. It's your car and you need to do what makes you happy, but if minor compromises would make the car far more salable, look at the big picture and consider going with the popular parts.

A person could build a car with a little V-6 and then install a V-8 when it came time to sell. The trouble with that plan is that it wastes money. If one of your goals with a bolt-together street rod is to keep spending under control, don't waste money re-doing things. Any time part of the car has to be redone, that's money down a cosmic rat hole, lost forever to a nebula of broken parts and exasperated expectations.

AFFORDABLE QUALITY

Affordability has to be tempered with quality. Your average street rod buyer doesn't shop by price alone. They don't want a pile of cheap, low-grade, poor-fitting parts regardless of how affordable it is. The trick is to buy quality parts where they count most without wasting money on superfluous items. This concept is detailed in other chapters including the one on blueprints for success.

Another way of looking at the affordability/popularity concept is to use parts that meet the minimum standard of acceptability, but don't go any farther above that than absolutely necessary. There is a very noticeable diminishing returns factor in high priced parts.

Paint and bodywork are a prime example of what we're talking about. Everyone admires a flawless paint job, but far fewer people are willing to pay

Everything about this Deuce coupe is first class. It's trick from front to back and top to bottom, but all that flash doesn't always translate into resale cash. There is a point of diminishing returns on trick parts.

It's also possible to drive too close to the curb on Cheap Street. Unless you're building a period-perfect fifties or sixties rod, potential buyers expect a certain level of sophistication like front disc brakes rather than drum brakes.

the high price tag attached to perfection. Street rod magazines feature stunning cars that are metal working masterpieces. Sometimes it seems like every square inch of the car was tweaked or altered in some fashion.

Many of those modifications are very subtle. The main thing you see is a beautiful car even if you don't know what it is that makes it so attractive. The car needs to be parked next to a totally stock-bodied version to make all the changes obvious, and you could still overlook modifications that cost thousands of dollars.

Top-notch street rods can easily have more money invested in paint and bodywork than the total cost of building a bolt-together street rod like this book advocates. Usually people who spend such large sums on their cars don't need or expect to recoup the money. If you were in that financial realm, you'd probably be out enjoying your professionally built street rod instead of reading about how not to take a financial bath in a fiberglass '32 Ford tub.

Sticking with the paint and bodywork analogy, going to the opposite extreme doesn't make sense, either. Poorly done paint and bodywork is worse than none at all. A bad paint job is a liability. It costs much more to strip and repaint a car than to start with the bare body. A bad paint job can easily kill a potential sale.

We're very big on leaving a bolt-together street rod in primer for a while. It's a good idea to drive the car in primer

to see if anything settles or needs to be adjusted before it's painted. If a fiberglass body was cured, prepped, and primed with quality materials, that's a usable base for whatever the next owner may decide to do. It's also work that will benefit you if you keep the car.

Doing the body prep work, adjusting gaps, aligning styling lines, and applying the correct primer/surfacer adds value to a street rod. That's an example of doing the minimum, quality work without overspending. There's a good chance that you will recoup most of the money spent on preparing a body for paint.

A street rod chassis and engine are littered with financial land mines. It's so easy to overspend by "hundred-dollaring" yourself to death. If a particular suspension part costs only a hundred dollars more in chrome, that doesn't seem like a bank-breaker. It might be only another hundred dollars to step up to a stainless steel version of the part. Again, no big deal, or at least, not until this hundred dollar hike repeats itself dozens of times.

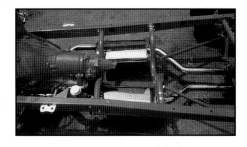

Don't expect to recoup your investment on overkill features like a fully polished stainless steel exhaust system. A well-designed system that doesn't hang too low is all you need.

Street rodders are always impressed with beautiful chrome or stainless steel components. They may gladly spend the extra money for those parts on their own car, but they won't spend the full difference when they're trying to buy your car. The same high quality component in its base steel form will get the job done every bit as well as the show quality stainless steel version. A little paint on the steel part will make it perfectly acceptable. The car is still a well-built

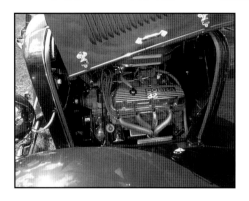

A small-block Ford engine often costs more than an equivalent small-block Chevy, yet most buyers greatly prefer Chevy power. For best resale value, stick with a 350 Chevy.

rod with quality components. It's just a little low on flash, but that can always be added later.

It's false economy to put drum brakes on the front of a street rod. People expect front disc brakes. They like rear disc brakes, too, but rear drums are still very acceptable. Super powerful aftermarket disc brakes with huge diameter rotors are high status items. They work wonderfully and they look great with the exposed suspension components of a highboy. The trouble with trick brakes is that they cost a great deal and its money that isn't easily recouped.

The difference in stopping power between the super brakes and the standard disc brakes that come with street rod chassis isn't too obvious under the easy driving conditions that most rods see. There's no doubt that the high performance brakes are superior, but the new, basic disc brakes easily meet expectations and are perfectly safe. This is a good example of buying quality components that are expected, but not overspending.

MODULAR MONEY MATTERS

How you manage your finances is your business, but we have a suggestion that can spread out the cost of building a street rod while making it easy to bail out on short notice. The concept is modular purchases. Instead of buying the vast majority of components at one time, buy what you need to complete various sub-assemblies.

Unless a street rod company offers you a package deal that's just too attractive to pass up, buying parts piecemeal isn't a bad idea. Besides spreading out the costs, you won't be crowded by a lot of parts that aren't needed right away.

You should adhere to the popularity precepts that we've been advocating. By picking your parts and sub-assemblies carefully, you'll have completed units that will eventually comprise the finished car, but could also be sold earlier if necessary.

An example of this modular concept is to start with the chassis. Let's say the car is a '32 Ford roadster. A '32 chassis works with any '32 body, so a deuce chassis is always a big demand item. If you installed the front and rear suspension systems (using affordable, but high quality parts) and then decided that building a street rod wasn't for you, you've still got a very salable item. Many companies sell complete chassis (less wheels and tires) so you'd be selling a very common and desirable sub-assembly.

If, after building the chassis, you're still enthused, move on to the next sub-assembly. The engine and transmission would be a good choice. If you needed to bail out after the engine was built and installed, you'd have a very universal combination that's always in demand. If you had a relatively minor financial emergency, you could sell the engine and put the project on hold until you could afford to get going again.

When you have a completed chassis and running gear, the next logical step is the body. The body can be the most expensive component so you're taking a

Unless you plan to run without a body, don't waste your time and money on things as excessive as a fully polished transmission case. A decent coat of gloss paint will serve just fine.

big step here. Still, you could stop at this point and sell the body and chassis or just the body by itself. There's usually a substantial waiting time for popular fiberglass bodies so it shouldn't be too hard to find another builder who will give you what you paid for your body (as long as you haven't altered it in some unusual way).

You will most likely lose a little when you sell an unfinished street rod.

The builder of this '32 roadster decided to sell before the car was finished. He did well to get it running without spending money on paint or upholstery. The supercharged engine could have been replaced with a less impressive unit to lower costs.

You can pretty well expect that your labor was free, but you were building the car for fun anyway. Even with the strong possibility of losing some of your investment, this financial scenario is much better than most hobbies.

As part of the planning stage, we recommend keeping detailed financial records for a variety of reasons. If you have a running total, anytime you're tempted to sell (or forced to sell) you'll know exactly where you stand financially. That can help you set a fair price and know when an offer is unreasonable. Knowing what you've invested may also make you rethink selling the car. If you're really close to the end of the big purchases, you might be able to find a way to push on to the finish.

By carefully planning your street rod and sticking with well-proven, popular, high-quality parts you should always have something that's pretty easy to sell. Hopefully, you won't want or need to quit before the car is finished, but knowing that you could without suffering major financial setbacks is reassuring.

DO-IT-YOURSELF, OR CALL IN THE PROS?

A good way to avoid problems is to know your limitations. If you get in over your head, you can sabotage the whole project. Careful planning should help you avoid most mistakes, as should sticking with the most complete sub-assemblies possible.

It's great to expand your skills. Hopefully, building a street rod will do just that. The key is to expand those skills gradually. As you master each new process, you'll gain the confidence to tackle ever more complicated tasks.

You're much better off seeking professional help before you mess up rather than afterwards. If there's anything that rankles professional builders and painters, it's dealing with someone who tried to save a few bucks, totally botched

Custom upholstery requires a walking foot industrial sewing machine and a lot of skill. Pre-sewn upholstery kits are easy to install. For a super budget approach, you can do some basic tucking, folding, and pinning with a colorful blanket.

the job, and then expects the pro to fix the problems for very little money.

You won't likely get a cheap fix, if you can even find a shop that will agree to tackle your mess. Many shops don't like to be responsible for correcting someone else's mistakes. If they will take on the job, expect to pay as much, and probably more, than it would have cost if you'd had the work done professionally in the first place. You can also expect some condescending words, or at minimum, a lot of head shaking and sighing.

The following points are things to consider when evaluating your skills.

Should I do any welding?

Unless you're an experienced, certified welder, no. There are lots of great MIG welders that are both affordable and capable of doing professional quality work, but it takes practice to weld well. Buy components that are either factory welded in a jig or can be bolted in place. Poor welds aren't something you want on your car or any vehicle that your family will ride in.

Can I build my own engine?

Yes. Building a small-block Chevy from an engine kit is pretty straightforward. There are a tremendous number of excellent books on the subject. We suggest that you buy a complete kit where all the machine work has been

done and one that doesn't require a core exchange. Before you commit to an engine-building project, compare the great prices on brand new crate motors.

Given the great deals on crate motors, building your own engine should be thought of as another aspect of learning new skills rather than saving money. It's possible to save money, but it's tough to beat the economies of scale that the professionals offer.

Should I do my own body prep?

Maybe. The quality of the reproduction body you buy has a lot to do with the amount of prep work that's required. Some companies finish their bodies to higher standards than some competitors.

Doing your own body prep and/or color sanding is an iffy situation. It's within the realm of a confident beginner, but you can also do a lot of expensive damage if you're overzealous. Most professional painters insist on doing the entire job so they can guarantee their work.

It's possible to do exhaust work at home as long as you use pre-bent pieces and don't mind clamping all junctions. There are kits, but you're probably as well off having a custom system welded up at a muffler shop that is experienced with street rods.

A body that needs a bare minimum of prep work is well worth the price difference over a down-and-dirty body.

Work like block sanding is within the realm of a cautious novice, but you might want to consult potential painters before you start. Prep work can make or break a paint job, so many painters insist on doing the prep work. If the paint looks bad, it's the painter who gets blamed, not the prep person.

There are books on fiberglass and metal prepping. The tools needed are simple and few. You will need a way to apply a catalyzed primer/surfacer. That could be the snag that sends the job to a pro. Before you start shooting paint, check out the local regulations regarding the use of hazardous materials in a non-commercial environment. You should be fully aware of any possible health risks from the chemicals and use top quality safety equipment.

Can I fit the body components?

Yes, but it might drive you crazy. The fit and alignment of body parts is a key gauge of the quality of a street rod. It takes a lot of patience and common sense to make the myriad of adjustments required to approach perfection. Full-fendered cars are obviously more involved than highboys.

Fitting body components is a classic case of cause and effect. Whenever you move one part, many other parts are affected. It takes a lot of compromising to find the combination of moves that delivers the best overall fit.

Probably the biggest challenge when it comes to fitting gaps is the hood. The hood is a high visibility part of the car and it has a lot of straight lines that accentuate any uneven gaps. You might consider having a professional fit the hood.

An important factor in body panel fitting is the use of high quality components. The chassis must be a precision base if you have any hopes of achieving an excellent fit.

If I can't paint my own car, can I save money by doing the color sanding and buffing?

Yes, you can save money. No, you probably shouldn't do it and we can't think why a shop would let you. Color sanding and buffing is an art form. It's too easy for an inexperienced person to burn through the paint and do more damage than good.

If you'd like to learn about color sanding, buffing, and related detailing operations, practice on an insignificant car. Try restoring the finish on a badly faded beater. Hone your skills on a car that doesn't matter before you attempt an expensive street rod body.

Is it possible to do upholstery work at home?

Yes, if there's an upholstery kit for your car. If actual sewing is involved, a commercial sewing machine and a fair amount of experience are required. Upholstery kits are pre-sewn so all you have to do is fit the covers to the base and secure the upholstery with hog rings. Carpeting is pretty easy to install (especially in kit form) as long as there aren't a lot of compound curves.

Very few tools are required to install an upholstery kit. The tools are inexpensive. A key to do-it-yourself upholstery is getting a tight fit. The vinyl needs to be as warm and pliable as possible. It often helps to have an assistant for the stretching process. The upholstery needs to be very taut on the cushions before it's secured with the hog rings.

You can do a very basic "tuck and baste" with a colorful blanket. Using a blanket or even a bedspread is easy because you're really sewing it in place. If you don't like the way it looks, it's easy to do it over. Colorful blankets constitute a perfectly acceptable upholstery style on unfinished cars.

Can I bolt together an exhaust?

Yes. You can buy exhaust components and "cut and clamp" the various pieces together. You'd probably be happier with a custom fabricated exhaust system that's welded together. Space is at a premium underneath street rods, so a professional tubing bender allows the fabricator to make bends you couldn't do at home. Tight bends are a key element of a first class street rod exhaust system.

Street rodders like their exhaust systems tucked up tight so there's as little visible as possible. The exhaust system needs to be properly mounted and insulated to keep everything tight and rattle-free. An exhaust shop familiar with street rods is your best bet.

Can I wire my entire car by myself?

Yes. Even though wiring can be imposing because of the maze of wires, street rod wiring kits make the job a no-brainer. If you can fill out the order form, you can wire your own car. The tremendous advances in the caliber of wiring kits have really taken a lot of hassle out of building a car.

Can I work on an automatic transmission at home?

Yes, but it depends on what you want to accomplish. When the transmission is out of the chassis, it's easy to access. If you want to do simple tasks like installing a shift improver kit, change the filter, switch torque converters, or add custom oil pan, those things can be handled with a minimum of tools. If you want to go deeper into the guts of the transmission and change clutch packs, you should probably see a transmission shop.

Can I polish aluminum parts at home?

Yes. You probably won't get quite the results of a professional metal polisher, but the do-it-yourself kits can come pretty close. It takes a lot of time and grunt work, and it is one of the absolute dirtiest jobs on the planet, but you can do it.

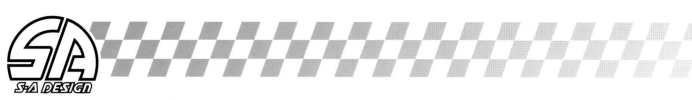

PROFESSIONAL ADVICE

Experience is one of the most valuable tools you can possess when it comes to building a street rod. If you're new to the hobby, you're obviously short on experience. Nothing beats actual hands-on experience, but you can learn a lot from people who are involved with street rods on a daily basis.

During the preparation of this book, many manufacturers and professional street rod builders were polled for advice. Much of the advice follows the same basic theme, which is to have a plan, but different people have unique perspectives on the process of building a street rod. There is lots of good information in the better catalogs. Some catalogs are little more than a price sheet with a few photos, but the best catalogs are mini reference sources.

Here are some highlights of our inquiries and research along with some random observations and opinions. As the news media is so quick to point out, "The opinions expressed here are not necessarily the opinions of the owners and management of this station." You should realize that there are several ways to build a reproduction body or fabricate a chassis, so the manufacturers will obviously give supporting evidence favorable to their style of building things. As with any research project, one should read as much as possible and then use that information to form their conclusions.

GENERAL ADVICE

Planning is at the top of almost every pro's list of best things to do when building a street rod. Without a carefully thought out plan, you're just asking for trouble. Know what you want and be realistic about your capabilities. Being realistic about your capabilities includes your financial resources as well as your building skills.

Pick a popular car and construction style. There was virtually universal agreement on this topic. Building your first street rod isn't a time to experiment. Stick with tried and true cars and construction techniques. A popular car like the '32 Ford is easy to find parts for and easy to resell, should the need arise.

KEEPING THE CAR COOL

Manufacturers of specific parts highlighted factors related to those parts. The cooling experts at Griffin Thermal Products feel very strongly about radiators and related parts. Besides their obvious bias, they're one hundred percent right about the extreme importance of a top-notch cooling system. Street rods often spend extended periods idling in stopped or very slow moving traffic during the warmest time of the year.

Street rodders tend to favor high performance engines, which generally run hotter than less potent power plants. The narrow grilles of street rods further hamper the flow of cool air. Combine these factors with warm weather and

Careful planning is the number one piece of advice our pro poll received. It takes planning and selecting the right car to build cars like the pros do. The tremendous appeal of this '32 highboy built by So-Cal Speed Shop is the result of decades of experience, but you can learn quickly by paying attention to what the pros have to say. (So-Cal Speed Shop)

slow traffic and the potential for over-heating is very real.

The Griffin people feel that an excellent cooling system should be part of the original planning, not some after thought. This includes knowing if you will use hood rod brackets or if an orig-inal style radiator cap will be used for appearance sake. Planning for air condi-tioning is very important. If your car has a modified grill shell, be sure the radia-tor will fit properly.

When it comes to Deuces and '33-'34 Fords, Griffin recommends using a small-block Chevy engine. Besides the ready availability of parts, Chevy engines are shorter which leaves more room for a heavy-duty radiator. A coolant recovery system is important. Griffin builds their '33-'34 Ford radiator with a built-in recovery system so an auxiliary unit isn't necessary.

The radiator and related cooling system components are vitally impor-tant to the health and welfare of your rod. Don't settle for anything less than a first class system. A hot rod that's too hot isn't cool.

KEEPING YOU COOL

Keeping you cool is the goal of Vintage Air. Some diehard street rodders think that air conditioning is for light-weights, but we'd bet that these critics have air conditioning in their family vehicles. Jack Chisenhall is the man in charge at Vintage Air. He's built some fine cars that have received lots of media attention. The company is located in San Antonio, Texas, so they know how to deal with heat.

Jack thinks the best tool a person can possess for building a street rod is a sharp brain. Like all the other experts, he stresses smart planning a key to suc-cess. Simplicity is another important consideration. In order for a street rod to be fun, it has to be a "real" car. That means all systems should function like they do on a modern passenger car. A cool running car is a real car. The radia-tor, water pump, and fan combination has to be well planned and executed.

In planning for an optimum cooling system, make sure that all the engine

Besides planning, all the pros stressed the importance of building a popular car. Their number one pick was the '32 Ford highboy roadster. A well-built car not only looks good, but also is very roadworthy. Andy Brizio's Deuce was built at his son Roy's shop. Andy has criss-crossed the country in the flamed beauty.

accessories are taken into consideration. Just mocking up an engine block won't tell the whole story. Air conditioning and other front-mounted accessories can take up valuable inches in a tight street rod engine compartment. Be sure that there is room for the accessories and a good fan.

Regarding the selection and pur-chase of parts, Jack advises against cut-ting corners on major components. Don't give up the best parts for a meager 15% savings. Buying the best parts will pay off in the long run. If you figure life span of a quality part versus a cheap knock off, good parts are usually less expensive in the end.

Vintage Air advises against used air conditioning components. The com-pressors and related parts from passen-ger cars are bigger than the special street rod versions. Space is always at a premi-um in a street rod, so the compact, high performance air conditioning compo-nents offered by Vintage Air and other street rod air conditioning companies are the best way to go.

Besides size considerations, used air conditioning components can be con-taminated, making them difficult, if not impossible, to clean. A lot of money can be wasted charging and recharging a

defective system. Start with new compo-nents to be sure of doing the job right the first time.

Continuing with the cooling theme, Pat Pennington of Koolmat Insulation, shared some advice relative to keeping a street rod comfortably cool. These cars are relatively small and the cockpit is close to the engine, transmission and exhaust system. All these systems gener-ate lots of heat.

A major mistake that many people make when it comes to insulating a car is not covering all areas. Even though sev-eral pieces may be needed to cover an area, it should look like one continuous piece when it's done. High temperature glue is needed to ensure that the insula-tion stays put.

Koolmat suggests using a bead of silicone to connect the pieces of insula-tion that were used to cover the floor, transmission tunnel, firewall, and kick panels. This seal stops heat from coming through the cracks into the upper breathing space of the interior. Sealing the insulation also keeps cool air-condi-tioned air inside where it belongs. Small amounts of silicone should also be used bond the carpeting to the topside of the Koolmat insulation. Koolmat's topside is silicone so glue won't stick to it; only silicone will. The bottom fiberglass side can be secured with any high temp glue.

Pat feels that many beginners make the mistake of insulating a car with inferior products in an attempt to save a few bucks. Then, when they find out that the stuff doesn't work well, they have to start over with quality insulation. In a unique spin on the trailered versus driven street rod controversy, Pat thinks cars are trailered because they can't take the heat, not because the owner is afraid of getting it dirty.

THE SO-CAL SPEED SHOP

One of the most informative (and visually appealing) street rod catalogs is the one produced by the So-Cal Speed Shop. It stands to reason since two of the principles, Pete Chapouris and Jim "Jake" Jacobs have extensive experience in street rod building and publishing. They are also excellent students of street rodding history. They've studied the best of the past and integrated that look with the best of modern technology. Besides their catalog, their excellent web site, www.so-calspeedshop.com is loaded with helpful information and great artwork.

Pete and Jake have built many world famous cars over the years. "The California Kid" '34 Ford 3-window coupe is probably the best known. They know all about stance and what elements provide the best "look." A good example is how they make their '29 A-V8 Model A roadster on a '32 frame. There's more to building one of these classic hot rods than plunking a Model A body on a deuce chassis. The frame rails need to be contoured to match the narrow '28-'29 A cowl. The rear rails need to be narrowed 1-3/4 inches in order for the body to sit our over the frame correctly. They leave the front crossmember as is, because the longer wheelbase of the deuce frame already stretches the wheelbase and improves the Model A profile.

So-Cal advocates the use of traditional hairpin radius rods on their traditionally styled chassis. Hairpin radius rods should be used with I-beam axles. Four-bar links are still the best method of locating a dropped tube axle. Four-bar systems can also be used with I-beam axles, but that isn't the look most people want.

So-Cal feels that a front Panhard bar is mandatory with Vega style cross-steering systems. The bar helps eliminate lateral axle movement and bump steer. A transverse front spring can move laterally on its shackles. This lateral movement of the frame in relation to the axle translates to steering gear movement. You don't want that, because unpredictable steering gear movement does not equate with pleasurable driving. So-Cal also recommends the use of a steering damper along with the Panhard bar. The damper improves overall steering smoothness.

Besides the Panhard bar and steering damper, So-Cal stresses the importance of obtaining and maintaining proper caster, camber, and toe-in. Caster is what affects how straight the front tires run and how easily the steering wheel returns to center after making a turn. They suggest between 5 and 9 degrees of positive caster. The caster angle of I-beam front axles can be adjusted with the radius rods, which is another reason So-Cal likes to use radius rods and I-beam axles.

Too much camber will cause tires to wear out quickly. They suggest camber settings of 0 degrees to +1/2 degree. If you buy a quality front axle, the camber should be correct from the manufacturer, as it's a function of the angle at which the kingpin hole is machined into the kingpin boss. An alignment shop may be able to bend a forged steel axle, but don't try to bend a cast iron axle.

Toe-in is the third factor in getting a smooth driving street rod. Toe-in is used to counteract the tendency of the leading edges of the tires to pull away from each other. So-Cal sets radial tires with 1/8-inch of toe-in by adjusting the tie rod ends.

So-Cal offered a couple tips regarding street rod bodies. They use both steel and fiberglass reproduction roadster bodies. They like to leave the door hinges in their stock location on traditionally styled highboys. Since door adjustments and panel fitting is so important to a quality street rod, they add turnbuckles to the inner quarter panels. This allows a greater amount of door adjustment. They also add extra

A good hot rod is a cool rod. A car that runs cool in hot weather and congested traffic will make the whole experience a pleasant one. A high quality radiator like one of these Griffin units is a must. (TCI)

A properly setup suspension will be a pleasure to drive. Caster is the forward or backward tilt of the kingpin on a straight axle car. Most I-beam or tube axles have a backward, or positive caster. Correct caster helps the car track straight. (So-Cal Speed Shop)

bracing to increase the rigidity of the bodies. Less flexing means less panel alignment problems. They add a steel tube and an X-frame structure around the cowl and between the interior area and the trunk. A seat belt mounting frame is also installed.

RON FRANCIS WIRE WORKS

Ron Francis' Wire Works is one of the pioneer street rod companies having been established in 1974. Ron attended the first NSRA Street Rod Nationals in 1970 and quickly saw the need for an easier way to wire street rods. His solution was wiring harnesses made specifically for street rods. Wiring is a part of street rod construction that intimidates many people, but when a quality wiring kit is used, it's a pretty simple job.

The Wire Works' catalog is digest sized, but it's a giant source of valuable information. There is also much solid information on their web site: www.wire-works.com. Ron Francis

offered the following advice about the electrical part of building a street rod. He also gave an overview of what's involved in wiring a typical street rod.

"Wiring a street rod is one of the last things to get done. It can be one of those tasks that you keep putting off in hopes that it will magically disappear. Well, it won't go away and the car won't go anywhere without electricity. Most people have decided on what their car will be made from, where to get the suspension, body parts, engine, what color to paint it and exactly which fabric you want on the seats. Rarely does anyone put forethought about where to put his or her fuse box…or the wiring. Believe it or not, I've actually had a customer say, 'But I don't have room for the fuse box!' Buddy, it's going to be real hard to push that car from rod run to rod run! It must be dealt with, and it's easier than you think.

"The hardest part of installing your wiring is deciding where to put the fuse box. Yes, I really do mean it. Once you've decided where to put the box, the rest is smooth sailing.

"Your second big decision is how to wire your vehicle. You have a couple options when wiring a car. One method is to re-use the harness from a donor car, if you bought one for the engine and transmission, etc. This option is not rec-

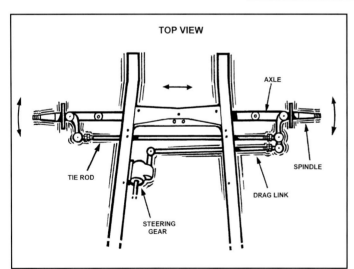

One problem with transverse leaf springs that are located by shackles is that the suspension can move from side to side. That moves the drag link, which moves the spindles and the tires, even though the steering wheel wasn't turned. This phenomenon, called "bump steer," is undesirable. (So-Cal Speed Shop)

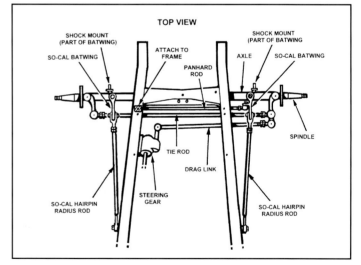

The solution to unwanted lateral movement is installing a front Panhard bar. So-Cal Speed Shop is very big on Panhard bars. They mount their bars behind the axle, thus improving the aesthetics of the dropped axle as viewed from the front. (So-Cal Speed Shop)

ommended because the technology is outdated, not to mention that car was a donor car for a reason. Also, wire lengths will be wrong, which means lots of cutting and splicing - a big no-no when wiring a "brand new" vehicle you just spent tens of thousands of dollars on. Wire manufactured prior to 1980 has plastic insulation that will crack with age. There will be circuits that you won't need in your car, leaving hot wires lying about or just snubbed off - a truly dangerous situation.

"The next method you may be tempted to try is to pay a wiring professional to do it. He/she could custom make a wiring harness. If you're rolling in money, this might be the way to go. But if you do it yourself, when you're finished you'll know how everything works - because you did it. If you happen to be on the side of the road with a problem, we hope you brought your wiring guy along. Can you troubleshoot it yourself because your wiring guy isn't with you? You know you want it done correctly, you want everything to work, and you want it to be reliable, technologically advanced, safe and most of all simple. You can do it yourself with a wiring kit."

The best method for wiring your car safely and simply, yourself, is to buy a "wiring kit." There are quite a few manufacturers in the market today making kits you can install yourself. What should you look for? A few of the most important issues include:

Simplicity – are the instructions easy to understand, and are they color-coded? Does the harness come as one big hunk of wiry confusion or is it broken down to its simplest parts? Does it come in sections so you can work with one circuit at a time? Is it color coded, or is the harness all one color? Are the wires printed (every few inches) as to where they go?

Safety – Is it fire-resistant wire? This wire is commonly known as "cross link." GXL is the recommended grade for wiring your car. The TXL cross-link is approximately the same quality as the old PVC wiring. Look for manufacturers who use GXL the most because it has the thicker insulation affording

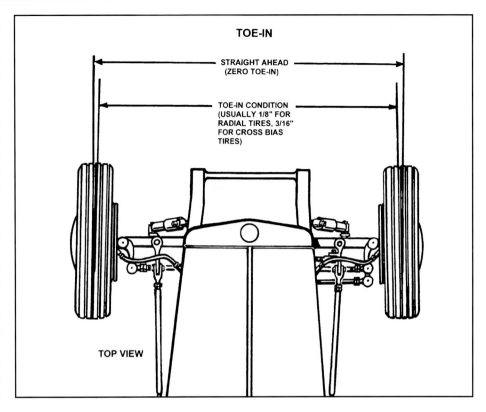

TOE-IN

STRAIGHT AHEAD (ZERO TOE-IN)

TOE-IN CONDITION (USUALLY 1/8" FOR RADIAL TIRES, 3/16" FOR CROSS BIAS TIRES)

TOP VIEW

Toe-in is another facet of building a car that is a pleasure to drive. Toe-in or toe-out is the angle that the wheels point when viewed from above. Street rods favor a slight amount of toe-in. The adjustments are accomplished by threading the tie rod ends in or out, thus changing the length of the drag link. (So-Cal Speed Shop)

more fire-resistance, and it also resists abrasion better.

Technology – Is it made from the latest components or is it made from parts that were originally used on older vehicles? They may be brand new parts, but is the technology new? Does the fuse box contain wiring and parts that may be subject to human error or quality issues? Were the parts in this automobile harness all originally intended for an automobile?

Upgrades – Will the harness/fuse box accept future accessories that you may want to add later? Will you have to cut and splice? Will adding these accessories and upgrades be simple, inexpensive and will they blend with the current configuration?

Accountability – Does the manufacturer offer any kind of warranty? Do they offer customer service and a trouble shooting phone line (or web site)? Is it live, or do you leave a recording where someone will get back to you later? Is the manufacturer able to track the prod-

uct and know exactly what you bought (i.e., serial number)?

Reputation – Ask your buddies. Ask more than one buddy. Who has been around a long time, who has name recognition? Who are people bragging about in their "Car for Sale" ads in the back of magazines? Ask about their wiring experience - were they satisfied? Did they think it went smoothly? And most importantly, is their car running well? Check with insurance companies for these types of vehicles to see if any discounts are offered for using any particular brand of product.

Once you have decided which kit to use, you will need to prepare for the ordering process. If you've made it this far, you can definitely handle the installation of your wiring. The Wire Works asks some pertinent questions in order to custom make a harness for your vehicle. If the company you are ordering from does not ask these questions, you are not getting a kit made especially for your car. (It will be universal, thus needing cutting and splicing, so now you better know what you're doing!). The following is a list of questions that must be answered in order for the Wire Works' staff to manufacture your harness:

1. Vehicle Year, Make and Body Style
2. Engine Year, Make, Induction?
3. Is your dash made of Steel, Fiberglass, Wood or other material?
4. Are your gauges Analog or Digital? Are you using an Ammeter or Voltmeter?
5. Do you have 2 or 4 headlights? Are you using LED or Halogen lights anywhere on the vehicle?
6. Do you have a Points or Electronic type distributor, factory or aftermarket, internal or external coil?
7. What kind of Alternator are you using, and has it been modified in any way?
8. What year and make steering column are you using? Which features are on it? What is the location of your ignition switch and your dimmer switch?
9. You can then tell them which accessories you would like to put in your vehicle, and their sales staff can guide you through the process of ordering what you need, without you having to purchase things you don't need.

Once the Wire Works is confident that they know everything about your vehicle configuration, they will build and ship your harness within 24 hours. It's shipped with a serial number, which identifies your harness as your own, and the information is kept for future reference, no matter who owns the vehicle. This way, if you have any questions or changes in the future, they can look up your personal information and help you solve any situation that may arise along the way.

When the kit arrives and you open the box, you will find a neatly packed assortment of items made just for your rod. Inside, you will find your Advantage Plus Fuse Box, configured to your specs. Surrounding that box is each individual section of the harness, bagged separately for ease of installation. There will be an "Orange Card" with your Serial Number and Tech Line phone numbers and a "Location Map" which explains how the fuse

panel is laid out, and recommended fusing specifications. You will also find your instructions, again fully personalized for your kit. There won't be a big confusing book or highly technical, confusing schematic drawings — just a few sheets of paper that are surprisingly simple to follow.

The Wire Works sends along a "General Guidelines" page to give you tips on running, cutting and crimping, as well as grounding, mounting and pre-installation procedures. A second sheet will define and explain the use of what the "Select-A-Circuit" fuses and connections are, as well as Maxi-Fuses, Color Cubes and the easy to use Zip-Lox Terminal Block Covers. The main instructions for the harness are two sheets of paper, with four printed sides. You'll start at Bag Number 1, and follow through from there.

You will find a new feature in the Advantage Plus kit that has made the simplest instructions in the industry even easier. They are called the "AccuLink Wiring Diagrams." Inside each wiring bag, the label folds out into a single sheet of paper which has a 'visual aid' - a drawing of how that particular section should be run. Hence, if the words don't do it for you, the pictures probably will, and vice versa.

Once you have read over the General Guidelines, and taken a peek at your instructions, it is time to begin. By now you should have decided where you were going to mount the Advantage panel, and have done so.

Starting with *Wiring Bag #1* (Alternator Section of Harness), you simply follow the written instructions. For example, the wires will have the terminals on them and you will do the following, "You will hookup the large RED wire to the 'bat' terminal of the alternator and run the other end to the starter solenoid. The white plug is connected to the alternator and the LT BLUE wire is run to #16 on the panel." Since the wire itself is Light Blue, and the Color Cube™ on the Panel is Light Blue, and "ALT FEED 2 16" is printed every 5 inches along the wire, it's hard to mess this up. Once you have trimmed the wires to length at the panel, and

crimped the terminals, you're finished wiring the first section of your harness.

Wiring bag #2, Engine Wiring (Starter and Distributor), is next. If you're considering starting the engine before the kit is complete, you only have two bags to go. There are usually only 3 to 5 wires in this section and you've finished the engine wiring. It will be set up for a points-style distributor, or an electronic/aftermarket, depending on your application.

Wiring bag #3 is the Ignition switch wiring for your column or dash mounted switch. It also addresses the Neutral Safety function. Your kit would include either a dash mounted ignition switch with the pre-wired plug, or the correct plugs to utilize the column mounted unit.

Wiring bag #4 addresses the gauge and dashboard wiring, including wires for indicators, radio, wipers, and clock. An enhanced accessory kit called the "Dash Gauge Wiring Kit" is also available with more elaborate, but very simple wiring with a quick disconnect plug. This allows you to pre-wire the gauges/dash on 'the bench' instead of on your back. Many builders find this option extremely attractive since it's so much easier to do this work outside of the car. If you ever re-do the interior, it's easy to unplug the dashboard.

Wiring bag #5 encompasses wiring for the turn signal switch, brake switch, and third brake light, including the steering column plugs. Wire Works supplies an adapter that links their harness to your column turn signal wiring making it one of the easiest parts of the kit.

Wiring bag #6 takes care of the Headlight & Dimmer switches, horn connection, high beam indicator, and dash light feed. This section contains the headlight cables with Sealed Beam Sockets included if necessary. Wiring bag #7 takes care of left & right front parking and turn signal wiring. Bag #8 contains left & right rear parking and turn signal wiring as well as the gas gauge sender and license plate light.

Each section is clearly explained, with a total of 8 sections to the average harness. With each section, you simply follow the written instructions, with the aid of the AccuLink diagrams . . . plug in the component then route back to the Advantage Panel following the printing on the wires, then trim, strip, crimp and slip under the appropriate screw and tighten. When you're finished, don't forget to replace the non-reversible Zip-Lox ™ cover strips. These will simplify any future troubleshooting.

Believe it or not, at this point, your car is wired. You should be able to drive it and pass inspection (depending on the state). Now if you'd like to go back and tie-wrap some of the wire, that helps keep it from hanging loose, reducing chances of abrasion or shorts. There is no need to wrap the harness in black electrical tape, since it is higher quality cross-link wire instead of the old PVC that used to have to be protected. Also, if you tape it, you won't be able to read the wires, which may become very valuable in the future.

Grounding is an issue that can confuse many folks, whether their car is fiberglass or steel. A properly grounded electrical system is imperative for the system to function as it should. Fiberglass cars need to be solidly grounded to the frame.

Now that you've wired the main system in your car, you can also wire the fuel injection with a Wire Works Telorvek Fuel Injection Wiring Harness. These harnesses are 'closed loop', running your vehicle at factory performance. Just as easy as the main harness, the Telorvek had two wires that run/feed it from the main Advantage Panel -and you're off. Whether carbureted or fuel injected, there is a kit out there for your application. It is simple, safe, and inexpensive, and you can enjoy the benefits of knowing exactly how your car works and runs because you did it yourself.

TOTAL COST INVOLVED (TCI)

Total Cost Involved Engineering, Inc., better known as simply TCI, is one of the superstars of the street rodding industry. As one of the oldest and biggest street rod chassis companies, more TCI frames and suspension components are probably underneath street rods than products from any other manufacturer. TCI started out in 1974 building Model A reproduction frames. Two years later they added '32 Ford frames and chassis to their product lineup. In 1982, they added 1933/34 Ford frames and chassis. Their current products cover a wide range of the hobby's most popular Ford and Chevy street rods and classic trucks.

The newest TCI product is their brand new '32 frame rails. Previously, they used stampings from an outside source. They felt the other stampings were getting on in years. They wanted to control the quality themselves. The new TCI frame rails are super straight with perfectly executed reveal lines. A new X-member replaces the old K-member. A big plus of the new X-member is that 2 1/2-inch exhaust tubing can be routed through it, instead of underneath it. That provides more clearance for a low uncluttered look.

In addition to pages and pages of glossy studio photos of street rod chassis and components, the TCI catalog ($5.00) has lots of helpful ideas about successfully building a street rod. Their web site www.totalcostinvolved.com is

Wiring a street rod can seem very intimidating, but it's really pretty straightforward when you use a well-designed wiring kit like those custom made by Ron Francis' Wire Works. Ron has a great deal of experience building street rods. The Wire Works catalog is loaded with helpful information. (Ron Francis' Wire Works)

another good information source. TCI's vice president of sales and marketing, Del Austin, contributed his valuable insights, also.

TCI cites a lack of planning as the number one mistake to avoid. It's critical to have a plan and follow it. In conversations with Del, he repeatedly stressed the importance of planning, planning, and more planning. A corollary to planning is to stick with your plan.

There are a lot of variables to building a street rod, so TCI suggests potential builders research and answer the following questions.

- What year and body style do you want to build?
- Steel or fiberglass body?
- Full-fendered or highboy?
- What engine, transmission, and rearend do you want?
- What gear ratio? Remember that transmission choice will affect the gear ratio choice. Tire diameter is another factor in choosing the best gear ratio.
- What kind of brakes — four wheel discs or front discs with rear drum brakes?
- Do you want chrome or stainless steel optional parts? TCI points out that these attractive additions can be very reasonable when purchased as part of a complete chassis package.

TCI advises against painting, powder coating, or chroming parts before they have been trial fitted. These things should be done after the initial assembly and fitting has been done. It's not a bad idea to actually drive the car for a while before doing the cosmetic work. Sticking to your original plans (with as few changes as possible) is a good way to stay on track, both time-wise and financially.

- Construction tips from the experts at TCI include:
- Assemble the chassis and install some "roller" wheels and tires. Try to use tires and wheels that are as close to the actual size and offset you plan to use.
- Mount as many components as possible.
- Run fuel, brake, and transmission cooler lines. If you try to install clamps after the frame has been painted, you run the risk of chipping the paint.

- Keep checking the fit of components as they're installed. Check them more than once. Things to check include: radiator to fan, firewall to engine (with distributor and induction system installed), floor to transmission, exhaust route, and fender (if used) clearances.
- On fendered cars, be sure that tire sizes and wheel offsets work well with the fenders. The relationship of fenders and tires is an important part of a perfect "look."
- On final assembly, apply quality white grease to all threads.

Del Austin passed along some advice on buying parts and what types of parts to buy. He's a big advocate of buying as many of the major components at one time as your budget will allow. You can save money and by buying major parts from the same manufacturer, you get parts that were designed to work together.

Mail order shopping or buying parts locally are both fine as long as you know exactly what type of car you want and the best parts to build it. References are important, both in regards to the quality of the parts and the integrity and customer service record of the company.

Del favors buying as many new parts as possible. Any safety-related parts should always be first quality, new parts. That includes all brake, suspension, and steering components. If the parts don't come with fasteners, buy premium grade ones. A quality part isn't any good if it falls off of the car. Del also likes to use new engines, unless you know the history of a used engine. New crate motors are such incredible values that they're tough to beat for quality, performance, economy, and cost.

As far as what tasks should be left to the pros, Del feels that welding and suspension modifications are the top issues. The easy way around welding is to buy an already welded chassis. By using top quality steering, braking, and suspension components that have been specifically engineered for your chassis, you can eliminate any potential problems in those areas.

A full set of sockets, ratchets, box-end wrenches, and basic automotive hand tools are on the top of Del's most

valuable tools list. Power sanding tools and a compressor are good if you plan to do much body work. On the paint versus powder coating subject, Del likes paint because it's much easier to match, should the need ever arise.

HERCULES MOTOR CAR COMPANY

Cecil Taylor is the driving force behind the Hercules Motor Car Company in Tampa, Florida. His many years of street rod building experience have resulted in a variety of street rod related products including their renowned "New Generation" 1933/34 Ford Woodie Wagon. Hercules makes all new stamped steel cowls and the other metal parts so there's no need to try to salvage some rust-eaten cowl.

The Hercules woodies are available as either phantom two-door models or the traditional four-door wagons. They also manufacture '33-'34 chassis that are available in several stages of completeness. Their body parts are well respected by professional street rod builders. This reputation is bolstered by the fact that Hercules builds turnkey cars as well as components, so they know what it takes to make good fitting parts.

Cecil has assembled so many street rods over the past 30 years that he's encountered almost all imaginable body fitting problems. He is especially proficient in fitting full-fendered cars. He shared his insights on body fitting and other tips.

Like everyone else, Cecil places a lot of importance on planning. Before starting a project, a person should explore the realities of building (and financing) a street rod to decide if it's a practical undertaking. First of all, you have to establish what price range is suitable for each individual case. Most people can't lay out the total amount all at once. The funding should be un-obligated money as these projects can take more time than originally planned.

Once a budget has been established, the next decision is to take a realistic look at what type of vehicle is going to best fit your needs in relationship to family size and what will make the whole family happy. Oftentimes a simple conversation with the family can produce a vehicle that is both practical and appeals to all involved (obviously, Cecil sees a lot of family value in woodie wagons).

Cecil advises people to attend NSRA or Goodguys events and talk to street rodders who have completed a component car (he hates the term "kit car"). Get their reactions and opinions about their project. Remember that all reproduction body manufacturers should feel that their product is the best. Otherwise, they're either terrible businessmen or painfully honest.

Buy a body and chassis that's as complete as possible. It's much easier and economical for a company to set up many operations on a vehicle, as compared to an individual doing it only once. The learning curve is very slow. If you're paying a shop to learn all these new twists to each vehicle, it can become very expensive. Shops that specialize in a particular vehicle can build superior cars quickly and affordably.

Cecil says that he cannot over emphasize that, regardless of what the brochures may lead you to believe, you will not be driving a new street rod in two or three weekends of work. Unrealistic expectations frequently lead to unfinished cars that end up for sale at fifty cents on the dollar in the local auto trader publication. If you know what to expect going into the project, you're much more likely to complete the car.

Many novice builders don't understand why it can take months to get a body or chassis from a well-known manufacturer. As Cecil points out, that backlog can be a good thing. A company that makes a worthwhile product is frequently several months behind. That's a sign of a popular product. Remember that street rod bodies and chassis are built to order, not stocked on shelves like camshafts or intake manifolds.

The important thing about production delays is to figure those delays into your planning. Be patient and wait for a superior product rather than impatiently settling for an inferior substitute. The time you save up front can easily be lost later when you have to fix something like an inferior fiberglass body.

Cecil strongly advises that entry-level street rodders buy the most complete body and chassis that their budget will allow. It makes sense to wait longer if that's what it takes to afford a more complete package. Don't buy a body that requires the customer to install the doors and trunk lid. It's so much easier for the pros to do these critical tasks than to risk them to an inexperienced builder.

Get as many parts together as possible before you attempt to assemble the car. It's very risky to use borrowed parts that are almost like the ones you will eventually use. There's no guarantee that the borrowed parts will fit the same as the actual parts. Even though Hercules builds the same style car every day, the cars all end up being slightly different. That's why you should only use the parts that are intended for a specific car.

Do not under any circumstance start painting parts as soon as you receive them. It's imperative to assemble the car in primer, drive it a little, and then disassemble it for paint and upholstery. It's too easy to scratch or otherwise damage paint during the initial assembly process.

There are many ways to assemble a street rod. Cecil can't say that any one approach is better than the others, but he knows what works for him. If you're building a street rod with full fenders and running boards, it's of utmost importance to properly install the running boards first. This may seem a little unusual, but the running boards serve as a central reference point for other body components.

Once the running boards have been loosely installed, the body can be set on the chassis in a position to align the rear fender well bead with the back of the running board. The running board, fender well and fender must all line up perfectly in order to have pleasing results at the end. Precision fit is highly desired in a street rod and the sign of a quality built car.

Do not install the front fenders or hood prior to installing the running boards and rear fenders. Do not attempt to mount the grille shell and hood until you have the radiator properly installed. There are many positions where the hood and grille will bolt together and appear correct, but there is only one location that is correct.

Cecil likes to use a 4-foot level or straight edge placed on top of the hood and extends it over the cowl vent area

Hercules Motor Car Company specializes in '33/'34 Ford woodies, both 4-doors and 2-doors. Speaking of doors, Cecil is big on buying a body that has factory-hung doors. That will save the consumer a lot of time and potential grief. The stance and panel fit is great on this woodie. (Hercules Motor Car Company)

A big benefit of having a professionally fabricated exhaust system is that by using a tubing bender the shop can get tighter bends than most pre-bent pieces. Exhaust pipes should go up and over the rear axle and all the way out to the rear of the car. (So-Cal Speed Shop)

until it almost hits the windshield. If the hood is in the proper plane, there won't be any air gap or daylight under the straight edge. If there's a gap at the point where the hood touches the cowl that means that the grille and hood are installed too high. If there's a gap at the back of the straight edge near the windshield, then the grille and hood are too low. When the grille and hood have been correctly installed, the bead that's stamped in the hood top should be running in a straight line with the body bead line on the body from front to rear.

A tip that Cecil passed on about '33-'34 hoods is that it's often necessary to cut the radiator mounting tabs on the chassis and lower them as much as half an inch. Lowering the radiator will help position the front of the hood just where it needs to be. The grille and hood are focal points any street rod and especially on '33-'34 Fords.

Cecil studied many original and beautifully restored '33-'34 Fords. He found that the hoods appeared to be high, leaving a gap of 1/2 to 3/4 inch between the hood and inner fender panels. As a result, the bottom front of the hood overbites the grille shell sides. This is a common problem, but it can be corrected with a little work. Remember, these early Fords were very affordable cars, not limited production luxury cars.

As such, the body fit tolerances weren't anything near as precise as what modern street rodders expect.

Cecil favors 4-piece hoods for novice street rod builders. The popular 3-piece hoods are much more complex to install than the 4-piece ones. Cecil figures that it can take up to 30-40 hours to perfectly install a 3-piece hood.

Cecil Taylor summed up his advice with the following major points:

Check with state and local officials to see if your dream car is legal for highway use. Check on what the registration and title requirements are. Some states require that all vehicles have some form of a fender to cover all four wheels. This regulation could very well spoil plans for a Deuce highboy or a T-bucket. Find out these things before you purchase a body. Insurance coverage usually isn't a problem.

Get the family involved. Find out what style of car fits your needs and those of your family. You want a mutually enjoyable car.

Do some research on the companies you have selected as potential suppliers. What kind of reputation do they have? Do they produce a quality part for a fair price? What kind of lead time can you expect on an order?

When it comes to engines, the small-block Chevy is the champ. It's by far the most economical motor to purchase and modify. Speed equipment is much less expensive for this engine than any other. Ford Motorsports is doing a lot to popularize the small-block Ford engines, but they're still way behind the Chevys in popularity. If you plan on doing any serious traveling in your street rod, Chevy parts are easiest to find in remote locations.

Don't overlook the importance of an efficient cooling system. Too many street rod events have congested traffic near the headquarters hotel and on the route to and from the event. Overheating is an unpleasant and embarrassing experience. Make cooling a priority and you'll avoid problems.

Check out local paint and upholstery shops as well as what name brand and style of paint you intend to use. Remember that some of the exotic paints like candies, pearls, and flip-flop colors are extremely expensive. The more exotic the paint, the tougher it will be to make any future repairs or touch-ups. A good solid or semi-metallic factory pack color is the safest way to go.

Tires and wheels can present a number of problems. Picking the right combination is very important to the success of a street rod. What I find works best is borrowing a wheel combination from a friend to see just how much back spacing and fender clearance you can come up with. There have been many sets of wheels bought prematurely that ended up being sold at the swap meet because they just didn't work out.

If you're working on a budget, as most of us are, it's very important to make a list of items as they are needed in sequence. Why buy the paint early on when you really need the motor long before the paint. Proper planning will always keep you working and moving forward with the project. A master plan is most important along with a sense of direction. A little common sense goes a long way. If you follow a set of guidelines and a game plan, the results can and will be quite rewarding.

Most people involved with street rods are very friendly and willing to help newcomers. That's especially true of the street rod component manufacturers. These companies know the importance of expanding their customer base, both to grow their individual businesses and to keep the hobby alive and healthy.

A major reason that street rod companies attend so many national events is to meet the public and get their products out where they can be seen. If you're contemplating building a street rod, spend as much time as you can checking out the manufacturers' displays. The people manning the booths are eager to talk to you. They're not hard-sell artists; they truly want you to make informed buying decisions because an informed customer is a happy customer. A happy customer is a repeat customer and one who tells his friends about good companies and favorable treatment. Street rod company employees represent a vast wealth of information. Don't hesitate to tap into their knowledge.

TOP TEN MISTAKES TO AVOID

Building a street rod should involve more fun than hassles. Avoiding common mistakes will make the whole project less stressful. The following mistakes are a general consensus of advice from experienced street rod builders. Much of this information is covered in other chapters, but it bears repeating. All of these tips are important.

LACK OF PLANNING

People who undertake a street rod project (especially their first one) without a well researched, carefully thought out, detailed plan are asking for problems and unnecessary expenses. Many of the following problems are related to a lack of planning. A solid plan will eliminate countless problems.

By planning, we mean write it down. Put the details on paper, make a commitment and try to follow through. Any plan is open to revisions, but changes chew up time and usually cost money. Thinking about your dream car is fine, but making a notebook or a folder of magazine photos, catalog references, prices, and other details is much more concrete.

Planning should also involve any sub-contracted work or parts with a long delivery schedule. Frames and bodies are rarely "off-the-shelf" items, so you need to plan for delivery time.

Street rod painters and upholstery specialists who are any good at all are booked up months in advance. The really high demand craftsmen can be scheduled a year out. If you want the services of one of these busy people, you need to have your car ready at the appointed time. Miss your time window and chances are good you'll be back at the end of the line. When planning for paint and upholstery, allow yourself lots of extra time for any snags or delays.

NOT HAVING A THEME

A key element of successful street rods is having and sticking to a theme. Not having a theme differs from a lack of planning. A theme should be part of the overall plan, but a theme is more about the "look" of a car than the logistics of building it.

You could have a well-detailed plan with time schedules that make the military look disorganized. You could have

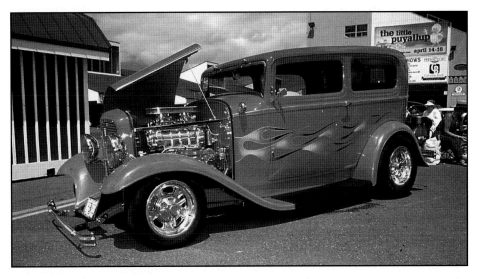

It's tough to criticize a car that has so many good features (like its stance, wheels & tires, nice chop, beautiful engine, etc.), but this Tudor mixes high-tech and traditional themes. The horizontal billet grille, billet mirrors, three-piece hood, and billet engine accessories contrast with old time features like rubber running board covers, stock headlights, cowl lamps, chromed door hinges, and stock bumpers.

a computerized price list with weekly updates, but you have to buy parts that look right together. Components, materials, colors, finishes, and even sounds (a street rod should have a performance exhaust note, not a wheezy, asthmatic vacuum-cleaner sound) need to belong together in order to have a theme.

If you spend some time at any old car event you can quickly spot major and minor theme mistakes. A question you should ask yourself is, "Does this part or modification make the car more cohesive, or does it look out of place?" For drill, you can silently ask yourself that question about various components you see on other street rods.

Probably the most common "theme" error is mixing different styles. Glaring examples are billet, slotted, LED taillights on a fifties style Deuce highboy or a banjo-style steering wheel on a smooth, high tech street rod. Most people make a number of small theme mistakes, but their total negative effect is far greater than you might think. It doesn't take much to tarnish the theme of a street rod. This is picky, subjective thinking, but that's what separates a good street rod from a mediocre one. Having a consistent theme is probably the most inexpensive thing you can do to create a sharp car.

Poor Stance

Without the right stance, you haven't got a chance of impressing the troops. We keep hammering away about stance because it is such a marker of a good street rod. Stance is the equivalent of posture. A person with poor posture and an expensive suit won't look as good as a person with great posture and a modestly priced suit. Just as good posture can help make a great first impression, stance can do the same thing for a street rod. Good posture conveys an aura of confidence. A good stance is a sign of a confident street rod builder.

Stance is elusive, but it's one of those things you know when you see it, even if you have trouble defining it. Study magazine photos of cars built by the rodding world's top professionals. Many hobbyists understand stance, but

The Joneses have way too much money so don't even bother trying to keep up with them when you're building your first bolt-together street rod. You could easily slip one or two more basic highboys in between the price gap of these two Deuces. They're both neat cars, which proves you can hang out with the Joneses and still keep your budget in check.

the really successful pros absolutely have to deliver it. Stance is one of those "experience" factors that makes pro builders worth their shop rates.

Since the cars we're advocating in this book are icon cars, there are lots of great ones around to study. Magazines with comprehensive spec charts can provide lots of insight into stance. Check the tire and wheel sizes, suspension parameters, and whose components were used. Hopefully, the body text mentions things like whether the frame was modified and how, if the body location was altered, and if the wheelbase is stock or modified.

Many pro builders make small chassis and body modifications that might sound insignificant, but they can have a big impact on the stance. If you're checking out cars at a street rod event, ask the owner if the wheelbase is stock or if the front wheels have been moved forward an inch. Also check to see if the rear of the frame rails were kicked up and/or if the front of the rails were pinched on a highboy.

Keeping Up With the Joneses

Unless you're a member of the Microsoft branch of the Jones family, don't waste your money and emotional effort trying to keep up with other rodders. There are a tremendous number of very affluent people in the United States.

Many of these successful people have become interested in street rods and they've had some phenomenal cars built for them.

Notice that we said, "Built for them," not "built by them." Typically, these high dollar rodders are very talented individuals, but they used those talents to build their businesses, not old cars. They've always had an interest in old cars, but only now in their middle or retirement years have they taken the time to get into the hobby.

The presence of these "deep pockets" street rodders has led to a vast array of very talented professional builders who gladly cash mega-digit checks as they build these rolling pieces of automotive art. Some people may scoff at these "checkbook rodders" but we think they're good for the hobby. They help keep the street rod industry solvent and they allow the rest of us to see some incredible cars.

There are also homebuilders that could well be professionals. These talented individuals are able to build stunning cars for a fraction of what a pro-built car would cost. If they had to charge for their time, though, their cars would be in the same thick checkbook arena as the pro cars.

You probably don't have the resources to pay for perfection. The current cost of perfection easily exceeds six figures. It's all about time and materials. It doesn't take a whole lot of 100-hour subassemblies at shop rates north of fifty dollars an hour to ring up a substantial bill. The hundreds of hours that go into flawless paint and bodywork alone can cost more than the average turnkey street rod. The neat thing about these high dollar cars is that they get lots of magazine exposure and they are prominently displayed at big street rod events. These cars help keep the hobby from stagnating. These cars are loaded with neat ideas that you might be able to use on your car. The ideas are free, so take advantage of them.

The biggest mistake about trying to compete with the high dollar cars is that it's a losing battle. The next trick car is already under construction by the time the current "It" car appears in a magazine. Realize your financial and talent limitations. Don't discourage yourself by striving for cars that very few people can afford.

BUYING CHEAP PARTS

It's tough to go wrong with quality parts. Quality parts may cost a little more (usually not a significant amount), but they quickly return their investment. People who try to save money by purchasing only the absolute cheapest parts often end up not saving much at all. It's far better to pay a little more for a part that you only have to deal with once than repairing and/or modifying a less expensive part that didn't quite do the job.

Quality parts don't have to be flashy parts; they're usually not. Quality parts tend to be made here and not in some third world country. They are built out of superior materials, they are engineered for specific applications instead of general ones, they come with the necessary installation hardware, and they're backed by a solid warranty. Companies who build high quality parts gladly stand behind them. They know their products are good and they want to maintain that reputation.

Buying quality parts is most important in terms of the chassis, brakes, running gear, and the body. If you want to cut a few corners, do it on the gingerbread stuff. A leaky chrome valve cover is no big deal compared to a faulty master cylinder.

Big thumping blower motors are cool. Hot rods are supposed to have impressive engines, but this much power is too much for a first street rod. Besides the added expense, this is more horsepower than you'll ever be able to use legally.

The costs of doing business are lower in some regions, but general costs are pretty comparable across the country. Street rod companies located in a rural area where land, utilities, taxes, and labor costs are lower than in big cities can produce quality products for less. Their products might cost a little less or they might retain more profit. So, when you see parts that are significantly less expensive than similar parts, you need to determine whether the savings are a result of lower overhead or lower quality components.

SPENDING ON THE WRONG THINGS

There is a difference between quality parts and expensive parts. You need to determine if you're paying for quality or just an image. Talking to other builders and inspecting the parts in person are good ways to gauge quality. Most "A list" manufacturers produce high quality parts, but there are cases where their parts costs more simply because of the label. The designer label part and the house brand part could even come from the same "ghost" manufacturer.

Street rodding isn't anything like the fashion world, but there are similarities. The consumer world is full of products that are made by big, relatively unknown manufacturers who make minor changes and install different labels on what are essentially identical products. Depending on where you buy the stuff, the prices and warranties can vary substantially.

Besides paying too much for "designer" products, many people also overspend on non-essential parts and overkill parts. The goal of a first time bolt-together street rod should be to build a safe, fun car on a reasonable budget. An interior stitched from near-perfect free-range hides where every possible surface is covered in leather is an example of overspending. A nice interior with all vinyl or leather seating surfaces with matching vinyl elsewhere is a better choice for your first car. Save the imported Italian hides for your Oakland Roadster Show entry.

Overkill parts are things like a bulletproof, racing strength rearend with

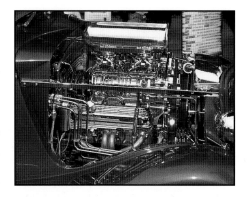

It's easy to spend a small fortune on chromed and polished engine parts. Besides the added costs, this much sparkle requires a lot of maintenance to keep it looking good. If you have the money for lots of chrome and the time to polish it, great. But keep your priorities in line if you're on a budget.

heavy duty everything, extra support braces, and steep gears or a 700 horsepower supercharged engine. A rebuilt 9-inch rearend and an RV style Chevy 350 with 250 to 300 horsepower will more than suffice in a bolt-together street rod. Buy quality parts, but don't buy more performance or flash than you truly need. You can always upgrade later.

TOO MUCH HORSEPOWER

Hot rods are supposed to be fast, but too much horsepower can be dangerous to your health and wallet. There's no denying the appeal of a nasty Willys coupe loping through a street rod event with open headers and a whining supercharger telling spectators that this isn't any sissy car. But, who needs that kind of horsepower to crawl through traffic at 5-10 mph?

If you crave horsepower, build a drag racer. Many of the fairground pounders are competitive in the power department, but they'd probably have a tough time hooking up that power at the track. It's easily too much car for an inexperienced racer to handle at the speeds the car can attain. What you have is a wild car that's not particularly good as either a street rod or a racecar.

Too much power can be difficult to control. There's no need for a car that leaps away from a stop or can haze the

The rearend and underneath side of this '34 Ford coupe is a work of automotive art, but it's far too much for a bolt-together street rod. This level of detail means the rest of the car should match. That means money and lots of it.

tires halfway down the block. You're just asking for an expensive ticket. You know the cops are aware of your car. Street rods don't handle or stop like Corvettes, Firebirds, and Mustangs. When you have a high horsepower car, it needs to be a total performance package capable of safely handling all that power.

TRENDY COLORS

Anyone want a pastel green car with pink, aqua, and peach graphics cheap? The popularity of trendy colors and paint schemes always fades long before the actual paint does. Fad colors tend to be very short lived. Unless you're a professional painter who loves to repaint your car, trendy paint jobs are a very poor investment of time and money.

Both colors and graphics themes can date a car. The trendier the paint the quicker you'll need to unload your street rod to avoid taking a huge financial bath. As quickly as fads become passé, you need to sell before the next fad comes along. Paint is one of the most expensive components of a street rod so choose colors wisely.

In addition to picking trendy colors, some novice builders make the mistake of using colors that are just plain odd. In a sea of red roadsters you may be tempted to explore the nuances of brown, but you'd better love brown because you'll likely own that car for a long time. As mentioned previously, build your first street rod as if you plan to sell it. If you keep it forever, great, but you'll probably bring out the for sale signs within a couple years.

Paint your car a universally popular color like red or black. Better yet, save a lot of money and leave it in primer until you've had more time to decide if you even want to paint this particular car.

YOU DON'T FIT THE CAR

A street rod that doesn't physically fit you is like a suit that's two sizes too small. Who cares how great either the suit or the car looks if you don't fit. Even if you can cram yourself into the suit before being shoehorned into the car, it's not going to be a comfortable experience.

Trying on a street rod isn't as easy as trying on suits. You can't go to your nearest J.C. Penney store and ask if they have a roadster in a '32 long. The bigger you are, the more important it is to check how you fit in a particular street rod. If you're over six feet tall, a street rod interior can be short on legroom. In general, the older the car, the more crowded the front seat is. Notice that we said front seat. Many sedans have outstanding legroom in the back.

A semi sneaky way to try out various cars is to attend a big street rod event. It seems like half of the cars are for sale at any given moment, so pretend like you're in the market for a Deuce roadster. You really are in the market, just not for someone else's car. You could be totally honest and tell the sellers, "I'm seriously thinking about getting a '32 Ford, but I'm not sure I will fit. Do you mind if I sit in your car?" You can also size up the seller and ask him how the car fits him. Temper his answer with the fact that he wants to sell you the car.

When checking out cars for fit, look carefully at the seat construction. A good upholsterer can find a couple extra inches if they plan ahead for a tall driver.

The thing to watch for with seats that have been squeezed down is whether the seat is still comfortable. Several reproduction street rod body manufacturers have altered their bodies slightly to offer extra room. An extra inch or two can make a huge improvement in comfort.

A chopped top can be a problem if you're tall. Depending on your height, you may end up looking right through the top of the windshield frame. Tops that have been chopped a couple inches are very common on open and closed cars, so check how you fit.

Your size might mean that a Tudor sedan is your best choice. In a sedan you have a great deal of latitude in where the front seats are mounted. Coupes and roadsters are limited by their design.

WRONG AXLE WIDTH

How the tires and wheels fit the car is a major determinant of a car's overall look and appeal. Choosing a good wheel and tire combination is important, but the best combo won't look good if it's six inches outside of the fenders. The wide track look is for new Pontiacs and Hot Wheels toys. On a street rod, you want the tires to be just inside the fender lip with enough room for suspension travel. Placing the wheels too far in is also a styling gaffe.

An underlying cause of tires that stick out too far is axles that aren't the right length. Axle width needs to be coordinated with wheel width, back spacing, and tire size. All of these elements must work together to achieve that perfect look. Some corrections for axle width can be made with the wheels, but changing wheels after the car has been built is expensive. The solution is to get the right measurements before you order the chassis.

Incorrect axle width can also be a front-end problem. The number of axle width choices is small, so it's tougher to go wrong with the front axle. A bigger front-end problem is a poor choice of wheel offset. Wheels with too little back spacing will place the wheels and tires too far outboard. Wheel and tire location is very noticeable on full-fendered cars, but it's also a big deal on highboys.

IT'S ALL ABOUT STANCE

Stance is something most street rodders want, but not everyone can get it right. Stance is both elusive and accessible. Stance is also rather subjective. It's one of those things in life that can be hard to define, but you know it when you see it.

Stance is how a street rod sits. Therefore, all street rods have some type of stance. When people discuss stance, they're really talking about cars with an excellent stance. Rods that look right (and "right" can be very subjective) are usually praised for their stance. A great stance is sort of like celebrities who are labeled as being cool, hip, or trendy. The arbiters of style are anonymous, but most often associated with the media. The same could be said about stance for street rods.

It's all about attitude, both the physical attitude of the car and the demeanor of the car. The car's psychic attitude is a direct result of its physical attitude. A street rod that sits right exudes a slightly arrogant, bad boy attitude, which is what hot rods are all about. Daily transportation cars have a stance, but they don't have much of an attitude.

Stance is also about proportions. The way the car sits is the main thing,

Stance is one of the most important aspects of a successful street rod. Stance is largely about the relationship of the wheels, tires, and body to the pavement or how the car "sits." John Carmody's '32 highboy has all the right elements of a classic Deuce highboy stance including the big 'n' little wheel and tire combo.

but how the various body parts look and how well they work with the rest of the car is also very important. There isn't any exact formula for proportions; things just have to look right. It's similar to what determines a beautiful woman. Proportions are a part of the beauty equation, but there are lots of women with "ideal" proportions that aren't generally considered beautiful. The whole package has to work well together.

Some builders favor top chops that are equal from front to back, while other builders like to take a little more off at the front. Depending on the car, a 3-inch chop at the windshield which tapers to a 2 1/2-inch chop at the back can give a subtle, but pleasing slant to the roof. A slant chopped top works with the overall rake of a car, but there's no guarantee that a slant chop will make a car a stance

superstar. How the finished car looks is far more important than any arbitrary set of measurements.

RAKE

Rake is the when the nose of the car is lower than the rear. Virtually all street rods are raked to some extent. Some builders like a perfectly level car, but they're a distinct minority. Rake can vary substantially, anywhere from a barely noticeable slope to the automotive equivalent of a cliff. The amount of rake is a big part of a car's stance. That amount, like most stance elements, is subjective and can vary from one region to another.

Using our first choice icon car, the '32 Ford highboy roadster, it's easy to see the role that rake plays in the overall look

Stance involves more than just the suspension and wheel/tire combination. It also involves the body modifications and the overall "attitude" of the car. Dan Petersen's '32 Sedan Delivery highboy has all the right elements. Even the windshield visor aids the look of the chopped top.

bows that are taller in the back than they are near the windshield. The forward slant of the top is another styling element that favors the raked look.

Full-fendered deuces also accentuate the forward rake. The different arches of the front and rear fenders work well with a rake. The rear deuce fenders are much more rounded than the front fenders. Rear fenders more closely follow the shape of the tire. The front fenders gradually slope back to the running boards. The leading edge of the front fenders has a slight downward slant that works very well with a raked stance.

Most of the rake elements were part of the original '32 Ford styling. Street rodders simply took advantage of those styling cues and accentuated them. The '33/'34 Fords also have a great natural rake that street rodders have capitalized on.

All the aspects of rake that have been mentioned contribute to a feeling of forward motion. Hot rods are all about improved performance and styling. Street rods are very active cars; they're not passive, so a forward rake is very natural.

of the car. Many elements of a deuce highboy combine to work with a forward rake. The big and little tires provide rake, both physically and visually.

Shorter front tires naturally place the nose of a car closer to the pavement than the rear end. The big rear tires closely follow the fender styling lines. That helps determine the height of the rear tires. Since the front tires are noticeably shorter, the big-to-short aspect draws your eyes forward and down.

Deuce frame rails have a natural rake. The smooth, flowing side rails arch up at the back. The front frame horns end on a downward slant. On a highboy, the exposed frame rails are a visual cue. The dropped front axle and short tires accentuate the natural flow of the frame rails.

The fact that deuce frames are noticeably narrower at the front further enhances the forward rake. The factory styling of the cowl, hood, and grille shell have a slight forward slope. The belt line styling reveal has a spear-like effect. It ends at the front edge of the hood side panels, again reinforcing that forward thrust look. Even the headlights on a highboy add to the raked look since they're traditionally mounted several inches lower than the stock headlights.

Highboy roadster windshields are usually chopped or leaned back slightly. Both techniques favor the forward rake. Convertible tops for roadsters have top

Body mods can influence stance. Craig Lang's bad boy '33 coupe has a slight slant chop which helps bring the eyes forward. The angle of the "A" pillars matches the leading edge of the doors. The car has excellent symmetry. The semi-gloss black paint, Halibrand wheels, and wild flames all contribute to the overall impact of the car.

The rear view is a great angle on '32 Fords. Notice how the big and little tires work with the natural design and flow of the fenders. This 3-window coupe has perfectly sized rear tires. They fill the fenders and leave just enough clearance for body movement.

GETTING THE RIGHT STANCE

Copy the stance of cars that most appeal to you. There's absolutely nothing wrong with copying another street rod. This is especially true with a bolt-together street rod. You want a car that's very well accepted by the street rodding community. The status of an ordinary street rod can be greatly enhanced with a great stance. That initial impression of how the car sits goes a long ways toward diverting attention from any budget aspects of a car.

You can copy another car's stance by taking measurements of the car (with the owner's permission, of course). Besides the actual measurements, make note of the car's components. A big-block powered car will sit lower than a small-block equipped car with the identical suspension components. Anything that affects the weight of a car will affect the stance.

Suspension components are very central to the stance of a street rod. All factors need to be considered. It's not enough to know that a car has a 4-inch dropped tubular front axle. You also want to know what type of spring was used and the makeup of the spring pack. Whether or not the main spring has reversed eyes is important. The type of front crossmember is a big determinant of stance. Many '32 Ford street rod frames use a Model A crossmember that places the nose closer to the ground than the stock '32 unit.

If you're measuring cars, you might find slightly different wheelbases on similar cars. Some builders and chassis companies are so tuned into stance that they go as far as to reposition the wheels. For example, some builders feel that '32 highboys have better aesthetics when the front crossmember is moved forward one inch. That increases the wheelbase by an inch.

Builders of full-fendered cars can also massage the wheel/tire location. Their goal is to center the rear tires within the fenders and to find the most attractive location for the front tires. Details like that might not be noticed right away, but they contribute to a perfect stance.

Besides measuring cars that appeal to you, a knowledgeable chassis builder can be a tremendous asset. These people deal with street rods for a living, so they know what works and what doesn't. Cars that have a great stance are rolling advertisements for their chassis. The builders need to know all the particulars of your car and how you plan to use it.

If you're concerned about the location of the wheels, ask the people at the chassis company. Ask them if they make any changes to the stock locations and if so, why? They should be able to point you to examples of cars with their chassis so you can compare their stance to that of other chassis builders.

SAFETY AND COMFORT

Some modified car and truck builders feel that there's no such thing

Sometimes it seems like there are almost too many perfect '32 highboys at major street rod events. That means there are lots of great examples to emulate. The fit, finish, stance and components are outstanding on this Deuce. Notice how the radical rake of the DuVall windshield works with the car's overall style.

as too low. Many magazine feature cars appear to be incredibly low. Terms like "in the weeds," "slammed," "laying frame," and "on the deck" are very positive in the view of magazine editors. A key element of magazine features cars is that they're most often parked for the photos. The car may have adjustable air-bag suspension, and you don't see if their height was raised for driving. If the suspension isn't adjustable, you can't see how rough the ride is or what a chore it is navigating the slightest road irregularities.

Ultra low cars are more for show than go. Since having fun is more about driving than parking, don't get too carried away trying to have the lowest street rod in town. The idea is to reach a nice compromise of stance, comfort, and safety.

A prime safety aspect related to stance is the vehicle's scrub line. The scrub line is an imaginary line between the lowest edge of any two rims. No steering, suspension, or chassis components should hang below this line. In case of a flat tire, you want the car to continue rolling on the rim, not skidding along on some chassis or engine part.

Suspension travel is related to both safety and comfort. The suspension has to have enough travel to absorb road shocks and keep the tires firmly in contact with the pavement. Road contact is also an important part of braking. You may think a rock-hard ride is tolerable, but it won't be for long. A comfortable street rod is one that's much more likely to get used.

By building an icon street rod and dealing with experienced, well-respected chassis manufacturers, obtaining a near perfect stance shouldn't be too difficult. Stick with proven combinations. People have been building great looking '32 Fords for decades so the winning combinations are readily available. You just have to pay close attention to details.

A street rod doesn't have to be a highboy to have a good stance. This resto-rod has a fine stance even though the tires aren't dramatically different from front to rear. It still sits low enough with a mild rake so no one will confuse it with a restored stocker.

A GOOD PLAN

Planning is a major theme of this book. Almost everyone consulted during the preparation of this book has stressed the importance of thorough planning. It's important for any street rod builder to have a plan and stick to it, but it's even more important for a first-time builder to have a solid plan.

There are many ways, from simple to complex, to gather information related to building a street rod. It can be as simple as marking magazine pages with Post-It notes and making lists on a yellow legal tablet, to having a multi-media computerized presentation. The main idea is to gather enough information to form opinions on what you like and dislike as well as getting a handle on costs.

VISUAL AIDS

It helps to be able to look at and study a variety of cars. Even though many of the icon cars discussed in this book seem similar, there are plenty of differences once you take a closer look. The more you learn about street rods, the more important these details will become. It's easy to agree that a '32 Ford roadster is the car you want. Once you make that basic decision, you'll be amazed at the variety of ways such a car can be built. The cars may be "bellybutton" cars, but like navels, there's a wide range of looks.

Whatever you can do to centralize your reference materials will make it easier to access and compare. A stack of magazines is a common reference source, but it's much easier to find what you want if you make an index of articles and car features. If you have categories for things like chassis and suspension, body, drivetrain, interior, wheels and tires, and miscellaneous, you can find a specific article quickly. We like to use those 1/2-inch x 2-inch neon Post-It notes on the magazine pages of interest. We use a different color for each major category.

Street Rodder magazine is an outstanding source of information. The issues are approaching the size of a rural phone book, so looking for a particular article can take a while. Each January issue includes an index of the previous year's content. This is a good thing to photocopy.

If you have access to a copy machine, you can copy articles of interest and keep them in file folders. That way you can quickly look through everything you have on a particular subject.

People who are very adept at computer programs like Photoshop will make concept illustrations based on your desires. These services are usually pretty reasonable if you can't do your own computer-generated concepts.

Most high-end street rods these days make use of an automotive designer. These talented artists can do very detailed illustrations of a car, offering multiple views and color themes. The best of these designers can be expensive, but people who spend over six figures on a street rod feel that the expense is well justified.

If you can't rationalize the cost of a "name" designer, check out local colleges or design schools. Often, you can find students who lack the experience to charge big bucks, but can still do excellent work. Many newcomers need and want exposure in the street rodding

A great thing about the popularity of '32 Fords is that there are so many to inspect at any decent sized street rod event. Be sure to bring a camera to record the features that appeal to you.

They didn't make any ugly '32 Ford body styles. Our suggestions for an icon Deuce are limited, but if you must have another body style, there are plenty to choose from.

community, so they're eager to design cars at affordable prices.

A designer (even a student one) can be a valuable asset, especially when it comes to choosing paint schemes, if you want anything other than a solid color. Given the high cost of custom paint jobs, it makes good financial sense to spend a couple hundred dollars more to know what you're getting. An ugly paint job costs a whole lot more to redo than paying a designer for some concept sketches.

Attending as many street rod events as possible is one of the best planning aids of all. Large national or regional events are the best because of the incredible volume and variety of cars. It's worth traveling to a major event because there's nothing as good as seeing the cars up close and personal. Besides closely inspecting cars, talking to the owners is an invaluable source of information.

Whenever you attend a street rod event (regardless of size), take along a camera. It doesn't matter as much whether the camera is a standard still camera, a video camera, or a digital cam-era. Film and videotape are cheap. The media cards for digital cameras are more expensive, but their creative flexibility is tough to beat.

When using a 35mm camera, try to use one with the widest possible lens. Street rod events tend to be crowded with spectators. Everyone want to get a close look at the cars, so if you're trying to shoot photos with an 80mm plus lens, you'll be so far away from the car that you'll have a very difficult time getting good total car shots. I use a 21mm-35mm zoom lens with a motor drive so I can get in close and shoot several frames if someone should step in the way. A macro lens is good for taking close-up detail shots.

Professionals who shoot for publications, use transparency film. They like the slow speed film (a low ASA number like 100 or less) for maximum color saturation. That's how they get those brilliant reds that you see in magazines. Pros often use a big flash even on sunny days. The flash fills in the shadows and helps make the colors really pop.

When you're taking photos strictly for personal use, color print film is the best choice. You can get oversized prints at a reasonable cost. Unless you're worried about accurate color representation, a faster film speed (like 200 ASA or 400 ASA) will give you more latitude in low light conditions without having to use a tripod. ASA numbers over 400 start to get grainy and colors can stray from accurate to abnormal.

You'll see lots of video cameras at street rod events. They're a great way to effortlessly shoot hours of video on anything that moves. You can use the audio feature to make notes to yourself. The downside to video cameras is that they're difficult to make comparisons with. Unless you do a lot of editing, you'll have examples of cars you want to study all over the tapes. We're all for video cameras, but we'd shoot still photos as well.

Digital cameras are the coming thing. They're revolutionizing the photo industry. Costs keep dropping while features and image quality keep improving. When you're just taking photos for personal use, you don't necessarily need some huge megapixel rating. You're looking for a record of ideas, not publication quality images.

Cameras that have either a movable lens or LCD monitor allow you to place the camera under cars for neat detail shots. Even on cameras that aren't that flexible, the fact that you can view the image before deciding whether or not to keep it means that you can shoot "blind" and if the shot isn't right, you can do it over. Zoom and macro lens features are nice to have so you can shoot a wider variety of photos.

With a digital camera you can do all kinds of neat things in terms of making reference files on your computer. The biggest limiting factor with digitals is the need for extra media cards. If you want to record a lot of images, you'll need costly extra media cards. Higher resolution images require more megabytes of storage. You could bring along a laptop computer and download images fre-

quently, but not many people carry laptops to car shows.

CONSTRUCTION PHOTOS

Once you start building your street rod, don't stop taking photos. A still photo or video record of the project will be both enjoyable to review later and instructional should you want to build a similar car in the future. Since we advocate building the car, fitting the pieces, driving it a while, and then taking it apart for painting and reassembly, a visual record can aid in the process.

If you get pre-assembled components, photograph them as you take them apart for painting or other work. That way you'll have an accurate record instead of trying to remember how the parts fit on an item that you disassembled three months ago.

Another benefit of construction photos is that you can give the next owner a set. The photos show the care of construction and the quality of the parts

you used. The photos can allay any doubts about how the car was built, especially on areas that are difficult to inspect.

Construction photos are fun to take to work or family gatherings. You can share your enthusiasm, which will help keep you motivated. When friends and family know about the project, they're more apt to ask you about it and that can be a subtle form of encouragement to keep the project on track.

NUMBER CRUNCHING

Visual planning aids are great for deciding what looks best and what type of features you want on your dream car. After you determine the elements of your ideal street rod, you need to figure out the costs. Get catalogs from several competing street rod companies. Compare costs (be sure you are comparing items similar in quality and degree of completeness) and include a "fudge factor" to cover price increases and general underestimating.

When people talk about little Deuce coupes, there are two different body styles, three-window and five-window models. The three-windows seem to be a little more popular, but it's a matter of personal taste as to which one you choose.

You can circle catalog prices or write lists on a lined tablet, but it's easier if you use comparison worksheets. You can customize your own forms to obtain information that's personalized or you can use some of the forms presented in this book. One of the biggest things about pricing worksheets is the need to be all-inclusive. Small parts can hundred-dollar the project to death. All too often, it only takes a handful of parts to blow a hundred dollar bill. That's another reason to buy the most complete kits and subassemblies. Kits are inevitably less expensive in the long run than buying things piecemeal.

Written forms are fine, but like the visual aids, it's even nicer if you can computerize the process. A few simple spreadsheets will allow you to compare prices and to keep running totals as the car is built. Cost analysis spreadsheets can help keep the budget on track. You can compare projected versus actual costs. You could even start with the total budget and work backwards.

Besides helping you as you go, such spreadsheets are a fine record of the project. They're an excellent way to show a potential buyer how much you've invested in the car. Spreadsheets may or may not be a good thing to show your spouse. Depending on the level of openness in the relationship, the spreadsheets will either show how responsible you are or reveal how much you spent on a silly old car.

Many '32 highboys look similar from across the street, but when you get up close you'll see lots of differences. These variations are things you can do to make your car unique while still staying well within the popularity boundaries.

YOUR PERMANENT RECORD

Well-executed planning aids can be more than something you use during the pre-building stage. Once you make your buying decisions, the worksheets can be converted to permanent records. You can also use them during the construction process. Keep records of what you ordered, whom you spoke to, how you paid for it, when the order was placed, and when it arrived.

When you make a permanent record of the parts used and any relevant parts numbers, you or a future owner will have a much easier time of finding any needed replacement parts. It's a good idea to make a smaller record of key mechanical parts and keep that list with the car. Then, if you have trouble out on the road, you'll know the part number of the item that broke. Since street rods are made up of many different make, year, and model parts, having the correct part number can save a lot of headaches.

Besides keeping a record of parts numbers, it's a good idea to include specifications. You should know these things when the car is being built, so why not write them down? Include things like front alignment specifications. Should you hit a monster pothole on a road trip, the alignment shop will know how to duplicate the original settings after they've done any necessary repairs. If any special engine tuning was done, repairs will be made correctly instead of relying on stock specifications.

Anything that helps you accurately plan your street rod is a valuable tool. Since careful planning is such a big part of building a great street rod, you're better off to err on the side of over planning. Don't expect to keep track of everything in your head. Dreaming about a street rod is lots of fun, but conscientious planning will help insure that those dreams do come true.

Besides saving time, buying a rolling car and chassis makes budgeting easier because such a big portion of the cost is tied up in one purchase. This '31 Model A full-fendered roadster is all steel and built by Brookville Roadster, Inc. (Brookville Roadster)

WHEELS AND TIRES

Adding wheels and tires to your street rod may seem like one of the easiest parts of the whole project. In many ways, it is, but it's also an area that can seriously detract from an otherwise great car. Wheels and tires are one of those "make-or-break" elements on a street rod. Choosing the right wheels and tires can be more important than picking the right color.

Painting a street rod one shade or red or another is a matter of personal preference. Within our rather arbitrary guidelines for building an icon rod, red is red. There are reds that are more popular (generally, brighter reds are better) than others, but you'd have to be pushing the limits of reddish-brown mud in order to go wrong with a red paint job.

Wheels and tires can be more important than paint color to the overall "look" of a street rod. Wheels and tires greatly affect the all-important "stance" and they also set the tone for what type of street rod you're building. Steel wheels go with the traditional hot rod look. Wire wheels are generally associated with resto-rods. Billet wheels are generally found on high-tech rods. And then, there are the "standards" that we so strongly advocate like the 5-spoke Torq-Thrust and Halibrand slotted mags (along with all the variants of these themes).

Even though we frequently mention the American Racing Torq-Thrust 5-spoke mag wheels and the slotted Halibrand Sprint wheels, there are lots of similar wheels made by other manufacturers. You can't go wrong with these two icon wheels, but if you don't want

to be just like half of the cars on the fairgrounds, you can pick a variation on these popular themes. Even American Racing and Halibrand make variations of their own marquee wheels. The key with using other wheels is not to stray too far from the classic look.

Like so many things in life, first impressions are very important. That may be shallow, but that's reality. Street rodders love the "neck snapping" aspect of a subtly executed super rod. That's where people are initially attracted to a car and then they notice some of the subtle modifications that make them

really pore over the car. That level of construction isn't something you should try to achieve with your first bolt-together street rod.

Even super rods rely a lot on first impressions. The car has to look right from clear across a large parking lot or people will walk on by. With a bolt-together street rod, first impressions are even more important, because you don't have tens of thousands of dollars worth of nuances that are commonly found on super rods. Wheels and tires are key elements of a good first impression as well as a good lasting impression.

A well-executed '32 highboy roadster is virtually a timeless street rod. Roy Brizio built this beautiful example in the late eighties, but it would still be admired at any contemporary rod run. The big 'n' little wheel/tire combination is a big part of the car's great stance. Like the car, the Torq-Thrust wheels are also timeless.

The large diameter wheel craze has crossed over from imports and sport trucks to the street rod venue. It takes the right style car for these huge rims to look their best. This super smooth '32 3-window coupe has lots of high-tech features that work well with the big wheels and low profile tires.

COMMON MISTAKES

You can learn a lot from the mistakes of others. Building a successful bolt-together street rod requires a fair amount of research. People who are students of street rodding tend to build the best cars. By studying existing cars in person (the preferred way) and in magazines, you can see which styles work and which ones don't. Remember, you don't want to build a trend setting street rod, you simply want to build the most acceptable car for the least amount of money. You're definitely building a "copy cat" car. Just try to copy the best cars.

The wrong wheels and/or tires on an otherwise nice car are like a few wrong notes by a symphony orchestra. If you wince, you know something wasn't right. Wrong notes or wrong wheels are a distraction from something that would otherwise be enjoyable.

You might not spot obviously wrong wheel and tire combinations.

Maybe you, like the builder of the car, think 12-inch wide wheels on all four corners give the car a neat Indy racer look. Everyone is entitled to their opinion, but don't expect to see cartoon styled cars in any national magazine or as the recipients of any event awards. If you're taste challenged, study the cars that win the awards and get the most magazine coverage.

One very serious mistake is mixing themes. The style of the wheels and tires need to match the theme of the car. We never cease to be amazed at how many people miss this point. Directional, billet wheels and ultra-low profile tires don't belong on a flathead-powered nostalgia rod. Likewise, painted Kelsey Hayes wire wheels and narrow, bias ply tires don't fit the style of a high-tech hot rod.

It might be possible to add a unique twist to a car by boldly blending building styles. Similar situations occur in fashion and home decorating. No laws state that you can't mix stripes, checks,

and plaids or have Danish modern and French provincial furniture in the same room, but it takes a bold person to pull it off. Edgy mixes straddle a fine line between wow and whoops. You don't even want to attempt such combinations on your first bolt-together street rod.

Probably the most common mixed themes mistake is putting some high tech wheels on a car that just doesn't need them. The latest euro-Asian 20-inch diameter alloy wheels might look stunning on a new sports car or sport truck, but that doesn't mean they'll look as well on a '32 Ford. Manufacturers tend to showcase their wheels on the types of vehicles that look best with the wheels. Pay attention to the types of vehicles used in wheel manufacturer's ads and catalogs. Don't let the flash of some new wheels cause you to make an expensive mistake.

Exaggerated sizes are another big mistake. Any wheel that's too wide or tall on either end of the car can look silly. Exaggerated sizes are a problem on highboys and an even bigger headache on fendered cars. Tires that protrude past the fenders don't look right.

A very common term around street rodders is "big 'n' little," which refers to large rear tires and much smaller front tires. There are definite limits to the size differential. T-buckets often have vastly different tire sizes and they probably handle it as well as any vehicle. Some deuce highboy builders achieve an almost cartoon look with exaggerated size differences, but on a bolt-together street rod it's best to be more conservative.

Other tire mistakes include the improper use of whitewall tires and raised white letter tires. Whitewall tires are acceptable on many cars including versions of the icon rods advocated by this book. The challenge is to use the right style and width whitewall to match the theme of the car. In general, whitewalls give a street rod a nostalgic look. Whitewalls look best with painted steel wheels, small hubcaps, and narrow trim rings.

Raised white letter tires were once quite popular, but so were six-inch wide paisley ties. Black sidewalls are the safest bet. You can't go wrong with black. Some fanatics have gone as far as shaving off the tire size information so they could have completely smooth, black sidewalls.

OFFSETS AND BACKSPACING

Getting the optimum wheels for your street rod involves more than just the wheel diameter and width. The wheel's offset is also very important. The offset, whether positive, negative, or zero, provides the "dish" or amount of recess from the outer rim to the mounting surface.

Offset is the location of the wheel center relative to the mounting surface, or the distance from the hub-mounting surface to the centerline of the wheel. A zero offset wheel is evenly centered. It's the same distance from the mounting surface to both outer edges of the rim.

A wheel is considered to have positive offset when more than half of the wheel is on the brake side. Conversely, a negative offset wheel had more than half

on the outside. Typically, modern front wheel drive cars have positive offset wheels. Even powerful rear wheel drive cars like modern Corvettes have positive offset wheels

Backspacing is another term used to describe the physical characteristics of a wheel. Backspacing is the distance from the wheel's bolt pad mating surface to the innermost part of the wheel rim. It doesn't matter if a wheel has zero, negative, or positive offset, it still has backspacing. Given an identical width wheel, the amount of backspacing would be different with all three types of offset. The positive offset wheel would have the greatest backspacing, followed by the zero offset and the negative offset wheels.

Wheel width is a misleading term when it comes to buying custom wheels. It would seem pretty obvious that a 15x7-inch wheel was 7 inches wide. It's actually 8 inches wide. Overall wheel width is approximately 1 inch wider than the stated width. That's because wheel widths are measured from bead seat to bead seat, not from outside edge to outside edge. The bead seats are where the tire is secured to the wheel.

Wheel width is one of those things like lumber sizing. A 2 by 4 is actually a 3-1/2 by 1-1/2–inch piece of wood. A 15x7-inch wheel is actually 8 inches wide, overall. You need to remember that a wheel will be one inch wider than its listed width.

Both offsets and widths are important when it comes to choosing the best wheels for your application. Street rods usually deal with very close wheel/tire/suspension clearances. In order to obtain the optimum look, builders strive to fill fender wells, keep the stance as low as possible, and still clear any suspension or chassis components. Offset variations of as little as half and inch can make a big difference in how a car sits, looks, and drives.

Sometimes, wheel offsets are referred to as the amount of front and back spacing. Backspacing is a far more common term than front spacing, although the amount of wheel on the outboard side of the mounting hub is the part most responsible for the "look" of the wheel.

Street rods have traditionally favored extra front spacing. That gives the wheel a deeper look. This look was popularized with the old chrome reverse wheels, where steel wheels had their centers removed and turned the opposite way. Most factory wheels in the fifties and sixties had more back spacing than front spacing, so by "reversing" the wheel, you ended up with a deeper wheel. That makes the wheel look wider even though the overall width hadn't changed.

Offsets and the amount of backspacing are important even on fenderless street rods. There aren't any fender lips to contend with, but a wheel that's nicely centered over the front brakes looks far better than one that's too far to either side. The straight-on front profile is a classic view of a '32 highboy. The size and location of the front wheels and tires are critical elements of this view.

CLEARANCES

Just as tires don't look right if they're too wide, tires that are too skinny also don't look right. This problem is most apparent on full-fendered cars. If there's too much distance between the outer edge of the tire and the fender lip, that gap won't look right. The goal is to fill the fender while leaving just enough clearance for suspension travel on most roads.

Large diameter wheels have a lot more space between the spokes. That leaves the brakes more exposed than usual, so it's nice to have good-looking brakes like these rear discs with polished calipers.

Body and suspension travel are important considerations when choosing wheels and tires. While a nice, tight fit is desirable; it's no good if you can't drive the car without constant chassis/body interference. The general rule is to leave a minimum of one-inch clearance between the widest part of the sidewall and the frame or fender.

You also need to allow for up and down suspension travel, especially when the car is fully loaded. A front seat passenger and two more guests in the rumble seat could easily add 500 to 600 pounds. What may appear to be ample clearance during construction could turn into a big rub when the finished car is loaded with passengers.

Front wheel width and offsets will affect the turning radius of a vehicle. You don't want the tires to hit the front four bar suspension links on hard turns. Yet, you don't want a wheel with too much negative offset (or limited backspacing) because that will give the car an extra wide track.

Dropped front axles are available is different widths. The axle width also affects the track of the car. Knowledgeable chassis manufacturers can help you pick the best axle width, wheel offset, wheel width, and tire size

This is a Halibrand Swirl, which is like the Sprint, but the spokes are slightly twisted. Al Clark has a super stance on his '32 Tudor. Notice how well the tires tuck up inside the front fenders.

so the whole combination works well together. The best time to make these decisions is when the chassis is ordered, rather than trying to correct mistakes after the chassis has been delivered.

WHEEL CONSTRUCTION

There are several different types of custom wheels with quite a wider range of prices among the different manufacturing techniques. As the builder of a first-time, bolt-together street rod, you should focus on buying a popular, affordable wheel that fits right, more than a particular style of construction. If you buy from a well-known manufacturer, you shouldn't have to worry about quality standards.

The more exotic wheels can have features that affect performance at the outer limits, but unless you plan on doing lots of serious racing, those factors shouldn't concern you. Terms commonly associated with custom wheels include billet, forged, cast, and one piece or two-piece construction. Even though custom wheels are called "mags," they're mostly made from aluminum. Alloy wheels are a more accurate term than mag wheels.

Cast wheels are usually the least expensive. Filling a mold with molten aluminum or aluminum alloy makes them. Billet is a big buzzword in street rodding, both as a description of chassis and engine components and as a type of custom wheel. Billet wheels are machined from a disc-shaped piece of aluminum that forms the wheel center. The center is then welded to an outer rim. Forged wheels place aluminum billets between dies and then form the wheel under very high pressure.

Even though cast wheels are the least expensive, it's usually easier to get custom offsets with billet wheels. This can be an important plus when you're dealing with specialized applications. With a standard bolt-together street rod, the normal range of offsets offered by cast wheel manufacturers should be sufficient. Two-piece wheels are easier to custom order offsets than one piece cast wheels.

Custom wheels come in a variety of finishes including painted, polished, natural, and chrome. With the wheels that we advocate, you're most likely to get either natural or polished finishes. Our first choice wheel, the American Racing Torq-Thrust wheel is available in natural cast finish, polished, and chrome. The

Solid wheels are a good choice for budget-minded builders. The wheels work well with traditionally styled street rods. They are most often used with wide whitewall tires. This side view of a '32 highboy illustrates the substantial difference in height and width between the front and rear tires. That is why they're called big 'n' littles. The front wheels are usually 14-inch and the rears are 15-inch (sometimes 16-inch).

chrome finish looks great and is much easier to maintain than a polished wheel, but there's a definite premium for chrome wheels. The polished wheels look almost as bright as the chromed ones, but you have to keep them cleaned and polished.

BEST BETS

There are three basic wheel designs that are always a good, safe choice for a popular, bolt-together street rod. These wheels have been popular for decades and should continue to be that way for a long, long time. The three designs are solid steel, five-spoke aluminum, and slotted aluminum wheels.

Solid steel wheels are pretty self-explanatory, but street rods rarely use the factory-issue steel wheels found on base model passenger cars. You paint a set of factory steel wheels from a Ford or GM passenger car (depending on the bolt pattern of the front and rear hubs), but these wheels are best used as "rollers" for moving the car around your shop before it's finished. There are companies that make special steel wheels for street rods. These wheels come in a variety of sizes and styles. Steel wheels are an affordable, conservative choice.

Custom wheels can be found for not too much more money than street rod steel wheels, especially when you include the costs of hubcaps and trim rings. Regardless of what type of wheel you're considering, include all the parts needed. In the case of steel wheels, caps and rings are extra. With alloy wheels, center caps and lug nuts may or may not come with the wheels. Special center caps like simulated knock-offs are almost always extra.

The two styles of custom wheels advocated here are generically known as five-spokes and slotted mags. Two well-known manufacturers' wheels are so often used to describe these wheels that their names are virtually synonymous with the generic terms. Torq-Thrust wheels are the classic five-spoke mags and Halibrands are the quintessential slotted mag wheel.

The five-spoke Torq-Thrust wheels are also known as "Americans" after the manufacturer, American Racing

In general, highboy rear tires tend to be wide, but not super wide. Some builders like to exaggerate the look with extra wide rear tires (sometimes they're referred to as dirt track tires after the style used by sprint cars). It's important that the tires are close to the body.

Equipment. Similarly, Halibrand makes many styles of wheels and their slotted mags are called "Sprints," but most people simply call them Halibrands.

There are many variations on the Torq-Thrust and Halibrand wheels. The two companies make variations and many other custom wheel manufacturers make versions, too. Halibrand makes a polished five-spoke wheel that resembles the Torq-Thrust design. Regardless of which brand you choose, the point is that it's hard to miss with classic wheels like the polished five-spoke or the slotted mag. These wheels are very popular and quite affordable.

TIRES

Tires are a critical component of any street rod. Besides their most obvious use, tires have a lot to do with the look, ride, and handling of a street rod. Tire size also affects the effective final gear ratio of the car.

Street rod tires tend to be on the conservative side compared to the latest "rubber bands" found on performance cars and trucks. By conservative, we mean tires with relatively tall aspect

ratios. The aspect ratio is the height divided by the section width. Low profile tires have smaller numbers for their aspect ratio. These numbers generally are in increments of five. There are

The slotted style wheels on the Carmody roadster are Billet Specialties Legacy models. The rears are 15-inchers and the front are 14-inchers. The rear tires are B.F. Goodrich Radial T/A, size 385-70R15.

There are many different styles of center caps and trim rings for solid steel wheels. From a distance they all look similar, but there are important differences so check out your options before ordering a set.

exceptions like the common 78 series aspect ratio tires.

Filling the fenders and achieving proper proportioning are important styling functions of tires. Tires are a part of that often elusive "look" that's so critical to successful street rods. Running a conventional 15-inch rim with tall tires can fill fenders or it could be done with 20-inch wheels and low profile tires. If the overall tire diameter is the same, the difference is in the style. For the type of cars advocated by this book, the 15-inch wheel and tall tire is the preferred way to fill the fenders.

Although there obviously aren't any fenders to fill on a highboy, rear tires need to look right in relation to the stamped, inner fender styling lines on the rear quarter panels. If the tires are too short, there will be an excess of the inner fender recess showing. That isn't part of the desired highboy look.

Tall rear tires are a factor in the stance. A rear-to-front rake is an integral part of the highboy stance. Tall tires in back along with considerably shorter front tires produce a "rubber rake."

Tires with a high aspect ratio, generally in the 70 series or higher, aid the ride of a street rod. The taller sidewalls have much more give than low profile tires. That extra flexibility helps absorb road shocks. A traditional highboy will have a ride that's rougher than the plush passenger cars most people drive on a daily basis. The tall tires help cushion the ride.

Tall rear tires also affect the choice of rearend gears. An average automotive tire might be about 25 inches in diameter. A truck tire could be in the 27 to 29-inch tall range. A highboy rear tires could be as much as 30 to 33 inches tall. The taller the tire is, the higher (numerically lower) the effective gear ratio will be.

If a hypothetical car was set up to cruise at an ideal rpm range with 27 inch tall tires, going to a taller tire would be like swapping in some economy gears. Switching to the shorter tires would be like installing performance gears. Since the tall highboy tires reduce the effective final gear ratio, it's common to see gear ratios in the 4.10:1 and higher range. A 4.10:1 gear set in a normal passenger car

would be a performance ratio, but in a highboy it could seem normal.

Rear tire size, rear axle ratios, transmission style (overdrive or non-overdrive), and optimum engine rpm at freeway speeds all affect the effective final gear ratio. It's very important to take all these parameters into consideration when you're planning a car. Do this before you start buying parts. The wrong combination could result in an engine that's roaring along at redline while cruising at normal posted speed limits or the opposite, an engine that's barely turning over so that transmission is constantly needing to downshift to avoid lugging the engine.

Front tires don't have as much of an impact on performance and styling as the rears, but they're still important. The majority of a car's braking is done with the front brakes. If the tires are too small, the road contact area is reduced which affects braking performance. Front tires also affect steering.

Tires are rated for their load capabilities. Smaller tires have lower weight ratings than larger, wider tires. Be sure that the front tires are adequate for the weight of the car. Looks are important in building a street rod, but looks should never compromise safety.

WHERE THE RUBBER MEETS THE ROAD

The bottom line with street rod wheels and tires is to follow the crowd. If you study a large number of cars similar to what you plan to build, you should notice definite trends. Tire diameters and widths will fall into a relatively narrow range. Wheel sizes are a function of tire sizes.

Within the range of tires found on cars you like, try to stay in the middle of things. Taking a middle-of-the-road approach will provide an excellent starting point. If you really want something different, you can change later. By choosing a popular tire size and wheel style, you'll be able to sell them without losing too much money. This is another example of how careful planning will allow you the maximum amount of flexibility without huge cost penalties.

BODY BASICS

When it comes to selecting a type of body construction for a bolt-together street rod, you have two basic choices (actually more like one and a half choices): fiberglass or steel. We do know of at least one very ambitious street rodder who fashioned a '32 Ford roadster body entirely out of wood, but you'll have to read *How To Build A Mortise And Tenon Street Rod* for the details.

We facetiously said there are one and a half choices because fiberglass is such an overwhelming favorite when it comes to the type of bodies used on most bolt-together street rods. The primary reason is availability. You can get a fiberglass '32 Ford roadster body (or almost any other two-door '32 model) from a number of fine manufacturers. The old days of long searches and/or expensive purchases are gone.

Some street rod builders still like to have the real steel deal, but there's no longer any real stigma attached to fiberglass-bodied street rods. Finding and restoring a gennie twenties or thirties Ford body is more work than you should attempt for a first-time street rod project. Even already built, older street rods can have a lot of hidden damage underneath a couple layers of paint. A major benefit of buying a new fiberglass body is that you're starting out fresh. There shouldn't be any hidden problems.

A relatively recent development in reproduction Ford bodies is the emergence of steel repro roadster bodies, and even coupe bodies now. A couple of companies manufacture excellent all-steel Model A roadsters (both regular roadsters and roadster pickups), '32 Ford roadster bodies, '32 Ford three-window coupes, and '33-'34 Ford roadster bodies. There's obviously no rust to contend with and finish bodywork before paint is similar to what's required of a fiberglass body. The biggest negative factor concerning steel repro bodies is their higher cost.

In the big picture, steel reproduction bodies don't cost a great deal more than comparable fiberglass bodies. Steel roadster bodies tend to be a couple thousand dollars more expensive than fiberglass ones. If you really want a steel body, spend the money, but if you're on a budget, a couple thousand dollars will buy a lot of other parts. You could probably buy a nice crate motor for the price differential of the two body types.

CHOOSING A MANUFACTURER

All fiberglass Ford roadster and coupe bodies look very similar, but that doesn't mean they're the same under the skin. There are price variations among different manufacturers of the same body style. Sometimes it's a matter of their pricing structure, but it can also be because of extra expenses related to a more complex construction process. It pays to do your research regarding how each company builds their bodies.

An important consideration that a first-time builder might overlook is authenticity. Not all fiberglass bodies are exact replicas of the original Ford products. Most street rod bodies have some common modifications like hidden hinges, recessed firewalls, filled

It's nice to be able to inspect fiberglass bodies in person. Major street rod events (the bigger, the better) are usually attended by the major body manufacturers. That means you can shop and compare before you place an order.

Checking out a bare body allows you to see what type of reinforcements (if any) are used, how thick the fiberglass is, how well the doors fit, and how straight the body panels are. The straighter the panels and the better the fit, the more money you will save on bodywork.

cowl vents, and chopped tops. Many manufacturers offer bodies with or without the above-mentioned features.

There are body manufacturers that offer stylized versions of popular Ford models. Some of these bodies are very popular because they resemble some famous, high-dollar street rod that was extensively massaged. Other stylized or supposedly stock bodies are just a shade off. They have one or more features that are just different enough to be annoying.

Looking at one of these "slightly off" bodies by itself might not make the problem areas noticeable. This can be a

It used to be that original steel bodies were all that was available. Even after the introduction of fiberglass '32 roadster bodies, most other Deuce styles were only available in their original (and often badly deteriorated) state. The current high costs of bodywork and paint make most original bodies an expensive proposition.

problem for a novice builder. Even if the novice builder doesn't notice or mind the styling flaws, they could become a very big problem later. We have frequently mentioned how fussy most street rodders are. These people will notice the body that isn't right and avoid it like the plague when you try to sell it. You might save money initially with a "slightly off" body, but it will come back to bite you later on.

Our suggestion is to use a fiberglass body that's as close to stock proportions as possible. Even if you like a modified body from some designer label builder, that's not the best choice for a first street rod. You want an early Ford body that's as mainstream as possible. A swoopy, hot ticket designer body might be all the rage for a few years, but there's no guarantee that it will still be popular in five years. You can't go wrong when you use an icon body.

Two main building techniques are hand laminating and chopper gun fabrication. Hand laminating is more labor intensive, but it yields a more consistent body. Chopper gun construction is much more automated and quicker, therefore bodies built this way are usually less expensive. As mentioned earlier, we recommend buying a top quality chassis and body. These two things are the foundation of a street rod, so they're not the places to cut corners.

Fiberglass resins and fibers come in different grades. Inexpensive bodies may use less than the best components. You should consult the manufacturers to learn about the products used in their bodies. Top quality body manufacturers will be proud of their materials.

An important area that can affect pricing is the amount and type of reinforcement used in the body. Some companies are proponents of steel reinforcement, some prefer wood, and some use a combination of the two. Builders who use the different reinforcement materials can make an excellent case for their choice. There isn't any government or consumer group testing standards, so you need to talk to people who have built street rods from different body manufacturers.

Professional street rod builders and

custom painters are all pretty opinionated. Street rod body choice isn't a subjective matter. Asking several builders and painters for body manufacturer recommendations can be confusing, but try to find a consensus. Some pro builders change favorites depending on which model you're talking about.

Besides talking to professional builders, talk to car owners at street rod events. Ask them about their experiences with the manufacturer of the body on their car. Even if the person had the car professionally built, they'll know if the body presented a lot of problems because the shop certainly charged for the extra work.

Street rod events are a great place to examine the bodies from different companies. Look very carefully to see how straight the body is. Check for signs of air bubbles or other finish irregularities. Pay particular attention to the areas around the doors and deck lid. Areas where hinges are mounted are typical spots for cracks and stress problems.

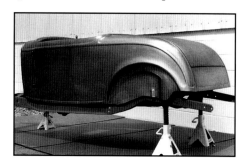

Now you can get a brand new all-steel '32 roadster body. Brookville Roadster makes beautiful reproduction bodies and fenders. The bodies are better than the originals because you can order them with various optional features installed at the time of manufacture. (Brookville Roadster)

Delivery time can be an issue with a fiberglass body. Due to the construction options such as door hinge style, firewall design, top height, and so forth, most bodies have to be special ordered. That can mean a wait of two or three months. You may be able to find a local dealer who has some popular bodies (like deuce roadsters and coupes) in stock, but you won't find much of an inventory.

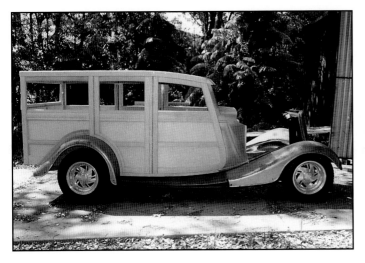

There is a viable wooden body option; Hercules Motor Car Company makes their beautiful "New Generation" '34 Ford Woodie. Besides the beautiful bodies (with hung and latched doors) they supply reproduction cowls and front sheet metal. Chassis in various stages of completion are also available. (Hercules Motor Car Company)

Besides their original style 4-door woodie, Hercules Motor Car Company also offers a phantom 2-door Slant Back Woodie. They call their cars component cars and they offer an extensive array of optional components all the way up to air conditioning and seats. (Hercules Motor Car Company)

There are benefits to custom ordering a body. They don't charge extra for standard options and special requests are reasonable when handled at the time of construction. One custom feature to consider if you're anything close to tall is a slightly stretched body. Cars like a '32 Ford phaeton can be ordered with the front seat moved back a couple inches. The change isn't noticeable from the outside, but those extra inches of legroom will be greatly appreciated. If you're tall, check to see if there are any such options on the body you want. In the relatively tight world of street rod interiors, every inch counts.

You may be able to find a body on short notice if you buy one of the package cars that are available. Some companies offer base body and chassis combos or rolling chassis and body packages. These "one-stop shopping" cars can be a good way to save time and money.

The best way to avoid long delays waiting for a body is to consult the manufacturers at the start of your project. Once you decide on a body style, find out how long it takes to get one. You should probably add a couple weeks to their estimate to be on the safe side. If you time your project well, the body could be on order while you're assembling the chassis and engine. Hopefully,

the body will be ready when the rolling chassis is finished.

The major fiberglass body manufacturers have been around for many years. That wouldn't be the case if too many customers were dissatisfied with the quality of their products. So, the final decision on whose body to use probably comes down to how soon you can get one and the consensus of present owners as to their take on quality.

BODY PREP

A new fiberglass reproduction body is in far, far better condition than a rusted original body, but that doesn't mean that the body is perfect. You could leave the body in its gel coat, but you probably don't want to. Even on the budget paint plan that we've proposed, you should prep the body for paint and get some primer applied. The gaps and seams should be checked for fit and alignment.

The better the quality of the body, the less prep work you'll need to do. The mold release agent needs to be washed off the body. The mold seam lines need to be removed. In order for primer to adhere properly, the body needs to be scuffed up. Any pinholes need to be filled and the body needs to be block sanded to make all the panels as straight as possible. If

there are any body reveals, like the one that runs from the tail of a Deuce to the grille, you need to be sure they line up perfectly. Body reveals that look like a graph of the stock market aren't attractive. Poor panel alignment is a sure sign of a marginal car.

Fiberglass bodies also need to cure. The chemicals in fiberglass cure to the highest temperature that it's exposed to. The darker the final color of the car is, the more important it is to thoroughly heat cure a body. A glossy black paint job will absorb more heat than the minimal gloss black color of the gel coat.

Great gaps are a sign of a well-built street rod. Ideally, the gaps should be no less than 3/32-inch and no more than 1/8-inch. Another critical area of alignment is the styling reveal that runs from the hood to the cowl. (Hercules Motor Car Company)

If fiberglass bodies aren't heat cured, they can continue to cure after the paint has been applied. The odds of a roadster being driven on a hot summer day are excellent. It's this type of day that can cause a post cure. Depending on how hot the body gets, some of the underlying fiberglass texture can show through. You don't want that.

Some companies suggest both sun curing and bake oven curing for bodies that are destined for black paint. Other companies suggest avoiding black and picking lighter colors. If you're concerned about post curing under a dark color, consult a painter is has done a lot of fiberglass street rod bodies and/or Corvettes.

Heat is the best way to cure a fiberglass body before any paintwork is done. If the weather cooperates, you can leave the body outside in the hot sun for a couple days. The body should be bolted to the frame and the doors should be installed and closed. You want the body to cure in its proper position on the chassis.

A quicker, more uniform way to cure a fiberglass body is in a heated spray booth. Many body shops have bake-oven style spray booths. The cost to bake a street rod shouldn't be too much because there isn't any labor involved. You might be able to save money by agreeing to have the body baked overnight or at a time when the spray booth isn't being used.

This is one of Harwood's '32 3-window coupe molds. The coupes include a one-piece headliner and removable garnish moldings. The bodies are cured and post-cured in the mold for up to two weeks. It takes time to build a high quality fiberglass body. (Harwood Street Rods)

Building durable fiberglass bodies is messy, time-consuming work. Each body component at Harwood Street Rods is meticulously hand laminated using fiberglass matt cloth. Parts made with a chopper gun are much less durable. (Harwood Street Rods)

Your best bet is to find a body shop that has cured fiberglass bodies before. The heat should be approximately 150 to 200 degrees. Heat curing a fiberglass body is one of the best things you can do to prevent paint problems later.

Gel coat sands easily so prepping a body for primer isn't too tough. Most people use 80-grit dry sandpaper on a sanding block or long board. The 80-grit sandpaper will leave an excellent surface texture for the primer to bond with. Gel coats don't require heavy sanding, you just want enough to provide a good base for the primer.

You should be on the lookout for air bubbles or pin holes. Sometimes these imperfections show up after primer has been applied. You want to find all air bubbles during the prep stage; they can be a considerable problem if discovered after the final color has been shot. One way to locate air bubbles is to run the round shaft of a screwdriver along all the body edges. Medium pressure should be enough to pop bubbles. Fill the divots with fiberglass compatible body filler.

FITTING FIBERGLASS PARTS

A fine fit is right up there with a great stance in terms of building a successful street rod. Most original, metal-bodied cars of the twenties, thirties, and forties were pretty generous in terms of gaps, panel alignment, and the fit of opening parts. Modern street rodders admire cars that have fit and finish standards equal to any contemporary luxury car.

Don't expect to achieve a micrometer fit on a bolt-together street rod, but don't ignore fit, either. Adjusting doors, trunk lids, and body reveal alignment takes time, but it's an easy way to make your car look like it was built by an experienced professional. As a home-builder, you can afford to spend the time it takes to make things right.

Street rods that are regularly driven should be assembled with looser tolerances than show rods. The razor thin door gap that looks so precise on a show rod is just an invitation to paint chips on a regular street rod. There needs to be about 1/16 inch clearance around the doors to allow room for road vibrations.

When setting gaps, remember that primer and final paint will add a little thickness. Gaps should be checked throughout the full range of motion of doors and deck lids. A gap that's fine when the door is closed might be too tight against the cowl when the door is all the way open.

Fitting a fiberglass car isn't rocket science, but it does require common sense and plenty of patience. Understand, that every time you adjust one part of the

Don't buy a body that doesn't have factory-hung doors. Door fit is a critical feature and not something easily accomplished by beginners. This is Harwood's '32 Tudor with the Sedan Delivery rear door. Notice that the Specialty Power Windows are factory installed along with the window glass. (Harwood Street Rods)

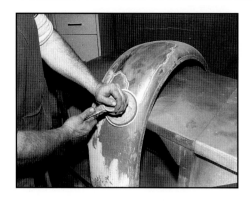

Original steel fenders can require an incredible amount of bodywork. This was actually a very solid Model A roadster pickup fender, but it still took two days to get it straight and ready for paint.

With reproduction steel and/or fiberglass fenders, bodywork should be minimal. The savings in body shop charges can easily pay for the fenders. (Brookville Roadster)

car, several other parts can be affected. It's not good to get the gap right at one end only to leave a huge, unacceptable gap at the other end. Compromise is a big part of fitting a street rod body.

The foundation of a good fitting fiberglass body is a strong chassis. Fiberglass cars, especially open ones, don't have a lot of extra structural reinforcement. Therefore, they rely on a rigid chassis to anchor the body. If there is too much flex in the chassis, items like doors and hoods will move around, leading to out of alignment gaps. Parts that don't fit right are prone to binding, and binding leads to nasty paint chips.

A problem that's related to securing the body to the frame is over tightening. You want a snug, secure fit, but too much force can lead to starring where the body develops small, stress cracks around the fasteners. Fiberglass doesn't do well with stress, so don't force parts. Find the cause of the interference and work slowly to solve the problem.

Starring can be a serious problem when attaching fenders and running boards to a car. Large body washers will help distribute the force. Using lock nuts instead of lock washers will allow the fastener to be secure without applying so much force that starring occurs.

Over tightening fasteners is asking for trouble. You want them tight, but it's better to err a little on the conservative side. You can cinch up the fasteners after the car is assembled the first time

and driven in primer. Using the car for a while before adding paint and upholstery allows you to shake out any problems including body fitting.

A benefit of buying a body and chassis package is that some companies build the fiberglass body on the very frame that will be used with the car. Getting your body built on your frame should save a great deal of fitting hassles. If you're considering a package deal, ask if the body is built on the frame or if the chassis and body are built separately (or acquired from different manufacturers).

Most bodies are built on original Ford frames or special jigs. The integrity of these foundations has a big impact on the final fit of your car. You hope that the original frame or jig matches the dimensions used by the manufacturer of your chassis. Having a body built on its exact frame avoids those possible inconsistencies.

Body parts should be fitted before starting in on the paint prep. Frequently, well-placed body shims will fix problems. Other times, door edges may need to be cut down a little or built up to make the gaps consistent. Be sure that you've exhausted all the adjustments related to shims and fasteners before you start grinding on door edges.

When you're fitting the body to the frame and using shims, you can save time in the long run by keeping a record of the shims. Make an accurate (or approximate) drawing of the frame. Indicate all the mounting holes and give each one a successive number, working clockwise from the right front to the left front.

On a separate list, you can note the number of shims and total thickness. This way you can keep track of where you're making adjustment and have a record of what was needed to make everything fit. Then, you can easily duplicate the shim combinations later in the mock-up and final assembly stages.

In addition to a diagram and list of shim details, you can duplicate the exact body location at any later time by installing two alignment pins. When you're satisfied with the body fit and location, make sure everything is properly secured. Then drill a hole on each

side of the car for body alignment pins. Drill the holes so that they're located in the door openings.

Drill through into the top frame rails. Then insert a dowel pin through the floorboard and into the frame. When you remove the body, leave the alignment pins in the frame. When the body goes back on, the two holes will place it exactly where it was during the fitting stage. The holes can be filled with body filler or just left alone and covered by the carpet.

Fitting and adjusting fenders and running boards involves many more variables than the body of a highboy. That's one of the reasons we advocate building a highboy for a first street rod.

Prepping and adjusting gaps on a reproduction metal body is similar to the fiberglass techniques. Surface prep and bodywork involve standard metal working skills as used on passenger cars. Starting with a rigid chassis is important, as is working slowly and methodically. When it comes to using any body filler, primer, or sealer check with your local paint supply store to ensure product compatibility.

A great deal of time and money can be spent on bodywork. That's another plus for leaving the car unpainted at first. Then, even if you don't get the panels to fit perfectly, you can do make more adjustments as time permits without damaging the paint. Fitting problems aren't quite as noticeable on a primered car as on a beautifully painted one.

Street Rod Tech

A trick to keep the ends of the webbing from fraying is to hold a butane lighter under the end. Pass the lighter back and forth until the plastic in the webbing gets hot enough to melt.

Protective webbing must be placed between the top of the frame rails and the body. The easy way to keep the webbing in place is by using the self-adhesive kind. To locate the holes in the webbing, Tim Divers, of Divers Street Rods, temporarily tapes the material along side of the mounting holes in the frame.

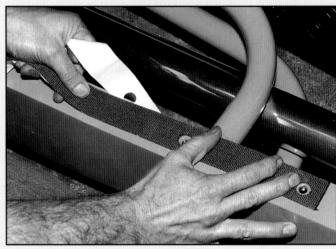

Center the first hole and start peeling away the backing tape. Remove small amounts of the backing as you go. Press lightly at first. Press down on the webbing so that it is perfectly flat. Don't let it bunch up or wrinkle.

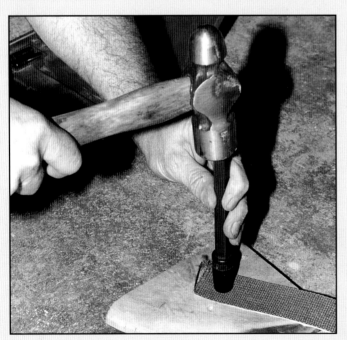

The trick way to get super clean holes is with a set of gasket punches. After marking the hole location with a Sharpie, the punch is centered over the mark and the material is placed on a block of wood. A ball peen hammer is used to make one decisive blow. The gasket punch leaves nice, clean holes. If you use a drill or a knife, the hole won't be as neat and there's a good chance that the webbing may unravel.

The mounting bolts were numbered during the initial fitting phase before the body was painted. Divers uses cut-down 1/8-inch industrial drill bits as locating pins. During the intitial fitting (before paint), 1/8-inch holes were drilled through the body and frame. After paint, these pins align the body perfectly so it can be bolted down for the final time.

Installing and Fitting the Body

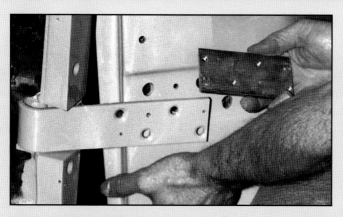

Most street rod door hinges are pretty rudimentary. They're basically big straps of steel that pivot. It's common to have a metal backing plate that fits inside the door skin. That way the doors don't need to be tapped for fasteners.

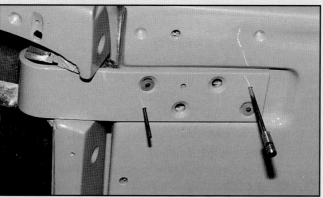

The hinges and doors were drilled with three locating holes during the preliminary fitting stages. The locating pins position the hinge while the tapered head Allen bolts are installed. The bolts are not fully tightened until the door gaps have been checked.

Low-tack masking tape protects painted edges during reassembly. The reason for using low-tack tape is to avoid the chance of lifting any fresh paint. You also avoid dealing with tape residue on the fresh paint. You can use regular masking tape – just stick it to your jeans a couple of times to remove excess adhesive.

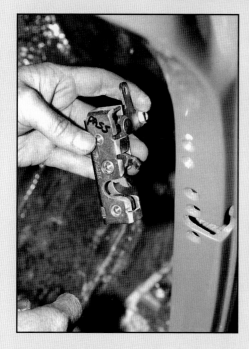

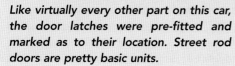

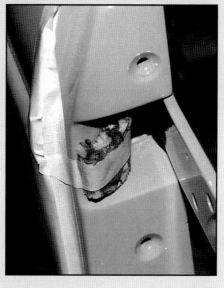

Like virtually every other part on this car, the door latches were pre-fitted and marked as to their location. Street rod doors are pretty basic units.

A pro trick when mounting doors is to tape a piece of foam inside the door-jamb where the hinge can make contact. The hinge will be moved a lot during this phase, but the proper rubber stoppers won't be installed until after the door is hung.

Installing a trunk lid is a two-person job. Someone has to be inside the car lining up the hinges. A big soft blanket was placed at the lower edge of the trunk opening. Again, it's nice that fiberglass is so light.

Street Rod Tech
Installing and Fitting the Body (continued)

The exact size rubber bumpers are important for achieving and maintaining proper door gaps and panel alignment. These common door bumpers are thick enough that they can be trimmed to the exact height needed with a razor blade.

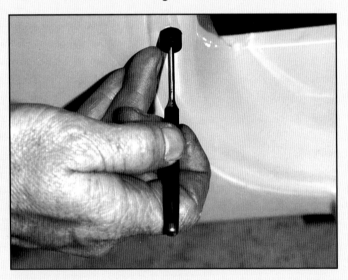

There is a small recess in the end of the rubber bumpers. Place a proper size flat-ended punch in the hole and use it as an installation tool. Gently push the rubber bumper into the hole with the punch. If you push too aggressively there's a chance the punch will pop out and damage the paint.

Even though this hood side panel was pre-fitted, it's still a good idea to work slowly while installing it. This expensive roadster was built to very close tolerances so it's easy to chip unprotected paint. Low-tack masking tape protects the contact areas.

Tim Divers uses small, thin pieces of plywood veneer as spacing guides while fitting hood side panels. They're most useful during the pre-fitting stage, but they can also be used to double-check gaps after painting. Remember when establishing gaps not to make them so tight as to not allow room for paint buildup.

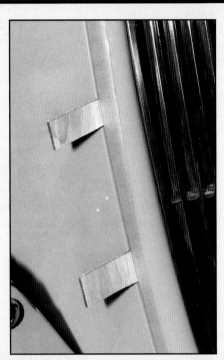

A well-built street rod shouldn't need a lot of body panel adjustments. Those problems should be resolved during pre-fitting. This hood panel and mounting tabs were custom built so only a small slot was necessary to allow for fine-tuning the fit.

Street rod doors should have some type of limiting device to prevent them from opening too far. This slide type limiter has two cotter pin holes to allow for different amounts of travel. Many roadster doors use a simple leather or vinyl door strap. These straps are visible inside the car as opposed to the hidden door limiters.

FRAME AND SUSPENSION

A solid chassis is the foundation of a good street rod. The chassis and all its related components are the most important aspects of building any street rod. A well-built chassis is a safe one and safety should always be a paramount concern. If you scrimp on safety, the only person you're cheating is yourself. A top quality chassis will make the whole project smoother because all the major components are tied to the chassis.

A first class chassis doesn't have to be an expensive one. Shop for quality and functionality first. Style should be secondary. This doesn't mean the chassis should look like the underside of a bridge, but the frame rails should be boxed and the cross members should be substantial enough to resist torsional forces. The chassis should be constructed in a precision jig. Experienced, qualified welders should do welding.

Quality construction shouldn't be a problem if you obtain your chassis from a reputable manufacturer. As a first time builder, you're probably better off going with a well-known, longtime manufacturer. It's easy to find examples of their products and talk to people who have used them. A new manufacturer might have an exceptional product, but it's easier with experienced builders to evaluate their workmanship and engineering.

Any time a chassis manufacturer comes out with something new and revolutionary, view it cautiously. It's not that street rod chassis can't be improved; it's just that the tried and true combinations have been working great for decades. As a first time builder, you want a proven winner. Let someone else experiment with new technology.

Besides the safety aspects of a solid chassis, a good chassis will make construction of the rest of the car easier. The chassis is the mounting point for body parts and driveline components. An uneven frame can make things like door

alignment and hood alignment a nightmare. You want as few variables as possible when it comes to body alignment.

Before you order a chassis, think carefully about the components you want. Street rod chassis are custom built to the customer's specifications. They're not a product that you can take back to the store and exchange for a different one if you change your mind about features. Decide on the style of car you want to build and stay the course.

Think about optional features such as chrome or stainless components. It's much less expensive to incorporate these options at the time the chassis is constructed than it is to make changes later. Do some comparison-shopping on options. Often, a little extra flash is only slightly more expensive than the plain version. This is especially true when you buy a package chassis.

Many chassis manufacturers offer package deals as stage I, stage II, and

A first class chassis is the foundation of any street rod. Buy the best quality chassis and components you can afford. We suggest buying from a chassis from a well-established company. This is the TCI '32 Ford chassis with an I-beam axle and 4-link kit. (TCI)

So-Cal Speed Shop likes traditionally styled street rods. Their '32 Ford chassis features Step-Boxed frame rails, hair pin radius rods, a dropped I-beam axle, rear ladder bars, a transverse rear spring, and a Currie Enterprises 9-inch Ford rear axle housing. The chassis is also available with rear coil-over shock absorbers. (So-Cal Speed Shop)

stage III. The higher the number, the more complete the package is. A complete, ready-to-roll chassis package can save both time and money. These high content packages are especially attractive for first-time builders.

FRAME RAILS

Frame rails are the most basic component of a chassis. They are the perimeter structure that the other components are attached to. It's possible to find a set of original Model A or '32-'34 Ford frame rails at a swap meet. The price might be very reasonable and extremely tempting, but don't buy them. Today, new, reproduction frame rails are the best way to build a bolt-together street rod chassis.

Original or previously modified frame rails are usually an invitation to big repair bills. Parts that are seventy years old are often bent, twisted, rusted, or otherwise compromised. New frame rails are mandatory.

A very small number of manufacturers actually make early Ford frame rails. It takes huge, specialized stamping presses to stamp '32 Ford frame rails. The authenticity of the frame rail design is most important when you're building a highboy. Full-fendered cars obviously hide the frame rails, except for '32 Fords. The styling lines on the outside of Deuce frame rails near the cowl area are very important. These lines should be stamped into the reproduction rails.

Some companies weld up '32 frame rails from flat stock. These frames usually don't have the rounded corners like the originals do. Fabricated rails can be missing the styling lines. Some companies make frames out of round tubing, but we don't recommend them for a bolt-together street rod.

Street rod frames should be boxed. The original frames were "C" shaped with the open part facing inward. Modern V-8 engines put too much stress on stock style frames. By enclosing the open side of the rails with welded steel plates, the torsional rigidity of the chassis is greatly improved.

A good set of frame rails should have the necessary body mounting holes in their proper locations. Cross-members and engine mounts should be set up for the engine and transmission you specify. Cross-members can be either rectangular like the rails or tubular. Different manufacturers have their preferences. We like the flat cross-members because they offer more surface area for mounting accessories. It's more difficult to drill holes and mount brackets to round tubing, but round tubing is very strong.

CROSSMEMBERS

Two terms used in conjunction with crossmembers are K-members and X-members. An X-member is in the center of the chassis, with two legs of the X projecting forward to the frame rails, and two projecting rearward. The X doesn't always meet in the middle, because there needs to be an opening for the drive shaft. The K-member usually consists of a transverse crossmember located near the back of the transmission, with two legs angled forward from the center of the crossmember to the frame rails. It looks like a "K" when viewed from above.

The front crossmember does more than just hold the two frame rails together. On a transverse-sprung front end, it serves as the mounting point for the front spring that is attached to the front axle. The design of this crossmem-

This close-up shot of a TCI '32 Ford crossmember shows how the brake booster and master cylinder are neatly enclosed. The crossmember provides torsional rigidity. TCI likes to uses square tubing since it is easier to drill mounting holes for accessories. (TCI)

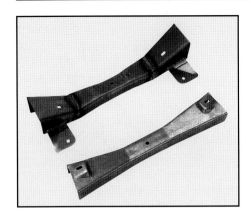

The front crossmember is very important to a good stance on a '32 Ford. The trick is to install a Model A crossmember (at bottom), which lowers the nose 1-inch. The crossmember has a 6-degree rake to provide the correct front-end geometry. The upper crossmember is a '33-'34 with tabs for mounting the radiator. (TCI)

ber affects the stance or the car and how the car handles. A trick that's so popular that it's virtually standard operating procedure is the use of a Model A crossmember in Deuce frames. The Model A crossmember is flatter, and lowers the front suspension by an inch.

Front crossmembers need to have about 6 or 7 degrees of rake (the figure can vary between 5 and 9 degrees). The axle's positive caster should net out at about 6 or 7 degrees. Depending on the amount of forward rake a car has, more positive angle may be needed to net the correct caster.

As the rear of the car goes up (like with extra tall tires), king pins that might have once been vertical now are tilted forward. That creates negative caster, so additional positive caster needs to be dialed into the crossmember in order to end up with the correct setting.

Straight axle cars favor positive caster. Positive caster means that the kingpins are tilted toward the rear of the car from true vertical. Correct caster will make the front wheels track straight instead of wandering. The proper caster adjustment also helps the steering wheel return to center after a turn.

The terms caster and camber are sometimes confused. Caster is the forward or rearward tilt of the kingpins from true vertical. Even though the

tires don't "tilt," the axle does and that affects steering geometry. Camber is when the tires tilt from side to side. Compared to true vertical, tires that tilt outward are said to have positive camber. Wheels and tires that tilt inward have negative camber. Most street rod front axles have the kingpin holes machined at zero degrees. Sometimes, there might be a slight amount of positive camber. Incorrect camber will cause the tires to wear prematurely.

A third front-end term is toe-in (and toe-out). If you look at the front tires from above and they are exactly parallel, that's called zero toe-in. If they point slightly toward each other, that's toe-in, and if the tires point away from each other, that's toe-out. Adjusting the tie-rod ends affects toe-in. Street rods with radial tires are usually set up with a slight amount of toe-in (about 1/8-inch).

The frame horns are an important part of a reproduction frame. The horns are the far ends of the rails. Depending on the exact style of car being built, the frame horns may or may not be left intact. For the type of '32 highboys that this books recommends, it's best to leave the frame horns attached. Builders who don't wish to use the stock style '32 gas tank usually bob the rear horns and install a rolled rear pan.

Some people might be tempted to paint the chassis or have it powder coated before it's assembled, but it's best to wait. A chassis should be assembled once

without paint or powder coating. Then, after you're sure everything fits and works properly, take it apart and paint things. Powder coating is a durable finish, but it doesn't like to be drilled. The finish can easily chip when you're drilling holes for brackets, clips, and accessories.

FRONT SUSPENSION

The front suspension is a key element of any street rod, but especially so with highboys. The front suspension is more visible than the rear, it supports more weight because of the engine, it controls the steering, and it has a major part in determining the all-important stance.

There are quite a few components and variables in assembling a complete hub-to-hub front suspension system. You can buy individual pieces, but the best option is to use a complete front suspension kit. When you buy a front kit (either by itself or as part of a complete chassis package), you don't have to worry about component compatibility. The manufacturer knows which parts work best together. You just need to pick the style of front suspension that looks and works best with your car.

There are two main categories of front suspension: traditional dropped axle and independent front suspension. For a bolt-together street rod, we suggest the simpler, less expensive dropped axle. We're not against IFS, especially if you're building a full-fendered car. If

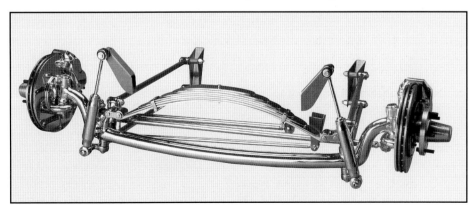

Here is a fully assembled TCI showroom model of a dropped tubular axle front suspension. Tube axles can't twist, and can only be used with a 4-link system. Unlike hairpins or radius rods, a 4-link allows the axle ends to remain parallel while the axle ends move through their suspension travel. I-beam axles, on the other hand, are designed to twist, so hairpins and radius rods are fine for them. (TCI)

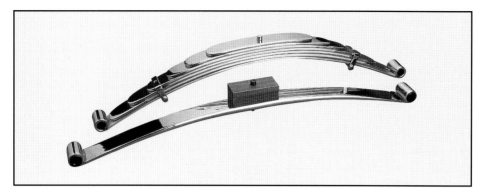

TCI offers two types of front springs for dropped axles. The top 7-leaf is the traditional style and the most common. The mono-leaf springs have reversed mounting eyes, as does the multi-leaf spring. Springs come in two widths to match the two standard axle widths. (TCI)

These are TCI batwings. They're available in stainless steel or stamped and folded steel. The stainless can be polished and the steel can be chromed. (TCI)

you plan to drive your car aggressively and are used to sports car-like handling, that's a good reason to consider the independent front suspension.

Within the dropped front axle category there are a couple variations. Those options deal with the axle and the locating rods. There are two basic axle styles: tube and I-beam. Axle style and the related mounting hardware should match the style of car you're building. A dropped I-beam axle and hairpin radius rods look best on a traditional style highboy. A tubular axle and 4-bar setup have a more modern flavor. A 4-inch drop is the most common configuration for both axle styles.

Dropped axles come in a couple different widths. The most common for the kinds of cars we're dealing with are 46 and 48 inches. There are also 47-inch axles. The narrower axles help keep the wheels and tires tight to the body when disc brakes are used.

The front spring and cross-member should match the axle style and width. In an effort to get the front of a street rod as low as possible, springs with reversed eyes are used. There are springs with hidden Teflon (or similar anti-friction material) buttons that make the movements of the leaves smoother. Some springs use strips of polypropylene between the leaves to eliminate the steel-to-steel contact. Besides the multi-leaf springs (usually seven leaves) there are single leaf springs called mono-leaf springs.

Keeping the front axle assembly in position is the job of the locating rods. There are three choices for straight axle street rods. Actually, there are three choices for I-beams and one choice for dropped tube axles.

Imagine a street rod driving over a bump with one tire – that tire goes up, while the other one stays on level ground. One end of the axle travels through an arc described by the locating link, while the other remains stationary. This imparts a twist on the axle. Tube axles don't twist, so using a four-bar or four-link locating system is imperative. The links form a parallelogram that allows each wheel to move up and down, but the spindles remain parallel, so the axle doesn't twist.

I-beam axles, on the other hand, can twist, so they can use single-bar systems like hairpin radius rods or split wishbones. Aesthetically, hairpin radius rods are favored because of their classic hot rod styling. Split wishbones are even more traditional, but for the purposes of this book, we suggest either a four-link or hairpins. Four-link systems can also be used on dropped I-beam axles.

Transverse front springs can move laterally because of the movement in the shackles that connect the spring to the two spring perches. Lateral movement of the axle can be translated into a steering input, leading to unwanted bump steer where the car over-reacts to irregularities in the road. A Panhard bar should be installed to prevent transverse axle movement. Panhard bars are typically mounted behind the axle, and attach to the frame at one end and the axle at the other. Panhard bars are also used on the rear suspension of many street rods.

The steering gear box is an important component of the front suspension system. Most modern straight axle street

Independent front suspension doesn't offer that traditional hot rod look, but it provides a nice ride. IFS looks best under a full-fendered car, unless the whole assembly is some ultra-trick billet unit. (TCI)

rods use a steering design known as cross steering. A favorite cross steering gear box (it's virtually the de facto box for street rods) is the Vega unit. This compact steering box has a recirculating ball mechanism that provides a smooth feel. The Vega unit is so popular that a couple of companies offer brand new, custom versions of the steering box. There are also new factory style boxes, so there isn't any reason to use a worn-out original.

The front shock absorbers need to be matched to the axle. The shocks need the correct amount of travel to provide a smooth ride. Like all the other front suspension components, you don't have to worry about choosing the right shocks when you buy a package chassis. A complete chassis kit will also include many items that weren't discussed such as the pitman arm, steering arms, spindles, drag link, and batwings.

Brakes are a vital part of the front suspension system. Do not cut corners on the front brakes. The front brakes are one of the most important safety features on a street rod. Since street rods have minimal (if any) bumper protection, you need to be able to stop before hitting anything.

Disc brakes should be considered mandatory equipment. A dual master cylinder is another must-have item. Early street rods like the ones covered in this book frequently use unassisted master cylinders. There are relatively compact power boosters for people who desire power brakes. Space can be at a premium in a street rod chassis, so you might decide to pass on a power booster.

A slick option for builders of traditional style highboys is a special front brake cover that looks like the popular Buick finned drums. These classically styled drums actually conceal modern disc brakes. They're a great way to combine looks and efficiency.

Brake lines are a vital part of any brake system. Some chassis builders include pre-fitted brake lines (and all the necessary fittings and clamps) on their complete chassis kits. Other manufacturers offer brake line kits for specific chassis.

A proportioning valve is another important brake system item. It regulates

Hairpin radius rods provide a traditional hot rod look to the front suspension. As discussed, they should only be used with I-beam axles. They've become very popular on icon style highboys. These TCI hairpins are available in plain steel, chromed or polished stainless. The hairpins attach to the axle via brackets called "batwings." (TCI)

brake line pressure relative to the front and rear brakes. The valve can be adjusted to fine-tune braking performance.

REAR SUSPENSION

Like the front suspension, a car can have either a solid rear axle or independent rear suspension. For the sake of this book, we're going to deal with the less exotic and considerably less expensive solid axles. Independent rear suspension systems look great with all their moving parts, but you can't see them when you're driving the car, so let the other guys pay for them.

The Ford 9-inch rearend is by far the most popular street rod rearend. As far as the cars featured in this book, it's virtually the only rearend. The smaller Ford 8-inch assembly can be used, too,

but keep in mind that performance parts are less common, and they aren't as strong. While the choice of rearends is pretty narrow, there are several options for mounting the rearend to the chassis.

Originally, Fords of the twenties and thirties used a transverse rear spring that was mounted behind the differential. The spring located the rearend laterally, eliminating the need for a Panhard bar. Two long radius rods were attached to the outer ends of the axle and to the torque tube (essentially the drive shaft). The result was a triangulated mounting system that worked quite well. Some street rods still use the transverse buggy spring, but the vast majority use coilover shock absorbers for springs.

The three most common methods for locating the rear axle are: a standard parallel four-link system, triangulated four-

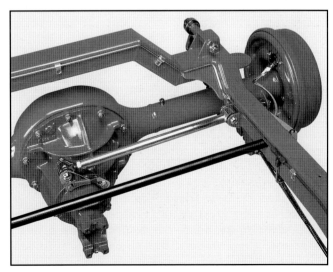

Front and rear Panhard bars are used to control lateral movement in the suspension. The Panhard bar connects the axle to the frame. In this photo the Panhard bar is the one closest to the rear axle housing. The forward bar is an anti-roll bar (commonly called a sway bar), which prevents body roll when cornering. (TCI)

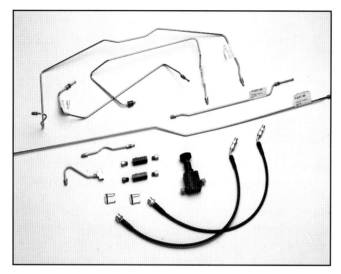

Bending brake lines can be a little tedious and you don't want to compromise the integrity of the lines. To make building a street rod easier, So-Cal Speed Shop developed an all-inclusive pre-bent brake kit for their Step Boxed chassis. The kit includes a Wilwood proportioning valve and residual valve. (So-Cal Speed Shop)

link, and ladder bars. The two different four-link setups are the most common.

Parallel four-bars require the addition of a Panhard rod to limit lateral movement. The triangulated four-bars don't need the Panhard rod because the two upper rods run diagonally from the sides of the center section outward to the frame rails. The rods form two triangles with the rear axle housing and the frame rails. The two lower links are mounted parallel to the frame rails, just like a conventional four-link system. There are proponents of both systems.

Ladder bars are the third option. They are essentially an updated version of the original Ford radius rods. Ladder bars are mounted farther forward than four-link bars, usually to the transmission crossmember. The ladder bars triangulate the axle housing to the frame. The bars themselves also form long, narrow triangles. At the axle housing the bars are separated like parallel four-links, but they converge at the front end where they attach to the crossmember. A Panhard bar is usually necessary with ladder bars.

Coil-over shock absorbers are

heavy duty, adjustable shocks that are encased in compact coil springs. The springs are much smaller than the large diameter coil springs used in regular passenger cars. They're available with different spring rates to match the weight of the vehicle.

Turning the base of the shock absorber changes the inner valving, which affects the ride characteristics. Adjusting the shocks usually involves getting under the car and turning the adjusters with a special spanner wrench. There is a coil-over system that can be controlled from the interior. Most people find a setting they like and leave it there.

The mounting angle of the coil-over shocks affects the spring rate. As the

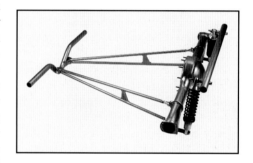

So-Cal Speed Shop likes to use ladder bar rearend kits with coil-over shocks. The system works well on the street and at the drag strip. The system is simple and allows about six inches of wheel travel. (So-Cal Speed Shop)

A great blend of traditional style and modern technology is the Buick-style front brake from So-Cal Speed Shop. The exterior housing looks like a vintage Buick finned brake drum, but hidden inside are all-new Wilwood dual-piston disc brakes with 11-inch vented rotors. (So-Cal Speed Shop)

This backing plate side view of the So-Cal brake assembly shows the built in air scoop that comes on versions that don't have the front ventilation slots. Some builders like to see the Buick drum ribs behind their custom wheels. (So-Cal Speed Shop)

The ubiquitous 9-inch Ford rearend comes in many configurations, both from the factory and in custom aftermarket units. TCI offers this trick unit with an aluminum center housing and seamless steel axle tubes with billet ends. Satin and polished finishes are available. (TCI)

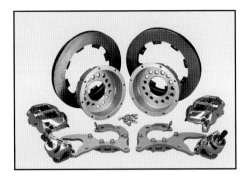

Great brakes are one of the best safety items you can have in a street rod. Front disc brakes are the most important, but there are also kits to add disc brakes to the rear axle. This is a rear kit with 4-piston calipers and aluminum hats and caliper brackets. (TCI)

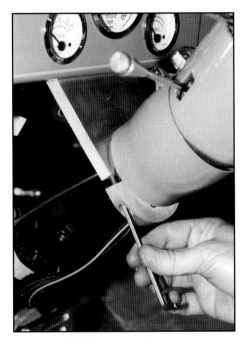

Steering column drops are used to secure either GM tilt columns or aftermarket columns. The billet aluminum drops are generally available with drops from 2 1/2-inches to 7 1/2-inches. The two halves of the column drop are held together with recessed Allen head bolts.

Two items that are sort of related to the steering column are the gas pedal and the brake pedal. The brake pedal location is generally a function of where the master cylinder is. The throttle should be installed after the steering column is in, so there is adequate clearance.

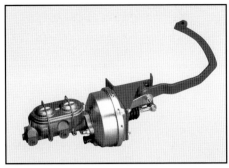

A dual master cylinder with a booster is the hot setup for easy braking. Street rod power boosters are quite compact so they fit in the crowded chassis. (TCI)

When an original GM steering column is used, the ignition switch is part of the deal. Aftermarket columns require a separate switch. Billet shifter knobs, turn signal stalks, tilt stalks, and emergency flasher buttons are available to dress up steering columns.

shock is tilted down from vertical, it loses some strength. Street rod rear coil-over shocks tend to be closer to each other at the top than at the bottom. This means the spring rate needs to be adjusted so it reflects the effective spring rate. This is another one of those math problems that you can skip when you buy a complete chassis.

Even though the front brakes do the majority of the stopping, rear brakes are also important. Drum rear brakes are very acceptable. Besides being less expensive, drum brakes are generally easier to hook up the emergency brake. Some rear disc brakes calipers have an integral emergency brake, but many don't have them. That means an aftermarket e-brake setup is required.

Some 9-inch Ford rearends came with factory disc brakes, but those units can be difficult to find. The old Lincoln Versailles and some loaded Mercury Cougars of the same era had a 9-inch with disc brakes that wasn't too wide for a street rod. Most Ford 9-inch rearends with disc brakes use aftermarket kits. These kits are great, but a set of factory-fresh drum brakes will work fine on a relatively lightweight highboy roadster.

The bottom line on frames and suspension systems is to buy as complete a chassis as possible. Let the experts do the engineering. Then, all you have to do is assemble the components.

It's best to use new universal joints when connecting the steering column to the steering box. Possible exhaust manifold interference should be considered when locating the steering column.

Street Rod Tech

All the parts were laid out for inventory after they were painted and powder coated. It's fun to have such a collection of clean parts to work with.

This pile of parts is typical of what you can expect when a complete chassis is delivered. The large assemblies like the frame, rearend, and front suspension are usually by themselves or attached to a pallet. The small parts are boxed.

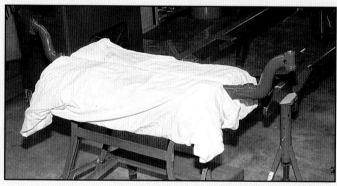

A tool that's most often associated with wood working projects, a Shop Mate adjustable vise/workbench, makes a great assembly stand for the front axle. The axle should be wrapped in an old sheet or several shop rags to protect the paint from damage.

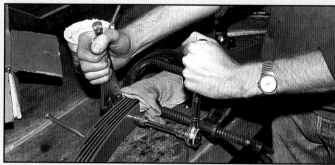

After the chassis was assembled and checked for proper operation and fit of all components, it was disassembled for painting and/or powder coating. Here the front axle, four-bars, and brake backing plates are being powder coated.

The spring leaves had to come apart for powder coating. Polypropylene strips were placed between the leaves for a smoother ride. It eliminates steel-to-steel contact as the spring moves. A large C-clamp was used to compress the leaves. Extreme caution should be exercised when working around any type of spring.

Assembling a Street Rod Chassis

Prior to installing the king pins through the spindles and spindle bosses in the axle ends, the pins should be coated with white grease.

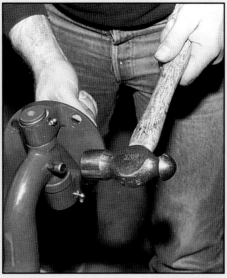

The lock pin is inserted through the axle end where it fits against the notch in the kingpin and holds everything is place.

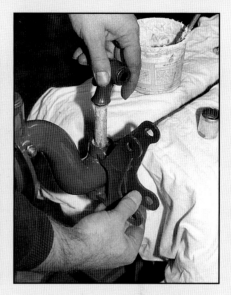

Coat the spring perches with white grease, then insert them from the topside of the axle.

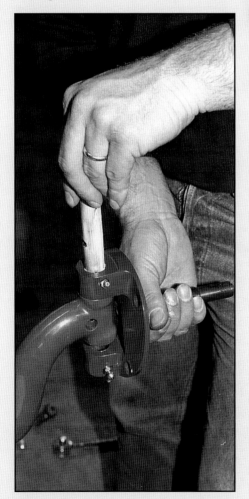

The kingpin is inserted through the spindle and the axle end. The kingpin has a notch about mid-point that needs to face the hole in the axle.

The completed front axle and spring assembly was placed on a padded floor jack and lifted into the underside of the front crossmember. This is must easier than trying to lift the axle.

The two U-bolts and the mounting plate secure the spring to the crossmember. Lock nuts are used.

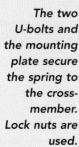

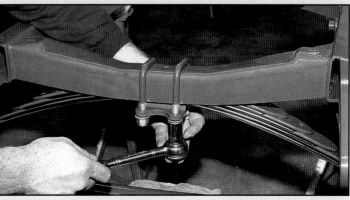

Street Rod Tech

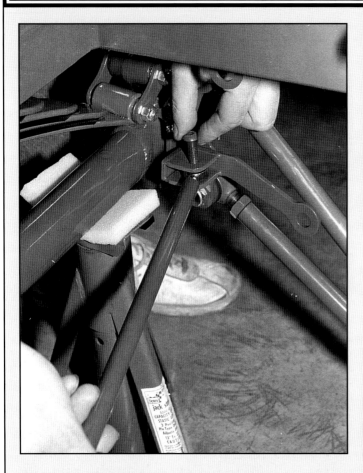

The front Panhard bar uses adjustable Heim ends and mounts behind the axle. It eliminates lateral movement of the axle on the spring shackles.

The front ends of the four-link bars are adjustable. They are set to the right length and the bars are bolted to the brackets on the frame and the axle.

Liquid thread lock, such as Loctite, should be applied to the bolts that hold the front disc brake caliper mounting brackets to the spindles.

The mounting brackets should be double-checked for security. You can't be too careful when it comes to the brake system.

The steering tie-rod is secured to the dropped steering arm with a castellated nut and a cotter key.

Assembling a Street Rod Chassis
(continued)

The wheel hubs need to be packed with bearing grease and the rotor and hub assembly can be installed on the axle.

Brand new brake calipers and brake pads were attached to the caliper mounting brackets.

The front shock absorbers were part of the whole front axle assembly from TCI, so their length is perfect for the application. The shocks are simple bolt-on items.

The brand new steering box is another bolt-on item, because the mounting bosses are installed on the frame at the time it is manufactured.

The pitman arm connects the steering box to the tie-rod. The arm mounting holes are tapered for a super snug fit.

Street Rod Tech

All the rearend components were spread out before assembly. The axles had to be removed from the housing because the housing was powder coated.

Coilover shocks serve both as the shock absorbers and the rear springs. The top of the shock is bolted to the mounting perch on the rear frame crossmember and the bottom of the shock is fastened to the shock bracket on the rearend housing.

The rear four-link bars are adjustable for length just like the front ones. A sure way to make sure the length is the same from side to side is to use a caliper to measure how far out the bar has been moved.

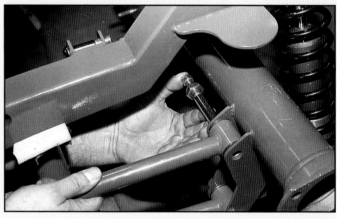

The four-link bolts go through the urethane bushings in the bar ends to secure the bars to the axle housing brackets. This is an upper bolt because it is specially designed to also mount the anti-roll bar.

The third member for the rebuilt Ford nine-inch rearend was reinstalled. It was installed dry so it's important to make a note to fill the housing with gear lube before driving the car.

Assembling a Street Rod Chassis
(continued)

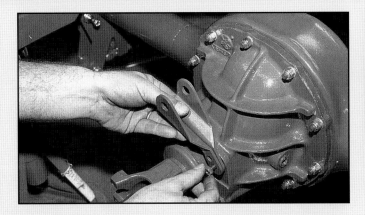

The third member needs to be in place in order to install the rear Panhard bar. The Panhard bar bracket mounts directly to the rearend.

The outer links of the anti-roll bar are aluminum. Short rod end linkage with bushings connects the anti-roll bar to the special mounting bolts that were previously installed in the upper four-link mounting brackets.

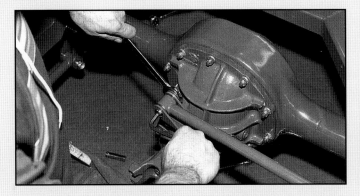

The Panhard bar is attached to the rearend bracket on one end and to a welded-on bracket on the inside of the left rear frame rail. The bar ends are fitted with urethane bushings.

The brake backing plates were powder coated the same color as the frame. That's a little overkill, but when you're having a lot of parts coated, it doesn't cost much more to do everything. Powder coating makes cleanup easy.

To help control body roll, a TCI torsion rear anti-roll bar was installed. On a Model A frame such as this, the bar goes through holes in the frame rails. Kits for '32-'34 Fords come with bolt-on tube mounts.

New rear axles were installed complete with all new bearings and seals. You can get away with used axles, but the bearings should be new. A bad axle bearing can leave you stranded.

Street Rod Tech
Assembling a Street Rod Chassis (continued)

All the rear brake components were also new. A trick way to make installing the brake drums easy is to measure the inside diameter with a brake drum gauge. Use the adjustment knob to lock the measurement.

Then assemble the wheel cylinders, brakes shoes, and springs. Use the flip side of the gauge to adjust the shoes with the drum off. The drum should fit right on.

Here is the completed TCI Model A chassis up and rolling. All the brake lines were installed and the exhaust system was also fitted before the roadster pickup body was mounted. The whole chassis was a bolt-together deal.

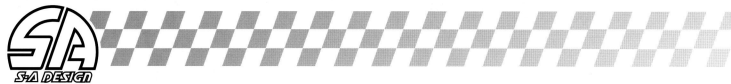

THE ENGINE AND TRANSMISSION

Small-block Chevrolet V-8; that pretty well sums up street rod engines. Since shortly after its debut in 1955, the small-block Chevy V-8 has been the default engine for street rods. Prior to the small-block Chevy, the Ford flathead was the engine of choice. After Oldsmobile and Cadillac brought out their new overhead valve V-8 engines in 1949, some of these big V-8's started appearing in hot rods, but not any substantial amounts.

The popularity growth of the small-block Chevy was phenomenal. It seemed like an overnight success, but it took a few years for used engines to filter down to the average hot rod builder. New, replacement engines were available, but hot rodding was a much more budget-minded endeavor in the fifties than it is now.

Speed equipment companies quickly saw the vast potential of the Chevy V-8 and were soon making more parts for the Chevy than the Ford flathead. The small-block Chevy was a natural performer from the very beginning. It was an impressive engine in stock form and it responded very well to modifications. Racers quickly learned how to make a small-block perform. Street rodders weren't far behind. The old saying about competition improving the breed was certainly true of the Chevy V-8.

As the small-block Chevy grew in size from its original 265 cubic inch displacement, bigger and bigger small-blocks became the engine to have. The 265 was only offered in 1955 and 1956. The 283, starting in 1957, and the 327 which debuted in 1962 were much more prevalent in street rods. The 350 cubic inch small-block first appeared in the all-new 1967 Camaro and was offered in all other Chevys in 1968.

Within a few years, the 350 small-block had become the dominant street rod engine. Over three decades later, the 350 small-block V-8 is still the world's most popular street rod engine. Total small-block Chevy V-8 production (counting all displacements) exceeds 40 million engines—that's popular.

The short, compact size of the Chevy engine makes it good for the relatively limited space available in street

The most popular engine in all of street rodding is the small-block Chevy V-8 in its many forms. Of all the displacements and induction systems, the 350 cubic inch with a four-barrel carburetor is the most common combination. The center valve cover bolts mark this engine as a late model ZZ3.

Modern Tuned Port Injection (TPI) systems are steadily replacing carburetors on many street rods. There are many aftermarket companies that make installing fuel injection relatively easy.

rod engine compartments. The Chevy oil sump is at the rear of the engine which means that the distributor is also at the rear.

CHEVY OR FORD?

We're strongly in favor of choosing a small-block Chevy engine for a first time, bolt-together street rod, but that doesn't mean a Ford engine can't be used. Some people like the idea of having a Ford engine in a Ford car. They might be fond of the small-block Ford engines due to favorable experiences in a Mustang or Ford truck.

Small-block Ford engines are a little narrower than Chevys, but they're also longer, with longer water pumps. The extra length can lead to firewall clearance problems, and the firewall may have to be recessed. Fords have front-mounted distributors, which makes servicing easy, but the front distributor location means that the oil pump is at the front of the engine.

A front-mounted oil pump means a front oil pan sump, which can get in the way of suspension components or crossmembers. There are short water pumps available and kits for moving the sump to the rear of the engine. Lots of great speed equipment has been developed for the 5.0-liter (302 cubic inches) Ford, although there isn't the variety that's available for the 350 Chevy. In general, Chevy performance parts are less expensive than their Ford counterparts.

WHICH SMALL-BLOCK?

Choosing a small-block Chevy engine depends largely on your budget, how much power you want, and whether you prefer a carbureted engine or a fuel injected one. Of all the various displacements, the 350 cubic inch version is by far the preferred street rod engine. Some conservative rodders go with the less powerful 305 cube engine, but the 350 is so much more versatile in terms of aftermarket speed equipment.

We'd hesitate to spend much money on a 305 engine. There's less performance equipment available and the added costs of bringing a 305 up to base 350 levels can't be justified. We're not against using a 305, but it had better be incredibly cheap. If it were our car, we'd upgrade to a 350 the first chance we got.

There is a larger displacement small-block, the 400 cubic inch version, but it's not a recommended engine for a bolt-together street rod. The small-block 400 has a reputation as a hot running engine. That's the last thing you want in a street rod. The engine isn't very common, so you'd have to go out of your way to find one.

Some early seventies Chevy pickups, Chevelles, and Camaros had 400 front fender emblems, but those engines were actually 402 cubic inch big-blocks. They're desirable engines for the originally equipped vehicles, but they're not often used in street rods. People who want a big-block Chevy usually step up to a 454.

A pretty popular hybrid is the 383 small-block, which is obtained by installing a 400 crankshaft in a slightly modified 350 block. This engine is known as a 383 stroker because the 400 crankshaft creates a longer stroke. It puts out lots of torque, which makes it a fun street rod engine, but it's the type of engine to upgrade to later if you feel the need for more power.

There were changes to the small-block during the eighties, including the addition of Tuned Port Injection in 1985. In 1986, the valve cover design was changed to eliminate leakage. Older small-blocks are well known for leaky valve covers. The oil pan flange and rear

main seal design were also changed in 1986. Hydraulic roller cam provisions were added the next year. The center intake manifold attaching bolt angles were revised in 1987. Pre-'87 intakes (and cylinder heads) have a 90-degree bolt angle. Cast iron cylinder heads from 1987 to 1995 and all Gen II aluminum heads have a 73-degree angle on the four center bolts of the intake manifold.

Even though they're still considered small-blocks, the engines changed considerably in 1992 when the Gen II LT1 engine debuted in the Corvette. A major

A great way to get a guaranteed new engine is with a crate motor. That's the general term for new, ready to run engines that are available from General Motors or companies like Jasper Engines and Transmissions. This is one of Jasper's 350 Chevy crate motors. (Jasper)

You can get crate motors in varying performance levels from RV type engines up to race motors. Jasper Engines and Transmissions offers big-block Chevys like this for people who don't think small-blocks offer enough excitement. (Jasper)

difference is the reverse-flow water pump. A new optically triggered distributor was also introduced. The block, cylinder heads, intake manifold, water pump, and distributor are all different on the Gen II engines compared to the older small blocks. The Gen II engines are wonderful engines; just make sure that all the parts you buy are compatible.

USED ENGINES

The low-buck approach to a street rod engine is a used engine purchased either from a wrecking yard or a private party. You have the best chance of getting some type of minimal warranty from a wrecking yard. With a private party, you're on your own as soon as the cash leaves your wallet.

A benefit of buying an engine from a private party is that the prices are lower than at wrecking yards. You could get a real bargain, but remember there is considerable risk involved in buying a used engine from a stranger. If it's such a great engine, why are they selling it at such a cheap price? It's very easy to overstate the condition and/or internal components or machine work on an engine sitting in the corner of someone's garage.

Don't assume anything or take anything for granted when dealing with used engines. The safest financial strategy when buying a used engine from a private party (unless they have paperwork to prove claimed machine work) is to try to pay as close to a core charge value as possible. If the price is close to that of a core engine, your biggest risk is time rather than money.

If you buy an engine from a wrecking yard, try to get one that's as complete as possible. Some yards try to sell the accessories separately. The accessories can cost almost as much as the engine. Buying a piecemeal engine is not the way to save money. You want a "carb to pan" engine, one with everything you need to make it run except a battery. Some yards may also hit you with a core charge. Unless you have a similar engine sitting around, a core charge can boost the cost of the engine. Determine the total, out-the-door, ready-to-run price before you hand over your money.

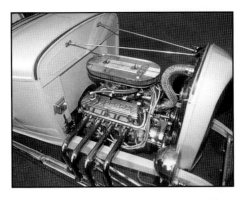

There's nothing inherently wrong with putting a Ford engine in a Ford street rod, it's just not as popular as a Chevy engine. Most chassis builders offer the option of small-block Ford engine mounts. Theses engines are a little longer than their Chevy counterparts.

A solution to the completeness and engine condition situation is to buy an entire, running car. This is a lot more work and your neighbors might not appreciate you parting out an old Chevy in the driveway. The good news is that you can get every possible part you need. If the car runs, you can run tests on the engine to assess its condition. You can get a good idea of what needs to be done in terms of repairs or rebuilding the engine.

It's always a good idea to rebuild a used engine. It will never be easier to do than when it is out of the car. You'll definitely want to thoroughly clean any used engine, so you might as well take it apart once it's clean. Depending on your view-

Since street rods (especially highboys) don't weigh a lot, you would think using a V-6 engine would be fine. You'd be wrong. V-6 and four-cylinder engines are very rare in popular street rods.

point, rebuilding an engine can be another fun project or tedious work that you'd rather leave to professionals. Rebuilding an engine can very easily add a thousand dollars to the cost of the engine. If you want high performance internal parts or require custom machine work, rebuilding costs can quickly escalate into the several thousand-dollar range.

Rebuilding a used engine isn't always the least expensive option. Depending on what needs to be done, how much you can do yourself, and how good you are at shopping, a rebuilt engine can approach the cost of a brand new crate engine. Like all other aspects of building a street rod, you should compare costs before deciding which way to go with an engine.

There is a great sense of accomplishment when you rebuild an engine and it performs far better than it did originally. Building a performance engine is sort of like a precision jigsaw puzzle. Unassembled, it's a pile of odd-shaped metal parts, but put together properly, it's a mechanical masterpiece. A street rod is a perfect location for a performance engine. The lightweight nature of street rods allows maximum use of the engine's potential.

An engine rebuild kit is a good way to go. Many well-known mail-order companies offer affordable kits for popular engines. By dealing in bulk, these companies are very competitive price-wise. The companies do all the necessary machine work so all you have to do is assemble the engine. An engine rebuild kit is the engine equivalent of a bolt-together street rod chassis—the pros do the hard work and you save money by doing the assembly work.

It's possible to avoid rebuilding an engine if you bought a relatively low mileage wrecking yard engine or if you got a complete car with an engine that checked out fine. You can save money by skipping the rebuilding process. With a reasonable amount of luck, you could simply clean the engine, paint it, change the fluids, and be on your way. This is an option for anyone on a very tight budget. You can always rebuild the engine later or buy a crate motor as your finances allow.

Big-blocks fit fine in '33/'34 Fords, as witnessed by this tri-power equipped one. There is room for an air conditioning compressor in this engine compartment.

Buying a complete, running car has other advantages in addition to getting the engine. If you buy the right car, you can get lots of other street rod components from it. Items such as an automatic transmission, tilt steering column, front disc brakes, driveshaft, and miscel-

Traditionalists are fond of the flathead Ford V-8, so named because of the design of the cylinder heads. The valves are in the block instead of the cylinder heads like OHV engines. Flatheads look neat with old time dress-up parts and speed equipment.

laneous interior parts can be salvaged from the right Chevy. We've saved lots of money using this approach, but it's messy and time-consuming. We also have the means to haul the remains to a scrap yard.

Most wrecking yards don't have any interest in a car that's had the most valuable parts removed. Before you take the big step of buying a parts car, make sure you can easily get rid of the remains. When scrap metal prices are severely depressed, it can be almost impossible to get rid of a hulk. Unless you want the world's ugliest planter, check carefully on the disposability of a parts car.

CRATE MOTORS

You can't beat a brand new engine for reliability and peace of mind. When you're driving your street rod a long way from home, you want to know you can get back home. Worrying about a 200,000-mile engine out of a wrecked taxicab can take a lot of fun out of a street rod trip. Most new crate motors come with a warranty. Since Chevy and Ford crate motors are the most popular ones, it's not too difficult to find a facility that will honor the warranty.

General Motors really got behind crate motors with their GM Goodwrench replacement engines. Street rodders quickly realized what great deals these brand new engines are. They're available without emissions equipment, which is fine since street rods don't have to meet contemporary emissions standards. If you use a fuel injection system, the engine should be almost as clean as a late model passenger car (few, if any, street rods use a catalytic converter).

GM Performance Parts (and many local GM dealerships) offers a wide range of brand new small-block engines that are ideal for street rods. The engines range in horsepower from modest to muscle-bound. You can get carbureted and fuel injected engines. They even offer fuel-injected engines that are designed to be used in pre-1974 cars without elaborate electronic controls. A GM Performance Parts crate motor known as the Ram Jet 350 is a 350 cubic inch small-block that produces

350 horsepower. In a lightweight street rod, 350 horsepower will really get your attention right now! The Ram Jet 350 has electronic-port fuel injection, Vortec cylinder heads, a wiring harness, a very compact control unit (computer), and the Ram Jet induction system. The small computer control unit was originally developed for marine applications. Boats are much less complicated than modern cars, so the system is perfect for street rods.

There are also big-block Chevy crate motors if you plan on pulling lots of stumps with your rod. Ford Racing Performance Parts is also getting into the crate motor game with its 5.0-liter engines. Many mail-order companies have their own versions of new crate motors, which may be better suited to your needs. Frequently, the mail-order versions can be equipped to produce more horsepower. Like other components, it pays to shop around to find the crate motor that best suits your needs at the most favorable price.

FUEL INJECTION BASICS

Modern fuel injection has become so pervasive in the transportation industry that it's tough to find a skateboard these days that isn't fuel injected. Unless you're drawn to the traditional looks of tri-power or a big four-barrel carburetor, fuel injection is the slick answer to all your fuel delivery needs. You can't beat modern fuel injection for efficiency and performance.

The scariest thing about adapting fuel injection to a street rod is the wiring. Modern cars and trucks are a maze of wiring, sensors, and various control modules. That level of complexity is counter to the simple essence of a street rod. Fortunately, several street rod and aftermarket performance companies took it upon themselves to simplify the installation of fuel injection on street rods.

One of the pioneers in the field of fuel injection wiring harnesses was Ron Francis' Wire Works. They were quick to offer full function, easy-to-install wiring kits for both General Motors and Ford fuel injection systems. The highly informative Wire Works catalog contains a lot of great material on fuel injection wiring and the key components of an electronic fuel injection system.

Although you don't need to be a fuel injection expert in order to install a system on your car, it can be helpful to understand some of the basic terms. The following definitions from the Wire Works catalog cover items that may or may not be found on your particular system. The year and make of the engine determine what components are used.

GM Fuel Injection Systems

GM fuel injection systems are the most commonly seen units in street rods due to the overwhelming popularity of small-block Chevy engines. There are a variety of differences on the injection systems used over the years.

The Wire Works harness for 1985-1992 GM Tuned Port Injection 5.0-liter and 5.7-liter (305 cubic inch and 350 cubic inch) small-blocks upgrades the '85-'89 engines by running them on a '90-'92 computer. The newer system uses a MAP sensor instead of a mass airflow sensor. This makes for an easier installation, because you don't have to install the MAF sensor, which is encased in a large, hard to route air intake tube. All the necessary computer controlled sensors are utilized as in the original vehicle. The transmissions that can be used with this system include the newer 700R4 and 4L60 automatics plus the older Turbo 350 and Turbo 400 units. Manual transmissions can also be used, but not many street rodders opt to row their own gears. The ECM requires a four thousand pulse per mile speed input.

The 1992-1997 GM LT-1 5.7-liter V-8 is a great engine favored by many street rodders. It can be found in various Corvettes, Camaros, Firebirds, plus some Chevy Caprices, Buick Roadmasters, and even a few Cadillacs. Depending on the donor car, horsepower ratings vary from 265 to 300. The 4L60 and 4L60-E automatics can be used on all of the engines. The Turbo 350 and Turbo 400 can be used on 1992 and 1993 engines. The '92-'93 ECM's require four thousand pulse per mile

Street Rod Tech
Fuel Injection Terms

Powertrain Control Module (PCM): The PCM is the computer or brains of the system.

EPROM: The EPROM is the memory chip. The Wire Works kits are designed to work with the factory PCM and memory chip.

Timing Disconnect: It facilitates base timing, but isn't required on GM LT-1 or LS-1 engines.

Data Link Connector (DLC): This connector allows for diagnostic evaluation of the system with a code scanner.

Malfunction Indicator Lamp (MIL): It indicates a problem in the EFI system. This light will blink trouble codes for diagnostic purposes.

Heated Oxygen Sensor (HO2S)/Oxygen Sensor: This sensor evaluates the air/fuel mixture and tells the computer how to make adjustments.

Knock Sensor: This is a very important sensor in a closed loop system (as used in street rods) because it tells the computer how to adjust the timing to eliminate knock.

Throttle Position Sensor (TPS): This sensor tells the computer how far open the throttle is and the related speed you wish to go.

Idle Speed Control (ISC): The ISC automatically adjusts the engine idle speed for changing conditions such as when the air conditioning cuts in.

Engine Coolant Temperature Sensor (ECT): It handles temperature indications for the computer.

Intake Air Temperature Sensor (IAT): It provides the atmospheric temperature readings.

Manifold Absolute Pressure Sensor (MAP): This is one of the primary sensors. It measures load changes placed on the engine for the PCM to adjust to the driving requirements.

Mass Air Flow Sensor (MAF): This is another important sensor. It measures the air intake used by the engine allowing the PCM to adjust fuel calibration to the driving requirements.

Fuel Pump Relay, Oil Pressure Switch, and Inertia Switch: These components work together to control the fuel pump operation. The oil pressure switch is important to this operation on GM engines while Ford uses the inertia switch to shut off fuel in case of a collision.

Fuel Injectors: EFI injection systems have a single injector for the Vortec V-6 and eight injectors on the V-8. Throttle Body Injection units have two injectors.

Exhaust Gas Recirculating System (EGR): This is an important component that helps prevent pinging, rough idling, and overheating.

Park/Neutral Circuits: They tell the PCM what gear the transmission is in. The PCM then controls the engine idle accordingly.

Speed Sensor: This sensor tells the PCM how fast the vehicle is going. It influences the idle speed control motor.

---

speed input and the newer engines require an eighty thousand pulse per mile speed signal.

The 1996 LT-4 5.7-liter SFI (sequential fuel injection) engine was rated at 330 horsepower and available in Corvettes with six speed manual transmissions. Although the computer isn't programmed for automatic transmissions, the Turbo 400 and Turbo 350 can be used. The ECM requires an eighty thousand pulse per mile speed input.

The General Motors LS-1 engine was introduced in the 1997 Corvette and

in the 1998 Camaro and Firebird. This is the new Generation III small-block V-8 with an aluminum block and cylinder heads. A noticeable difference from previous generation small-blocks is the individual ignition coils for each cylinder. The Firebird and Camaro versions are best for street rods. The transmission is the 4L60-E automatic. This engine utilizes the OBD II (on board diagnostics) diagnostic system. That means all emissions control devices must be connected to the system or trouble codes will be set.

GM engines with throttle body injection (TBI) can also be used in street rods. Ron Francis' Wire Works makes harnesses for them, too. The throttle body injection systems are found on GM trucks. The system used on 1985-1991 5.0-liter, 5.7-liter, and 7.4-liter (454 big-block) is upgraded to use the '88-'90 CK truck computer. Two fuel injectors mounted on top of the throttle body inject fuel into the motor. GM uses most of the same sensors on a TBI unit as they do on a tuned port (TPI) engine. Throttle body injection uses a MAP sensor for fuel calibration. This computer controls the engine only, so an electric shift transmission can't be used with this computer. The available transmissions are the 700R4, Turbo 400, and Turbo 350, plus the manual transmissions.

The GM Throttle Body Injection 5.0-liter, 5.7-liter, and 7.4-liter engines from 1991-1995 added a computer command to the 4L60-E and 4L80-E automatic transmissions. While the engines look the same and use most of the same sensors as the 1985-1990 engines, the ECMs don't have the capability to control the electronic transmissions. Wire Works harnesses incorporate the wiring necessary for the electronic transmissions. The CK series truck computer is used in this application.

Ford Fuel Injection Systems

Ford engines aren't nearly as popular as Chevy engines when it comes to powering street rods. That doesn't mean they aren't a viable choice. The later model fuel injected engines are a fine alternative for people who want their rods to be all Ford.

The most popular Ford street rod engine is the 5.0-liter (302 cubic inches) V-8 and the 5.0 HO (high output) version. The engine was introduced in 1985. It uses a speed density, multi-port fuel injection system. An EEC engine control computer handles engine management chores. The HO version can be found in Mustangs, while the regular 5.0 V-8 was used to power Thunderbirds, Lincoln Town Cars, Cougars, and the full size Ford Crown Victoria.

The HO engines have larger fuel injectors and more of a performance camshaft. In 1986, the HO engine became available in Ford light duty trucks. In 1988, Ford switched from speed density in California to mass airflow in Mustangs. The following year all 5.0-liter Mustang engines adopted the MAF system. Non-Mustang versions remained speed density systems. The AOD and AOD-E automatic transmissions were used with the 5.0-liter

Most small-block Chevy engines are mounted relatively low in the chassis of '32 Fords. That means there's ample room for a Roots-style supercharger (also called a blower) and a four-barrel carburetor underneath the hood.

engines, but the older C-4 can also be used. Mustang manual transmissions also work with these engines.

Builders seeking more cubic inches can use Ford's 5.8-liter (351 cubic inches) V-8. Fuel injection was added to this series in 1988. A high performance version with improved cylinder heads and a different intake manifold was introduced in 1993 in the awesome, limited edition Lightning pickups. The engine uses a MAF type injection system. The E40D, E40D-E, C-6, C-4, and manual transmissions can be used with this engine.

A less common Ford engine is the 1993 and newer "modular" V-8, which displaces 4.6-liters (280 cubic inches). Depending on the version, the engine either has a dual overhead cam or a single overhead cam design. Horsepower ratings range from 205 to 280. The DOHC version is found in the Lincoln Mark VIII. The Mark VIII engine has intake manifold runner control solenoids that operate plates that are closed below 3000 rpm, so the engine is running on two valves per cylinder instead of four. With no air delivered to the secondary intake valves, fuel economy and emissions are improved at low rpms. Above 3000 rpm, the plates open for more power. The 4.6-liter modular engine has two ignition coils, with each one serving four cylinders. The 4R70W automatic transmission is used with the 4.6-liter V-8.

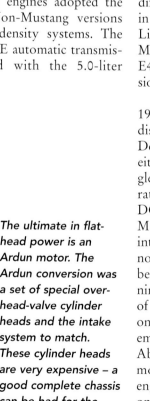

The ultimate in flathead power is an Ardun motor. The Ardun conversion was a set of special overhead-valve cylinder heads and the intake system to match. These cylinder heads are very expensive – a good complete chassis can be had for the price of an Ardun setup.

TRANSMISSIONS

An engine without a transmission is an expensive noisemaker. You need to effectively transfer the engine's power to the pavement via the transmission, drive shaft, and rearend. The original hot rods all had manual transmissions, simply because that's all there was. The original, mass-market automatic transmissions like the GM Hydra-Matics were big, awkward units not well suited to street rods.

Even as automatic transmission technology improved and the units became more compact, hot rodders resisted automatics because of their low performance image. Some rodders still cling to the idea that a car isn't a hot rod without a 4-speed, but those shift-it-yourself guys are the minority.

When the street rodding resurgence happened in the mid-seventies, automatic transmissions quickly took over. Whether for ease of installation, added floor room, or just laziness, street rodders opted for automatic transmissions. As modern automatic overdrive transmissions became more prevalent, they were quickly embraced by rodders. The overdrive units allow for good off-the-line acceleration and comfortable, economical cruising. That's an unbeatable combination.

The GM Turbo 350 automatic was the long time street rod standard. It still is a very popular unit although it's losing ground to the overdrive automatics. The Chevy versions of the Turbo 350 are the most popular because they have the same bellhousing bolt pattern as the small-block Chevy engines. Other GM divisions' units (Buick, Olds, and Pontiac, commonly abbreviated BOP) have a different bolt pattern. They can be adapted to Chevy engines, but it's much easier to use a Chevy transmission.

In addition to being the transmission attached to most 350 small-block Chevy engines, the Turbo 350 is a good size and shape for the limited space available in a typical street rod. The Turbo 350 is relatively short (there are different tail shafts; 6-inch and 9-inch lengths are the most common) and not too wide. It fits well in narrow street rods and doesn't require a massive hump in the floor.

The Turbo 350 was offered in Chevy passenger cars from 1969 to 1986. Examples from the first ten years had traditional torque converters. The later units had lockup converters. Like the 350 engine, the Turbo 350 transmission is plentiful, easy to work on, and a strong performer. There are lots of aftermarket products to improve shift points, raise torque converter stall speeds, and provide better cooling. Heat is an automatic transmission's worst enemy, so using a radiator with a built-in transmission cooler is a must.

The big brother of the Turbo 350 is the Turbo 400. It can be found in lots of street rods, especially those with big-block engines. Turbo 400 transmissions are slightly bigger in all dimensions than the Turbo 350. Most street rod chassis can be ordered to fit the Turbo 400, but the Turbo 350 or one of the newer overdrive automatics will work as well.

There are a variety of GM automatic overdrive transmissions that can be used in street rods. They include the 700-R4, 200-4R, 4L60, and 4L80 models. The 700-R4 replaced the Turbo 350 and is the most common street rod application. It has four forward speeds and a lock-up torque converter. The converter clutch system uses a solenoid-operated valve that is controlled by the ECM. At approximately 45 miles per hour, the ECM signals the converter to lock up.

The 4L60 automatic replaced the 700-R4 in 1991. It's very similar to the 700-R4 with a few internal modifications. The 4L60-E version is computer controlled. The "E" usually designates an electronically controlled transmission. The engine computer controls shift points depending on the throttle angle, speed, and transmission temperature.

The 4L80-E automatic is the heavy-duty computer controlled unit. It replaced the Turbo 400. The ECM controls shift points the same way it does on the 4L60-E transmission.

These overdrive transmissions have become standard equipment in modern cars and trucks. The overdrive fourth gear is great for fuel economy and the first three gears are designed for quick acceleration.

The later versions of the 700-R4 transmissions are a better choice than the first models. In general, the 1988 and newer models are superior to the early years. All of these transmissions can be upgraded with aftermarket parts. Your main concern should be to match the transmission's capabilities with the engine's power.

Ford's answer to the Turbo 350 and Turbo 400 are the C-4 and C-6 automatic transmissions. These two automatics were widely available during the seventies and eighties. They're durable, well-proven transmissions. The C-6 is known as a heavy-duty tow package transmission. The less stout C-4 is fine for most small-block Ford engines.

An impressive engine that you'll see at street rod events (and one that has no place in a bolt-together street rod) is the Chrysler Hemi. The engine has a rich racing heritage and it looks neat, but it's not a particularly practical engine.

Better choices for Ford powered street rods are either the AOD (Automatic Overdrive) or AODE. In 1984, the AOD replaced the C-4. The AOD has four forward gears, but no converter lockup feature. These fine transmissions are found in most late-model Ford products including the popular 5.0-liter Mustang GT, which is a great donor car for a street rod. The overdrive transmissions cost more than the C-4 and usually require electronic controls, but the improved performance is worth any necessary wiring.

Another variation of the Ford automatic transmission is the E40D that was introduced in 1989 in light trucks. The

Just as the 350 small-block and Turbo 350 automatic have long been the default units, so has the 9-inch Ford rearend. It is by far the most prevalent rearend found in street rods. Currie Enterprises is the leader in 9-inch rearends for street rods and other modified vehicles. Their units are better than new. This one is equipped with rear disc brakes. (Currie Enterprises)

EEC controls shift points, but the converter doesn't have a lockup feature.

In 1992, the AOD was replaced with the AODE automatic transmission. This unit does have a lockup torque converter. The EEC controls the shift points.

Ford introduced the 4R44E and 4R55E automatic transmissions in 1995. Both units have lockup torque converters, and the ECM controls shift points.

REARENDS

The third member of the drive train triumvirate is the rear axle housing. The default rearend is the venerable Ford 9-inch. This street rod standard is probably more universal than the ubiquitous small-block Chevy. Unless a car has independent rear suspension, odds are overwhelming that there's a 9-inch Ford rearend sending the power to the rear tires.

Durability, affordability, and availability are all key reasons for the extreme popularity of the Ford 9-inch rearend. Ford made millions of them from 1957 to 1987. The units were found under a wide variety of cars, trucks, and vans, so there are a lot of differences among them. The most important variable is width.

Passenger car rearends are favored by most builders, in particular some of the earlier station wagon units. The 9-inch was used in cars from 1957 to 1973. Pickups used the rearends until 1984 and the last few years limited their use to Ford full-size vans.

There are cosmetic differences among the various 9-inch rearends. Ones with smoother "pumpkins" or center sections are the most desirable. The 9-inch is so popular that aftermarket com-

panies custom build new housings. The new housings have smooth backsides and can be ordered to almost any width. The new rearends have lots of other benefits like the ability to have them fitted with high performance components of your choice. They can be had with any bolt pattern you desire and there's the ability to use either drum or disc brakes.

The Ford 9-inch rearend is so popular and versatile that you can get one outfitted to your exact performance needs. The rearends are plenty stout in stock condition, but bigger axles, special bearings, and limited-slip differentials can be installed to handle very high performance engines.

Other Ford rearends are sometimes used in street rods. Foremost is the 8-inch unit, which is a smaller, less rugged version of the 9-inch. The 8-inch came in many Ford products with lower horsepower engines. The 8-inch will work fine in street rods that don't have monster motors or drivers with over-

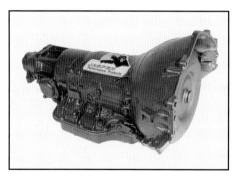

Besides crate motors you can also get ready-to-run performance transmissions like this one from Jasper Engines & Transmissions. For the longest time the GM Turbo 350 was the most popular unit, but the various GM automatic overdrive transmissions are challenging the venerable TH 350. (Jasper)

weight right feet. There aren't as many gear ratios or performance options for the 8-inch as the 9-inch, so you're better off with a 9-inch rearend. Even if you're a very conservative driver, people expect a 9-inch in a street rod. It's one of those "must have" parts.

Late-model Mustang GTs are good engine and transmission sources for people who desire an all-Ford street rod. Most of these donor cars were equipped with Ford's 8.8-inch rearend. These rearends hold up well to all the abuse given the average Mustang GT, but they just don't have the cachet of the venerable 9-inch.

If you buy an older Chevy parts car for the engine and transmission, the vehicle will most likely have a GM 10-bolt or possibly a 12-bolt rearend. The 12-bolt units are more desirable for high horsepower applications. They will work in a street rod, but very few '32 roadster builders use them. They're not as easy to work on as the Ford 9-inch and they're not quite as strong. Most importantly, they're not popular and you want popular components in a first-time street rod. If you end up with a GM 10-bolt or 12-bolt rearend, sell it to someone with a Camaro or a Nova. The narrower versions of the 12-bolt are very popular with Camaro owners and street machine builders. Narrow 12-bolts can be quite valuable, so if you get one, sell it and buy a 9-inch Ford rearend.

There are other specialized rearends like the quick change. These classic hot rod rearends look great, but they're expensive and only racers really need to change gears in a hurry. Like independent Corvette and Jaguar rearends, quick-change rearends are better choices for people who have built several street rods and want to step up a notch in sophistication. Some companies make quick-change falsies to make a Ford 9-inch look like a quick-change.

For a first time bolt-together street rod you want dependability, affordability, and popularity. Those characteristics are well represented by the default trio: a small-block Chevrolet V-8 engine, a GM automatic transmission (preferably, a late-model overdrive unit), and a Ford 9-inch rearend.

IT'S ALL IN THE DETAILS

A street rod is kind of like a movie. The stars (chassis, body, engine) are the most obvious players, but without the supporting cast and crew, there wouldn't be much of a show. In the case of street rods, there are lots of subsystems that aren't especially glamorous, but you can't build a useable car without them.

The subsystems and "little" details can consume a lot of time during a street rod buildup. Whenever possible, it's best to buy subsystem packages. When you have to buy individual components, hardware, and miscellaneous stuff, it increases costs and time.

Gauges are an example of the value in buying a package. A totally complete gauge kit should include all the instruments, bezels, mounting brackets, wiring, and sending units. When you're dealing with the little brass fittings that connect senders to gauges, you can waste a lot of trips to the parts store searching for fittings and adapters. With a gauge package, everything is matched at the factory.

Speaking of component packages—don't be fooled by seemingly lower costs of some so-called packages. Frank Hettick of Classic Instruments, Inc., has run all the numbers and has thoroughly done his homework. He knows the differences between excellent quality and passable products and the true costs of installing a complete gauge package. The really good packages can even have a few extra parts to cover all contingencies. An incomplete kit can end up costing more than a really good one due to all the extra purchases needed to finish the job.

Price those little blister packs of fittings and fasteners the next time you're at an auto parts store. It often seems like you're paying more for the packaging than the actual product. When you buy a well-thought out, all-inclusive kit, the manufacturer passes bulk quantity savings on to you. And, you save an incredible amount of time and hassles.

HOT AND COLD

Heat (and sometimes, cold) can be a major issue in a street rod. If you've never owned a street rod before, you need to realize the huge differences between them and modern passenger cars. Contemporary cars and trucks are so loaded with comfort and convenience items that we tend to take them for granted. You have to buy a really stripped car these days to not get air conditioning.

In terms of creature comforts, street rods, especially roadsters, are very basic.

The original idea of a hot rod was to strip a car down to its essential elements. Performance was valued over comfort. Modern street rods are much more comfortable than their predecessors, but they're still basic compared to the average family car or truck.

There's a certain attraction to being "out there" in a roadster. It's part of that rebel image. The environment of a street rod makes you an active participant in the driving experience, not a cocooned autopilot. Many people have compared driving a roadster to driving a motorcycle, but with more wheels. That whole ethereal Zen thing is fine, but the odds are great that you'll eventually wish for slightly cooler surroundings.

The whole heat issue of street rods is compounded by the when and where that most street rods are used. Except for some real hardcore rodders, these are fair weather cars. Street rods see the most use during the warm, summer

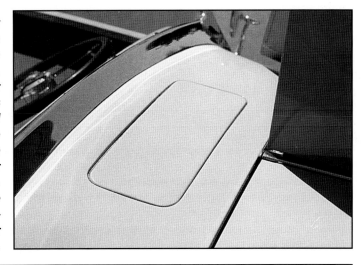

A majority of early street rods fill the cowl vents for a smoother look, but you can order fiberglass bodies with functional vents. When the car is moving the vent directs air into the cockpit. It's not the same as air conditioning, but it's better than nothing.

Another original method of cooling was the swing-out windshield. Both closed and open cars had this feature. Vehicles with stock style windshield posts can still take advantage of this feature.

parts of the country are almost always hot and humid in the summer.

Even west coast events tend to be in sunny California or places like Nevada. A prime example of how hot a hot rod happening can get is the huge Hot August Nights event that's staged in Reno, Nevada, at the peak of summer temperatures. When "Hot and August" are part of the name, you can bet you're gonna sweat.

Not only are street rod events held in hot locations, the very nature of these events generates lots of traffic. Long lines of street rods can mean traffic jam (albeit, an enjoyable traffic jam) temperatures. The pavement sizzles, your engine radiates heat, and the sun beats down on your head until you feel like a human heat sink.

We're not trying to belabor the heat issue, but if you have realistic expectations, you'll have a better time. By taking heat problems into consideration during the original construction period, you and your car will be better equipped to handle the heat.

months. The overwhelming majority of street rod events are held in the summer. Rain is the nemesis of street rod events.

The bigger the event, the hotter it usually is. Organizers know the huge economic difference weather can make,

so they plan events with the smallest odds of bad weather. The really huge street rod and general old car events tend to be produced in central parts of the country. Centralized venues allow the maximum number of participants to attend. These

KEEPING YOUR COOL

There are two aspects to increased cooling: you and the car. Keeping you cool involves both active and passive measures. We define active measures as things that increase cooling like air conditioning. Preventing heat from reaching you, like with insulation, is an example of passive cooling.

Air conditioning used to be relatively rare in street rods. Given the fairly tight confines of a street rod engine compartment and the large size of O.E.M. air conditioning systems, it was a challenge to adapt a passenger car A/C system to a street rod. Using smaller components and making your own custom system took a lot of engineering and work.

Several companies saw the need for specialized air conditioning systems made just for street rods. They developed compact systems to fit crowded engine compartments. They also made the interior components attractive and sized them for street rods. The result was a large increase in the number of air-conditioned street rods.

The basic '32 dash is available in several styles from the reproduction body manufacturers. This Deuce features the wall-to-wall look with eight symmetrical gauges. A tilt steering column is a virtual must in the tight confines of a street rod interior. GM columns with no shifter (usually from GM vans) are getting tough to find, but brand new custom GM style columns are available from several manufacturers in a variety of finishes.

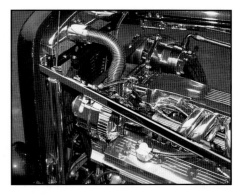

Finding a place for a gas tank can be a challenge. The trunk will obviously work, but that means giving up valuable luggage space. The neat thing about '32 Fords is that the stock style tanks are mounted behind the body between the rear frame horns. There are oversized Deuce tanks for people needing a few extra gallons of gas.

There are several vintage taillights that work well with Model A and '32 Ford street rods. This compact unit is a reproduction '47-'48 Chevy unit. The blue dot center is a popular add-on, but they're not legal in all areas. A better idea is to use high intensity bulbs so the brakes are as visible as possible to other motorists.

This car is well equipped for cooling both the engine and the passengers. It has a heavy-duty radiator with the biggest electric fan that will fit, a tubular coolant recovery system (on the left), and a compact air conditioning compressor on the right side of the engine.

Installing air conditioning in a roadster might seem like an oxymoron, but it's not a bad idea. The ability to have some cool air flowing over your warm body is refreshing. Of course, you can't contain the cool air in an open car, but just having the breeze effect when you're crawling along in traffic is great.

Air conditioning is affordable, but not inexpensive. You should figure on spending at least a thousand dollars for a basic street rod A/C system. If you're on a tight budget, you might want to postpone the purchase. Air conditioning can be retrofitted, but it's easiest when done during the original buildup.

If air conditioning is a luxury in an open car, it's virtually a necessity in a closed car. In a list of priorities, we'd place air conditioning ahead of other extras such as a trick sound system, high performance engine modifications, and expensive wheels.

There are plenty of things besides air conditioning to help maintain your cool. Continuing with the cooling theme, there's the issue of having a cowl vent. Most reproduction body manufacturers offer the choice of a functional cowl vent or a filled one. The filled ones look better, but the vents do increase air movement when you're under way. They don't do anything in traffic jams, but they worked in the thirties and they still do today.

We'd place a higher value on having a working cowl vent in a coupe or sedan than in a roadster. Airflow might not make you a whole lot cooler, but the movement can help psychologically. Another way to improve airflow in a non-air conditioned closed car is with a power rear window. There are kits that allow the rear window to be opened.

Depending on the type of windshield you choose, you may have one that's hinged at the top. This is how they were originally. You can tilt out the bottom edge of the windshield frame to get some more air in your face.

Light colored upholstery will help keep a roadster a little cooler. As good as black looks, it absorbs more heat than lighter colors. Black is easier to maintain (especially with kids) so there are a number of trade-offs to consider. A soft top can provide protection from the sun, but a top on a sunny day kind of defeats the appeal of having a roadster.

Preventing excess heat from reaching you is another key component of

Rain protection isn't very high on most roadster owner's priority lists. There are a couple alternatives. One neat solution is this compact, storable top called "The Topster." It has a two-inch chop and fits the original '32 Ford mounting points.

There are removable fiberglass tops that you can get for roadsters. Most of them look pretty good. The problem is storage. You can't take them on and off in the middle of a trip.

building a cool car. Street rods don't have anywhere near the amount of insulation that new cars have. A prime reason that new cars and trucks are so quiet is that they are so well insulated, both for sound and heat.

There are lots of high-tech insulation products available for street rods. These products are well worth their cost. The goal is to keep as much engine and road-generated heat away from the cockpit as possible. The floor and fire-

wall are key areas to insulate. There isn't much between you and the engine in a street rod, so it's easy for all that heat to reach you. Heat will find its way in through openings that you might not have considered, like around the steering column and the brake pedal. It's important to seal off the interior as tightly as possible.

Besides the engine, another source of heat is the exhaust system. Due to the limited room between the frame rails, you usually don't have a lot of choices as to where to mount the mufflers. They frequently end up in the middle of the chassis, right under the cockpit.

Insulating the floor will help keep out exhaust heat, but you can further reduce the radiated heat with heat shields. By mounting a metal shield between the muffler and the floorboards, heat will be deflected. Heat shields can be a squeeze to accommodate because street rodders like to have their exhaust systems tucked up tight to the floor. Exhaust systems that hang down noticeably are a sign of a sloppily constructed car. There are special flat mufflers to help fit in the mufflers and heat shields.

Street rods that have things like a fuel injected engine, air conditioning, power accessories, and a trick sound system can generate some pretty substantial bundles of wiring. Advance planning is needed to make sure there is adequate room in access holes where the wires run. You don't want chafed wires.

KEEPING THE CAR COOL

The less heat the car generates, the cooler you and the interior will be. The prime heat generator is the engine and its related components. As mentioned previously, there isn't much between you and the engine so it's easy for heat to be transferred.

Over and above your personal comfort is the anxiety of watching a temp gauge flirt precariously with the 280-degree mark. No one likes it when his or her car overheats, but it's especially embarrassing when you're cruising through a congested street rod event. Favorable attention quickly plummets to sardonic pity and you have to deal with the mess of overflowing antifreeze.

Conditions associated with street rod events generate lots of heat and so does the design of the cars. The big V-8 engines used in modern street rods are shoe-horned into spaces that were designed for much smaller and much less powerful engines. The narrow design of street rod grilles means that narrow radiators must be used. That doesn't leave a lot of radiator exposed to fresh air. To get the cooling capacity needed for the engines, thick high performance radiators are required.

Things like smooth hoods contribute to engine heat buildup. The heat

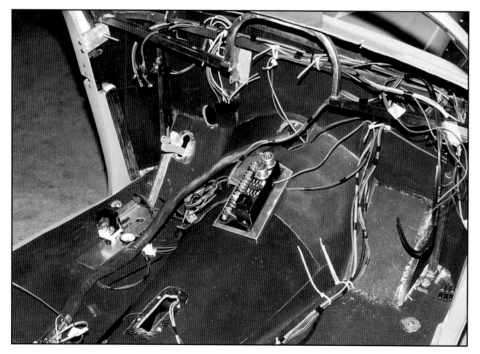

Modern street rod require quite a lot of wiring to run all the electronic components that people want in their cars. This interior looks like an explosion at a wiring factory, but it's really not that bad. Modern wiring kits are so well designed that you mostly just connect pre-labeled wires.

needs to escape, which is a good reason to use a louvered hood. Louvers also impart that traditional hot rod look.

Many things will help keep engine-operating temperatures in the low anxiety range. The primary factor is a top quality radiator. A street rod radiator is not a place to cut corners. If you install air conditioning in the car, be sure that the radiator is set up for A/C.

Fan shrouds can aid radiator efficiency. There are special high-flow water pumps that are ideal for street rod engines. It also helps to keep compression ratios at conservative levels. A radical engine is much more likely to overheat than a less muscular one. As we mentioned earlier, it doesn't take a Top Fuel motor to make a street rod quick. A small-block Chevy V-8 that would be sluggish in a full-size passenger car will move right along in a lightweight street rod.

There seems to be a difference of opinions as to whether an engine driven traditional fan or an electric fan works best. Fat-fendered street rods that have space between the grille and the radiator often use an engine fan to pull in air and one or more electric fans in front of the radiator to push in extra air. Given the design of the grilles on the cars this book suggests building, there isn't the option of a front-mounted electric fan.

If you're using a computer controlled fuel injection system, finding space to mount the CPU can be a challenge. A common location is up under the cowl on the passenger side of the car. You will usually have to fabricate a mounting bracket.

This three-window coupe has lots of power accessories like windows, door locks, trunk release, truck lift, antenna, etc. so a lot of extra relays are necessary. This Hotronics Commander 9000 unit was mounted in the back corner of the cab on the passenger side. The function of every different colored wire is listed on a label on the Commander 9000.

There are two main factors related to fan selection: space and air movement. Space problems take precedence, but that sometimes leaves the engine with insufficient cooling. Factory-style, engine driven fans move large volumes of air. They're very efficient, especially when used in conjunction with a fan shroud. Besides the space considerations, another engine fan problem is its location relative to the radiator. Due to the way that engines are mounted relatively low in street rods and the radiators tend to be tall and narrow, the fans can be too low to do the most good.

A coolant recovery system should be used to maintain coolant levels and prevent spillage. Instead of the ugly plastic recovery tanks used in modern passenger cars, there are handsome polished stainless steel tanks for street rods. These tanks come in several sizes, but they're all long and thin. The tanks mount on the side of the radiator and they're pretty unobtrusive.

Besides cooling the engine, it's wise to keep the transmission cool, too. Some people use engine oil coolers, but it's hard to find enough room for too many coolers. Auxiliary transmission coolers are also tough to locate. There are special, compact coolers designed for street rods, but getting sufficient airflow to them can be a challenge. Some builders fashion scoops to direct air to the coolers.

Paint choice can affect engine compartment temperatures. Black and other dark colors absorb more heat than light colors. This isn't to say that people who live in Arizona should paint all their cars white, but paint color is a factor. The combination of lots of little factors can significantly raise engine-operating temperatures.

Hot Seat

The original topic was hot and cold, but more accurately it should have been mostly cold and a little hot. Heating a street rod isn't anything like cooling concerns, but there are times when heat is neat. Roadsters are usually plenty warm on sunny days, but in the early morning and evenings, an open car can get very cold. Coupes and sedans are better, but they can also be rather chilly.

Even with a heater, most roadster owners pack a heavy coat in the trunk. If you don't have a top, a waterproof heavy coat is a better idea. Street rod air conditioning units can be had as cooling

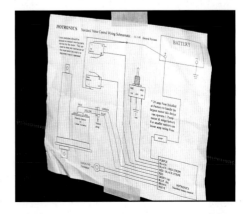

Hotronics supplies clean wiring diagrams with their kits. Tim Divers tapes the diagram inside the car near where he's doing the wiring so it's always available for reference.

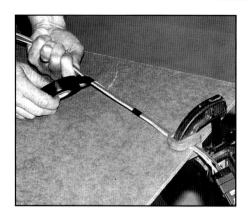

A neat trick for obtaining very tight wiring harnesses is to clamp the end of a particular sub-assembly to a board or workbench. Then pull the wires taut and wrap them with electrical tape approximately every six inches.

only, cooling and heat, and cooling, heat, and defrost units. Adding heat is very inexpensive, so it's something you should get. Defrosting ability is a moot point if the dashboard design doesn't allow room for vents. The typical street rod coupe defroster serves double duty as the driver's shirtsleeve.

An often-overlooked source of on-demand heat is a heated seat. Heated seats are becoming quite common in new cars. It wouldn't be difficult to integrate heating elements in the upper and lower seat cushions. The types of heaters that use a rheostat instead of a simple off-on or high-low switch are preferable. There are also aftermarket heated seat kits.

GETTING WIRED

A street rod won't run without some type of basic wiring system. Even if all you want to do is fire the engine in the chassis, some wiring is necessary. If you want lights, music, gauges, air conditioning, and all of a car's other amenities, you're going to need a wiring harness.

Wiring a car from scratch is one of those tasks that seems so overwhelming as to make you abandon the whole project. Fortunately, several people who understand the mysterious comings and goings of electrons have developed easy-to-use street rod wiring kits. The development of street rod wiring kits was one

of the best things to ever happen. Wiring kits are especially important with modern fuel injected engines that rely on computers and sensors to run efficiently.

A wiring kit will save huge amounts of time and they make it easier to neatly run the wires. A snake pit of loose wires is a scary sign of a poorly built street rod. Since wiring is tucked away, the goal is to install it once and forget it. Tracing wiring problems can be very frustrating, so save lots of potential future problems by using a quality wiring kit.

Wiring kits can be customized to your specific car. In order to do that, you need to know in advance what components you'll be using. This is one more example of the importance of careful planning.

DASH AND GAUGES

The dashboard is one of those things you look at every time you drive your street rod. Yet, many builders seem to just randomly install the gauges and accessories. It doesn't cost much more to do a nice job; it's mostly a matter of planning.

Studying the dashboards of similar cars is always a good place to start. Dashboard styles vary from ultra simple to overly cluttered. Our suggestion for a first-time bolt-together car is to stick

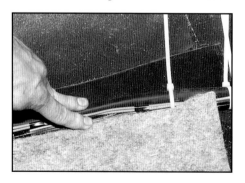

It's common for wiring harnesses to be routed under the carpeting. To get a professional look, you want the wires to be as unobtrusive as possible. These wires are being run along the driveshaft tunnel. They are tightly bundled and run along the edge of the carpet padding. If they were under the padding, they might make a bump. The cable ties are positioned so the ends are against the floor. You don't want bumps in the carpet.

Cutting wires and attaching your own terminals can be done is a simple, inexpensive multi-purpose wiring tool. Putting the wire in the numbered groove that matches the gauge of the wire strips the excess insulation. The other part of the wiring tool is used to crimp the terminal after the stripped end of the wire has been inserted. You only want to strip enough wire to make contact inside the terminal.

with clean and simple. Depending on where you buy your fiberglass body, there are a few different dashboards available. On '32 Fords, the most common choices are completely flat, the stock style center oval, the larger, centralized "Auburn" rectangular dash, and a shortened version of a 1940 Ford dashboard.

Whatever dashboard style you choose; try to make the gauges work with the style of the car. For example, digital gauges don't look right in a traditionally styled highboy. Conversely, vintage design gauges look out of place on a high tech street rod.

There are five important gauges that should be included. They are the speedometer, water temperature, oil pressure, fuel level, and voltage gauges. The most common combination of these gauges is a large speedometer and four smaller gauges. Some builders like to include a tachometer that's the same diameter as the speedometer.

A compact variation of the "big five" gauges is a normal sized speedometer and a similarly sized four-in-one gauge that contains small temp, oil, fuel, and volts gauges. The compact size is a neat idea, but the gauges are a little small for easy, accurate reading. They're fine for getting a general reading.

A must-have gauge for street rods is a programmable speedometer. Given all the variables in a street rod's tires and gear ratios, an electronic speedometer can easily be adjusted for accurate readings.

Glove boxes are pretty rare on non-fat-fendered street rods. Unless a '40 Ford style dash is used with its built-in unit, glove boxes are seldom cut into a Model A or Deuce dash (the exception being the '32 three-window coupe dash, which originally had a glove box). Many builders gain some valuable storage space by installing a package tray underneath the dashboard.

SOUND SYSTEMS

Good music enhances the whole street rod experience. The challenge is where to mount the equipment. Some people build the control unit into the dashboard, but it's more common to mount the main unit under the dash or even under the seat in the seat riser. A better idea is to use a stereo that has a remote control unit. Then the hardware can be mounted out of the way in the trunk. Even if you have dash-mounted controls, a 6-disc remote CD changer is a good idea.

Heat shrink tubing is a neat product for protecting the ends of wires and their terminals, especially on items that are prone to corrosion like battery cables. Shrink tubing comes in various diameters. Heat from a heat gun or hair dryer will cause the tubing to shrink. A quick way to install the tubing is to fabricate a little heat shield out of aluminum and clamp it to the end of the heat gun.

Here is the negative ground cable with its shrink tubing protection. This heavy-duty cable was made out of welding cable. A solid ground is important in a fiberglass car. This cable will be attached to a substantial bolt that goes to the frame.

Open street rods don't have a lot of room for big powerful speakers. Available depth is as much a problem as overall speaker size. You need to research what is available in the way of small speakers. When you're out on the open road, it can be difficult to hear any music, so you crank up the volume. Then, when you slow down, the music is way too loud. A neat solution is to get a stereo that's speed sensitive like the ones they use on many late model GM vehicles.

The sound system should be planned in advance so it can be installed along with the wiring kit. You don't want a lot of extra wires running underneath the carpet.

LIGHTS

Headlights and taillights on street rods are slightly different than their counterparts on newer cars. The types of icon cars that we advocate don't always have their lights in the same places. This is especially true of highboys, but it also applies somewhat to full-fendered cars.

The original headlights on these cars were mounted on the fenders instead of in them. When the fenders are removed, new light locations are needed. Headlight choice and location are some of those seemingly little touches that can have a substantial impact on the overall look of the car.

There are a variety of aftermarket headlights. The most common ones are aftermarket units that are smaller than the original lights. Typical early Ford headlights were 9-10 inches in diameter. The aftermarket lights, which are often referred to as King Bee lights, are usually 7 inches in diameter. The aftermarket lights work well with the stripped down, lean look of a hot rod.

Aftermarket lights aren't always used on highboys. There are plenty of builders who like the larger, stock style lights. Study the profiles of headlights you see at events and in magazines to help you determine the best ones for your car.

Headlight mounting brackets are as important as the style of light. There are a variety of custom brackets that mount to the frame rails of fenderless cars. Not everyone sets their lights at the same height or the same location relative to the grille. This is another example of little details that help set the overall look of a car. The most important thing to check regarding headlight height is local vehicle codes. You want to be legal and you want the lights to be effective.

Full-fendered street rods have lots of headlight options, too. Most cars use some form of the factory headlight-mounting bar. The most popular version is a dropped bar. These bars lower the headlights a couple inches. There are various styles of dropped headlight bars. Some builders use cut-down headlight bars so there isn't a bar going across the

This street rod's compact Optima battery can be accessed from the trunk. The heavy-duty angle iron mounting bracket is attached to the big bracket that secures the gas tank.

front of the grille. Headlight choices are the same as for fenderless cars.

Almost all street rod headlights use powerful quartz halogen bulbs for better visibility. There are super bright bulbs for the taillights, and even red LED kits that fit inside conventional taillight housings as well. Most street rod taillights are rather small, so you want the brightest possible bulbs. You will need a headlight dimmer switch. You can get universal floor mounted switches, but most builders prefer the steering column stalk type switches. You need a high beam indicator light on the dashboard to be legal in most states.

There are a lot more options with taillights than headlights. People have stuck almost every imaginable taillight on the back of street rods. The preferred look is something small and subtle. You don't want some big, garish lights to detract from the simple lines of the body. As far as location goes, taillights can either be mounted in the lower rear deck panel or fastened to brackets. Body mounted lights seem to predominate, but there are also lots of slick brackets.

Taillight brackets are usually some variation of a stock bracket. Builders like to use brackets and lights from other year Fords. Shortening stock brackets so the lights tuck in closer to the body is a popular trick.

Even though taillight selection is virtually unlimited, a few standards are used most of the time. Probably the

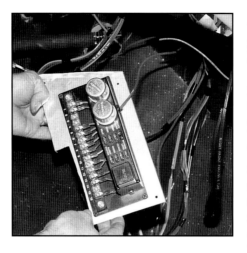

For optimum space utilization underneath crowded dashboards, it's often necessary to fabricate a custom-mounting panel for the CPU or fuse panel. Brackets are easy to build with a sheet of relatively thin aluminum. Here is a typical mounting bracket for a small, very basic fuse panel on a minimalist roadster. All the fuses are neatly labeled for quick repairs should you ever need to replace one.

most popular taillight is the '38-'39 Ford teardrop unit. They're usually called just teardrop lights or '39 Ford taillights. The lights are usually mounted on the surface with their stainless steel trim rings, but some builders choose to recess or "French" them into the lower rear deck panel.

Another very popular taillight for Model A and Deuce highboys is the '50 Pontiac unit. These simple, round taillights are bigger than the teardrop lights, but not so big as to overpower the rear of the car. The Pontiac lights are also available in reproduction form.

Two popular rectangular style taillights are the '41-'48 Chevy and '42-'48 Ford units. The Ford unit is rounder than the Chevy, but the Chevy light is more commonly used. There are reproduction stainless taillights for all Model A and thirties Fords. Using the stock style taillights is always a safe choice.

Late model passenger car taillights have been integrated into the rear deck panels. The trend is to use thin lights and recess them into the body. Modern third brake lights are a popular choice to use as street rod taillights. There are also a lot of different custom taillights that use

the thin, horizontal look. Some builders go to the extra effort to make the taillights totally flush with the body.

Third brake lights are a good idea if you can work them into the body in a subtle fashion. Third brake lights are easier to blend into coupe and sedan bodies. The challenge is to have good brake light visibility to alert following motorists without looking like an emergency response vehicle. Street rods attract a lot of attention. Following motorists might be more focused on checking out your car than paying attention to the fact that you're stopping, so be sure you have good taillights.

Turn signals should be a part of your lighting system. It's easy to incorporate turn signals in the taillights. It's tougher up front, but it can be done. Some builders put little turn signals in the lower part of the headlights. Others put small ones in or on the frame rails.

A rear license plate lamp is required in most states. There are nice little lamps that are incorporated in license plate frames so they serve a dual purpose. Stock Model A and '32 Ford taillights have a clear lens in the bottom of the light housing, but in order to take advantage of this feature, the license plate has to be mounted under the taillight.

FUEL SYSTEM COMPONENTS

Once you figure out which side the gas door is on, you can forget about the

Small bundles of wires, like these temperature gauge sending wires, in the engine compartment can be made neater by bundling them with plastic spiral wire wrap. It's inexpensive and available from Ron Francis Wire Works.

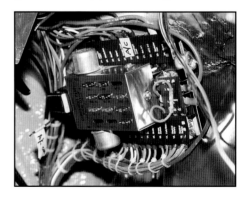

Here is another style of fuse panel that was installed in a sedan. It was mounted under the cowl on the driver's side because the main wiring harness runs over to the kick panel and along the doorjamb.

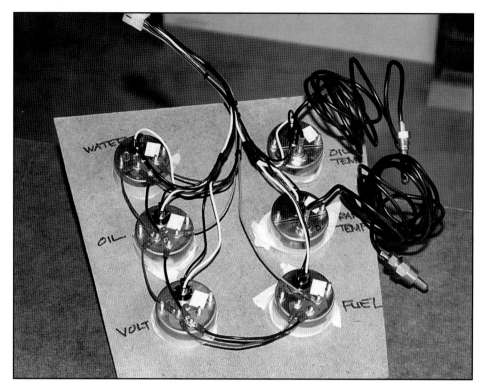

These Auto Meter gauges will be installed in a custom console in a '33 Ford coupe. To make wiring the gauges easier, they were placed in a piece of hardboard the same size as the console. The wires that connect the gauges to each other were cut to exact lengths and the terminals crimped on, so there's no excess wire. The gauges will be easy to rewire when they're installed in the finished console.

limited storage there is in a street rod.

Model A Fords originally had their fuel tanks in the cowl. Many older, steel rods kept this location, but we've never been comfortable having 10-12 gallons of gas sitting between the engine and us. Full-fendered Model A street rods can use twin, sidesaddle tanks that reside under the running board splash aprons. Highboys need to place the tanks behind the seat or in the trunk.

Deuces and '33-'34 Fords can use the traditional rear-mounted tank location between the two rear frame horns. Cars with bobbed rear frame horns need to use a trunk-mounted gas tank. For a first time, bolt-together street rod we recommend the stock tank location. There are stock and slightly oversize '32 tanks.

Running fuel lines is another mundane but necessary task. Fuel lines and fittings aren't difficult to make, but a clean installation requires careful planning. The lines must be securely mounted, and well away from any moving parts, heat sources, or anything that might abrade the line. A trick for getting bends in the right place is to make patterns with coat hangers or other relative-

fuel system of your family car. The fuel system of a street rod requires a lot more involvement. Car choice dictates general gas tank locations, but there are some variations. Since we advocate the use of new parts, we'll forget about stock gas tanks. Old gas tanks can be rust receptacles, resulting in clogged fuel filters, mucked-up carbs, and even leaks. A brand new gas tank is the best way to go.

Street rod gas tanks are available for most popular cars in steel, stainless steel, or polyethylene plastic. The choice is a personal one. A bigger consideration is the fuel tank capacity. In general, street rods don't have very large gas tanks. Modern fuel injected engines deliver very respectable fuel economy figures, but older, high performance engines can rival SUVs for poor fuel economy. A limited fuel range can mean lots of extra stops on long trips, but for the average weekend drive, it shouldn't be a problem.

Some builders place a fuel cell in the trunk. The safety factor of fuel cells is a good idea, but it's tough to give up what

A classic dashboard technique is to cover part or all of the dash with engine turned aluminum. This material can be obtained in sheets. The gauges are properly spaced and holes are cut. Many builders like a smaller turned aluminum insert like those used on '32 Ford coupe dashboards.

ly stiff wire. Then you duplicate the bends on the actual fuel lines.

GETTING EXHAUSTED

Exhaust system components can take up a lot of room in a chassis. The vast majority of street rods run dual exhausts, for both performance and sound. You could save a little space by running a single muffler, but you'd still need a crossover pipe. Some builders have run dual pipes back to a single cross-flow muffler behind the rear axle. This modern passenger car configuration saves space in the middle of the car, but finding enough room out back can be tough.

A consideration regarding exhaust systems is what size tubing to use. Rods with blown big-block engines like to impress the troops with sewer pipe-sized tubing, but average small-block engines are better served with relatively small diameter pipes. The common tubing sizes are 2", 2-1/4", and 2-1/2" diameter.

There are countless ways to mount headlights. Where they are in relation to a Deuce grille is a topic for considerable debate. The small aftermarket lights on Craig Lang's stunning '32 appear to be floating, but the back of the light bucket is attached to the fender in the approximate location of the original headlight bar base. The V'd spreader bar might be considered a bumper by some people, but it's really more of a design element.

You can buy exhaust components and fashion your own bolt-together exhaust system. This is one way to go, but you're probably better off having a muffler shop build the exhaust system.

Muffler choice is a personal matter, but most builders like a relatively quiet muffler that still has a good rumble when the gas pedal is mashed. There is a contingent of street rodders who like as little sound dampening as possible, but all that extra noise can be tiring.

Muffler size can affect how quiet the system is. There's a trade-off between how quiet a muffler is and how easily it can be fitted to the tight confines of a street rod chassis. There are new "flat" mufflers that help conserve space and prevent the dreaded "hanging muffler syndrome."

Street rodders like to display their creativity with exhaust outlets. There are lots of slick custom exhaust tips available. It's best to run the exhaust pipes all the way to the back of the car. You want to keep exhaust fumes away from the passenger area, especially on open cars and cars with rumble seats.

As for material, if you're building a full-fendered car, aluminized steel tubing will do the job. But remember that highboys are easier to look under, and people expect to see a nice finish underneath any street rod. If the budget allows, consider a stainless steel exhaust system, or get the regular steel exhaust system coated with a permanent, high-temp exhaust coating. These coatings prevent heat transfer, look good, and prevent rust.

SPARE TIRES

Spare tires are very rare in the types of street rods this books advocates. The limiting factor is space. Full-fendered street rods with bigger trunks (like '40 Ford coupes) have room for at least a space saver spare tire. It is possible to fit a space saver tire in the trunk of a '32 roadster, but it's the same trade-off as with gas tanks. Given the pretty slight chances of getting a flat tire, most Deuce roadster owners go without a spare.

There are a few alternatives. The two best things you can do if you don't carry

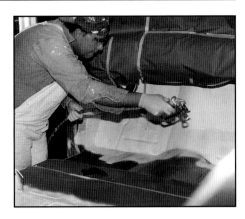

Good insulation is one of the best investments you can make in a street rod. It helps keep heat down and makes the car quieter. There are many types of insulation and some builders use more than one. An easy to apply high-tech insulation is Cool Car Ceramic. It can be sprayed or brushed on.

a spare are have a cell phone and belong to a roadside service organization like AAA. For lots of reasons besides flat tires, a cell phone and AAA should be mandatory street rod equipment.

Run-flat tires are available, but expensive. They come in limited sizes, too. There are special inner liners that offer added safety in the case of a blowout. Buying quality tires, keeping them properly inflated, and checking for signs of excessive wear or damage are other ways to minimize the risk of a flat tire.

You should carry a limited selection of tools so you can deal with things like flat tires. Many custom wheels use special lug nuts so you need to carry the right size socket wrench. Street rods tend to be very low with limited jacking points. There are special low profile street rod jacks, which are a good thing to have. Remember, the car will be lower than normal if it has a flat tire.

BUMPERS

Street rods don't offer a great deal of crash protection. Bumpers aren't used too much. Some full-fendered or fat-fender cars use them, but the most you're apt to see on a Deuce highboy is some abbreviated nerf bars. These little mini bumpers offer minimal protection.

Many people use them as much as a styling element as a safety item.

The best things you can do regarding safety are proactive measures. You need great brakes so you can stop before you make contact with the car in front of you. You need top quality suspension components and tires so you can take evasive action instead of hitting another vehicle. You need to use seatbelts at all times.

MIRRORS, WIPERS, HORNS, AND OTHER LITTLE STUFF

As simple as street rods are, they still require a lot of basic accessories that every vehicle needs to be safe and legal. These items include mirrors, windshield wipers, horns, emergency flashers, gear indicators, sun visors, and emergency brakes. Given the limited space available and the desire to keep a street rod as uncluttered as possible, finding a place for all this stuff calls for some creativity.

Mirrors tend to be a sore spot with many street rod builders. They hang off the car and don't do anything to enhance the desired smooth look. Mirrors are especially important on coupes and sedans because of their restricted rear vision. Ideally, your car should have right and left outside mirrors and an inside rear view mirror. All street rod mirrors tend to be on the small side so you need all the help you can get. As with other accessories match the mirror style (traditional or high tech) to the style of the vehicle.

Street rodders try to avoid rain, but you can't always predict the weather. Plus, you need some type of wiper to

Electric fans are almost standard equipment on street rods. Except for fat-fendered cars, which have space between the grille and the radiator, most street rods must use pull-through fans. An open engine will dissipate heat better than one enclosed in solid hood panels, but it still needs the fan.

comply with vehicle codes. Closed cars aren't as difficult to fit with wipers as open cars. There are specialty wipers designed for street rods. The goal is to find one with a motor that's as compact as possible. The other challenge is to make the wiring as unobtrusive as possible. Some roadster owners devise removable wipers with plug-in wiring harnesses so they only bring them out if they get caught in the rain.

Street rod windshield wipers don't use very big wiper blades. The usual size

is 10-inches. That doesn't clear a very big area, even on a chopped windshield. A backup idea is to treat the windshield with one of those rain repellant solutions, like Rain-X

A good, loud horn is a vital piece of safety equipment. You need to be a defensive driver in a street rod. Other drivers can drift awfully close to you in their desire to get a better look at your neat car. Don't use a novelty horn. You need a powerful horn.

Emergency flashers should be part of the turn signals and steering column package. They should also be included in the wiring harness. Modern tilt steering wheels or the special street rod models include these features so you don't have to cobble them in elsewhere.

Interior sun visors are nice, but they're rarely seen on twenties and early thirties street rods. Open car drivers and passengers should always carry sunglasses. Coupes and sedans can accommodate sun visors, but they shouldn't be very tall. A visor that extends down too far will block too much of a chopped windshield. Street rod windshields are

This is a classic '32 Ford grille and grille shell with the stock emblem and radiator cap. It's more common to see filled shells. You can get a new radiator that fills through the original opening, but even cars with the cap usually have the filler neck behind the top tank of the radiator.

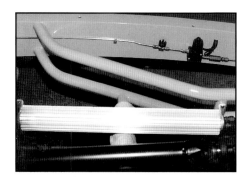

Given the limited space available in a street rod chassis, it can be hard to find room for things like a transmission cooler. Also, since these cars tend to be super low, the traditional finned style coolers can pick up a lot of road debris. A slick looking solution is to use a heat sink style transmission fluid cooler. They are long and skinny and their ribbed aluminum outer shell looks better than the old style coolers.

almost vertical, so there isn't any room to flip the visor up against the windshield like on modern vehicles.

An emergency brake is a mandatory item. Space is always tight in a street rod cockpit so early cars favor center-mounted, pull-up style e-brake handles. There are suspended pedal style emer-gency brakes, but they're more often used in fat-fendered cars. If you don't want a column shift, several companies make transmission shifters for automatics. These shifters mount right on top of the transmission and give the appearance of an old manual transmission. There are matching emergency brakes that also mount on the transmission.

Some type of gear indicator should be employed. Depending on the style of steering column, you may have an indicator right on the column. There are several styles of LED shift indicator kits. There are ones that mount in the dashboard and ones that mount on the floor on the left side of the floor shifter. At minimum, a shifter knob with the pattern on it should be used.

SECURITY AND INSURANCE

A street rod is supposed to be about good times, so we hate to inject any negativity, but you shouldn't overlook security. Given the basic nature of street rods, there isn't much to prevent a determined thief from taking your car. Most rodders are very particular about where they park their cars. At big rod runs, the motel rooms closest to the cars are always in big demand. Some people lock their cars inside their trailers, but thieves have been known to take the trailer and its contents. A thief towing a trailer down the road is much less noticeable than one driving a street rod.

There are people who use the steering wheel clubs and other steering wheel devices. There are special steering wheels where the wheel is removable. You actually take the steering wheel with you when the car is left alone.

Alarms are OK, but people often don't pay much attention to car alarms. Try setting off your daily driver's alarm system in a mall parking lot and watch how few people even give it a second glance. A problem with electronic alarms is their sensitivity. You want to adjust it so it registers an intrusion, but you don't want it going off all night long at the motel every time another rod goes by with a loud exhaust.

A security device that immobilizes the electrical system is a good idea. An activation switch can be hidden if you're clever. Many people wire a dummy switch or make something that is counter-intuitive. Sears has a trick battery with a built-in security system.

Another possibility is a brake system lock. There are devices that use a solenoid (like a line lock in drag racing) to lock up the brakes. This is another device that needs some clever hiding to work best.

The final security item is good insurance. Too many people make the mistake of trying to save a few dollars up front and don't properly insure their cars. That's fine until you have a loss. If you want stated value insurance, you have to take care of that long before you file a claim. There are specialty insurance companies that cater to street rods. These companies know street rods, unlike your local all-purpose agent. The specialty companies realize how little the average street rod is used and they can tailor rates to reflect the actual usage. This means that good coverage can be less expensive than marginal coverage from a company that doesn't understand special interest cars. The specialty insurance companies advertise in the major street rod magazines.

A top quality radiator (the only kind you should consider) isn't cheap. The fins can get damaged during the construction process if you're not careful. As a free safety measure, Tim Divers tapes a piece of cardboard to the radiator while he is working on a car.

Detailing on a Budget

Detailing is what separates one street rod from another. Since the thrust of this book is how to build an icon car with a big emphasis on popularity, it would be easy to build a carbon copy car. We're all for emulating the key elements of successful, highly popular street rods, but it's also nice to personalize your car.

Street rods are much more personal than daily drivers, but there is a sameness to many rods. Detailing is the name for the small, subtle touches that distinguish your Deuce roadster from the six parked near you.

You can always make any street rod stand out with outrageous modifications, but there's a huge difference between positive and negative attention. Wild modifications, especially in the hands of a beginner, can easily lead to disaster. Properly done detailing should bring positive attention to your car.

A great thing about detailing is that much of it can be done after the car is assembled and on the road. You can make little upgrades and changes while you're enjoying the car. Doing it this way can stretch your budget and extend the building fun.

Color and Contrast

The creative use of paint is one of the best ways to detail a street rod. Even though we strongly advocate painting a first-time street rod a popular color like red, other colors can be used for accent. Contrasting colors are a major way of accenting a paint job. Most paint detail-

ing needs to be done during construction, but some tasks can be done later.

The first area to consider for color is the chassis. It's fine to drive around in a primered car, but you should consider painting or powder coating the chassis before components get too dirty. It's easier to paint frame rails and major chassis components when they're nice and clean. You also want to protect these parts from rust.

If you're thinking of powder coating the chassis, be sure that the color will

work with whatever body color you eventually use. There are so many shades of red that it's very possible to get a shade that is just different enough from the body color as to be terribly annoying. When it comes to matching colors, close isn't good enough. Some local powder coating companies can match (or at least get very close) their colors to the body color you want.

When you paint a chassis and you're sure you will paint the body the same color, talk to your painter about the

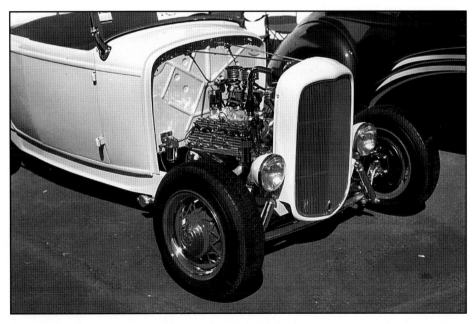

The use of contrasting colors is one of the easiest ways to make an icon car stand out from all the other similar cars. It's hard to tell in a black and white photo, but this traditionally styled '32 roadster makes excellent use of a moderate amount of bright red to contrast with the pure white body. The wire wheels, grille bars, engine block, finned cylinder heads, and upholstery are all red. The red really adds some zip to the white car without overpowering it.

Contrasting colors can be used in places that aren't always obvious (sort of the automotive equivalent of lingerie). John Foxley very patiently applied a red and white checkerboard pattern to the firewall of his '34 Ford.

benefits of buying all your paint at one time. It is possible for different batches (or custom mixed colors) to vary a little from each other. If you don't plan on painting the body for a couple years, wait to buy the paint.

Most highboy builders paint the frame rails the same color as the body. A popular exception is a red chassis on a primered car. The bright red contrasts nicely with the dull primer (or semi-gloss black). If you eventually paint the body red, great, but if it stays in primer, it still looks good.

A black chassis works with most colors, although it's pretty conservative. Many builders like black because it's easy to maintain. A car that's driven a lot

Engines are a natural place for detailing. This small-block Chevy deserves to be out in the open. The bright red block and copious amounts of chrome contrast nicely with the brilliant yellow body. Red was used between the valve cover fins, inside the carb scoops, on the carb bases, and on the blade supports of the fan.

is a good choice for a black chassis. Black also looks good with components that are either chromed, polished aluminum, or painted a contrasting color.

Color is the least expensive way to add some interesting contrast to a chassis. It's considerably cheaper than chrome, stainless steel, or polished aluminum parts. The choice of a contrasting color depends on the primary chassis color. In general, people usually pick a lighter or darker shade of the main color. You can get paint that looks like aluminum. That gives a nice machined look to the parts. Check out the chassis and component colors of cars you like at street rod events to get ideas for your car.

Besides contrasting colors, you can use contrasting finishes. The best example of this is chromed suspension parts against a black background. Metal parts like rear axle housing, shock absorbers, brackets, and front axle can easily be painted with aerosol spray paints. You won't get the same job with spray cans that you get with professional painting equipment, but it will work fine for a while. You can always touch-up or completely re-do any problem areas.

ENGINE AND TRANNY DETAILING

A good, strong engine is a vital component of any street rod, so it makes sense to want to show it off. Unless you're going the ultra low buck, super-slob route, you'll want a clean, painted engine and transmission. If you take your time to thoroughly clean and prep the engine block, the resulting paint job will look better, last longer, and be easier to maintain.

There are things you can do to an engine that require more time and grunt work than experience or specialized skills. Some of these detailing tricks fall into the "how much time do you have?" category, but we're just presenting ideas.

If you look closely at many show cars, you'll probably notice that the engine blocks, cylinders heads, intake manifolds, and related parts look much smoother than the same parts on your car. Meticulous builders make the parts look super smooth by removing casting lines. Some go as far as to cover the

rough block castings with body filler. Removing casting flash is fine, but covering a block with body filler can affect cooling ability.

Casting details can be removed with a die grinder and special carbide burrs and abrasive rolls. The carbide burrs are used to do the preliminary grinding and the abrasive rolls (they come in cylindrical and conical shapes) are used for the finish work.

An example of how grinding off casting marks can save money is with exhaust manifolds. Custom exhaust headers are nice for their extra power, but many street rodders prefer cast iron exhaust manifolds because they're noticeably quieter. There are some slick, custom-made cast iron exhaust manifolds, but when you're on a budget, why not use some inexpensive stock ones.

Cast iron exhaust manifolds in their stock form aren't very attractive, but with some grinding and painting, they will look quite nice. Depending on the exact manifold style, there are lots of bumps, numbers, and webbed areas that can be ground smooth. There's brush-on or spray paint that's specifically made for exhaust systems. Typical colors include factory gray, matte silver, stainless steel gray (a popular choice), and black.

Besides the exhaust manifolds, the whole exhaust system can be detailed and protected with high temperature paint. If the main components are a light

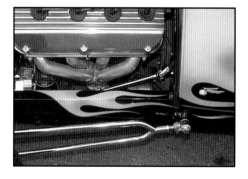

Flames are a hot rod staple. They can be used to advantage in many places other than the hood and doors. These interesting flames start inside the frame rails and come up and over with a couple little floating licks going back below the cowl. The placement of the flames by the exhaust manifolds works well.

Traditional pinstriping is a popular way to decorate the entire car, but larger, more impressive designs look neat on trunk lids. Depending on the amount of contrast, the designs can be either subtle or bold.

color, you could add detailing by painting the fasteners and hangers black. Simple, little touches like this give a chassis more definition and interest.

The grinding and smoothing techniques can also be employed on parts like the transmission case and cast iron intake manifolds. Most transmission case flashing is on the topside, so smoothing out the case is sort of overkill, but it looks good while the body is still off.

The intake manifold is one of the most visible parts of an engine, so a little massaging here is time well spent. Once the intake manifold has been smoothed, it can be painted the same color as the block or a contrasting color. Using aluminum or stainless steel colored paint can make the manifold look more like an aluminum one. This trick can also be used on cylinder heads. Real aluminum cylinder heads are a desirable and expensive, but you can emulate the look for a couple bucks worth of paint.

Aluminum intake manifolds look great when they're polished. You can save money by doing your own polishing. This is a very messy, labor-intensive task. Professional polishers really earn their pay. It's not too hard to polish the big, relatively flat top surfaces, but the deep little pockets can be a bear.

Street rod magazines and parts catalogs offer lots of trick chrome and aluminum engine accessories. The really slick billet parts can add up quickly. The inexpensive alternative is to paint the

stock brackets either the block color or a contrasting color. You can always add the fancy parts as your budget allows.

Carbureted engines need some type of air cleaner. This is a great place to express your individuality. There are lots of trick aftermarket air cleaners that can be used right out of the box. You can use paint to make these ready-made parts more unique.

Air cleaners with some type of flat top panel make a nice little "canvas" for your artistic attempts. Traditional air cleaner decor favorites are pinstriping and flames.

Engine hoses are one of the least attractive features of any engine compartment. The bucks-up beauty tip is to replace the stock hoses with braided stainless steel hoses and anodized AN fittings. There are also less expensive braided hose covers. They go over your stock hoses.

One thing to be careful about when using any non-stock water hoses is leakage. Depending on the style of the cover "fitting" you might not get a perfectly good seal. This weakness probably won't manifest itself until you decide to go for a July cruise through Death Valley. For added peace of mind, you might want to have a radiator shop pressure test the whole system.

Goodyear makes some special hoses that are a bright blue color. Depending on your engine's color scheme, they can add a neat contrast. The least expensive trick

This tip is as much an interesting detail as it is detailing. Steve Wright gained several very valuable inches in the cockpit of his '32 highboy roadster by placing the seat just underneath the beltline reveal. Most roadsters have seats that roll up to and/or over the reveal.

Storage is always at a premium in street rods. Notice the very simple shelf underneath the dashboard of this Deuce. A more compartmentalized storage shelf would distract from the car's clean lines.

you can do to rubber hoses is to spray some clear aerosol paint on them before you install them. That's an old used car lot detailing trick for making a steam-cleaned engine compartment sparkle.

EXTERIOR DETAILING

Paint or polished parts can be used to detail the exterior of a street rod. Even a car that runs around in primer can be spiced-up with a little paint. Most exterior detailing tricks are best done in moderation. The idea is to make your car look good, but not gaudy.

Tasteful pinstriping is a very traditional exterior detailing item. Several professional pinstripers attend most major street rod events if you can't find a suitable painter locally. The mark of a really talented striper is their ability to pull super thin lines. A neat application is to have two or three different colored lines painted right next to each other. From a distance, it looks like a single stripe, but up close you can appreciate the different colors.

Adding some type of decoration to primered bodies is a popular trick. Flames are very popular on primered cars. They exude that bad boy, hot rod look. If you don't want to spring for a full flame job, a pinstriper can apply just the outlines. You can also save money by putting a few strategic flames on the body instead of covering the whole front half of the car.

Possible locations for smaller flame jobs include the belt line of the car,

Another solution to the limited storage problem is this '40 Ford style dashboard in a '32 roadster. The dash has a glove box already built in. Contrasting colors were used on the dash. The top of the dash is black (like the body) and the lower part is bright red (like the upholstery).

down low near the frame rails (or even on the frame), or just on the fenders of a full-fendered car. Painting flames on just the front fenders can be a reasonable way of seeing if you want to flame more of the car at a later time. If you want conservative flames, check out getting some pearl ghost flames.

Wheels are a big focal point on street rods. Paint can be used to accent aluminum wheels. Slotted style mags can be painted inside the slots or "windows." If you paint aluminum wheels, a good clean surface is important. Care must be taken when masking off the sections of the wheels that you don't want to paint.

Painted steel wheels can be detailed with chrome or polished stainless steel

There are interesting compromises between an Italian leather interior and a milk crate. This unfinished roadster had some colorful "Route 66" material sewn into a very basic seat cover. The cover is straight and plain which helps keeps costs down.

trim items. Trim rings and hubcaps are the most common items, but you could skip the caps and use chrome lug nuts. You can get a variety of custom hubcaps. A detailing trick from chromed steel wheels is to leave the outer rim alone, but paint the center of the wheel to match the body. That gives the look of a smooth trim ring.

Good looking tires are important to complete the wheel package. Some people get carried away with the liquid protectants. The most desirable look is a little less shiny and more like a brand new tire. Some detailing extremists have been known to shave off all the raised size information on the sidewalls. Those people have too much free time.

INTERIOR DETAILING

There isn't a whole lot you can do to tastefully detail a street rod interior. Things like upholstery and carpeting are considered part of the overall interior phase. The same goes for the column, steering wheel, and instrument panel.

A common interior detailing trick is to have the dashboard pinstriped. This is particularly effective on a traditional style high street rod. The type of gauges you pick make a difference on whether or not to use pinstriping. Digital gauges look too modern for traditional pinstriping. The best gauges for pinstriping around are the traditional style black with white numbers gauges.

A unique shift knob is an easy way to personalize a car. There are lots of wild ready-made knobs or if you're the artistic type, you might be able to whittle your own.

Interior accessories that we advise against include fuzzy dice, cartoon character floor mats, furry steering wheel covers, and any type of stuffed animal or doll. Let your street rod stand on its own merits and leave the dolls and stuffed animals in your child's room.

To an outsider, a street rod is a street rod; they don't appreciate the subtle differences. The more time you spend around street rods, the greater your appreciation of those unique details will be. Detailing is an easy way to personalize your street rod.

You can't get much more do-it-yourself basic than a pair of aluminum aircraft bucket seats with a chunk of bare foam for the bottom cushion. This look fits with the old time hot rod/lakes racer theme, but it's not for long trips.

The Mexican blanket in this chopped Deuce Tudor was very casually installed. It was loosely fitted to the cushion and any excess fabric was trimmed.

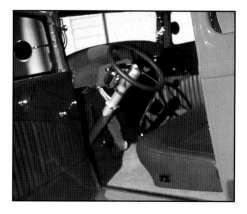

The same Deuce Tudor was later professionally upholstered in handsome gray leather, but the same seat cushions were used that were under the Mexican blanket.

TOOL TIME

Bolt-together street rods involve a fair number of nuts and bolts. Experts did all the difficult welding and fabrication work, but you still have to do assemble the parts. To do that you need a modest selection of mechanic's hand tools. You also need an appropriate place to build the car.

People who like street rods usually like tools, too. You could very well already have more than enough tools to build a street rod. If you don't, this chapter will help you focus on the most useful tools, how to set up your shop, and how to keep track of all the parts to your project car.

YOUR HOT ROD HAVEN

A spacious, well-lit, comfortable place to assemble your street rod will make everything go better. When you have space to spare, things don't seem as tense. Ideally, it's nice to have full use of a double garage. Street rods aren't very big; they're smaller than the average family car, but you want room to work around the car. Expect your project to take several months. Make this clear to other family members so they'll not expect much usage of the garage until the project is completed. If the family is as enthusiastic as you are about the car, they'll be more understanding about losing their share of the garage.

If the family garage is loaded with neglected junk, take this opportunity to thoroughly clean the garage. Donate stuff to charities or have a garage sale. If necessary, consider buying a storage shed to keep the normal garage clutter in for the duration of the street rod buildup. You could also rent a storage locker. The extra workspace is well worth the added costs.

People who really get into the street rod hobby often build a separate shop for future projects. That's a great luxury if you can afford it and have the extra space. Pre-fabricated metal buildings (often called pole buildings) are usually less expensive than wooden garages. When they're properly insulated and heated, metal buildings can make excellent workshops.

With a two-car garage, you can spread out sub-assemblies so you're not always tripping over things or constantly having to move one part to work on another. We like to put the chassis or car in the middle of the workspace. That way, there's lots of room on all sides of the car. We use storage shelves to store parts.

Good lighting is important. A bright environment is more cheerful and enjoyable to work in. Four-foot long, basic, fluorescent shop lights are very inexpensive. The ones with heavy-duty ballasts work better in cold tempera-

Street rods aren't very big when they're fully assembled, but they can take plenty of space when they're apart. An extra big work area makes the whole project more enjoyable.

Besides work space, it's nice to have ample storage. Mike Miller's shop has lots of room around the car and plenty of workbenches, parts bins, and storage cabinets. It's also well lit and heated—two highly desirable features.

tures, but hopefully your garage has some heat source.

The fluorescent lights are so reasonably priced (it seems like they're always on sale somewhere) that you can get lots of them. They're lightweight so you can move them around to provide the most light wherever you're working. If you have room on your garage walls, you might consider mounting a couple fluorescent lights along the wall at about the mid-point. Lots of professional shops (especially ones that do bodywork) employ wall-mounted lights.

Wintertime is prime street rod building time, so a heated garage is pretty much a necessity, especially in northern climes. If you use a portable heat source, be sure it's safe and meets all building codes. It would be tragic to have your new street rod go up in flames along with the building. It's a good idea to use a carbon monoxide detector.

Any amenities like a TV, small refrigerator, or sound system will make the garage more like a mechanical den. When the environment is pleasant, it's a lot easier to leave the living room behind and spend an evening working on your street rod. A couple stools or old chairs are nice for guests. A well-equipped shop is a magnet for guys, and it's fun to have company while you work on your project. Visitors are handy for holding things and fetching tools.

An item that most people overlook is insurance coverage. You should check with your insurance agent to see if you need a special policy rider to cover your unfinished car in case of fire or theft. Most companies won't insure a car until it's a completed, licensed vehicle. An expensive collection of street rod parts might be more than your normal comprehensive insurance covers. Any additional insurance premiums will seem insignificant in the event of an actual loss. Check first so you won't be sorry later.

PARTS STORAGE

Bolt-together street rods are essentially full-scale model cars. As such, there are a lot of loose parts. Big storage shelves are great for storing and organizing parts. Within those shelves, use different size containers and bins to further segregate the parts. Assorted plastic freezer bags are great for storing parts and fasteners. You can see what's inside and write specific information on the outside of the bag.

If you don't have enough built-in shelving, consider purchasing a couple of roll-around wire storage shelves. These sturdy shelving units have lots of space and the parts are readily visible. The big casters make it easy to move the units out of the way or keep parts close to where you're working. The rolling shelves are available in warehouse buying clubs and at home improvement centers. They're reasonably priced and still useful after you've finished the car.

We've had excellent results buying shelves, cabinets, and workbenches at public auctions. Prices tend to be high at automotive-related auctions. We've done better at large office and manufacturing facility auctions. These places usually have substantial quantities of storage items. The best deals tend to come near the end of the auction when most of the used office equipment buyers have bought all they want. Storage cabinets and shelves that are more banged up than the rest of the inventory might not be good enough to resell at a store, but they're fine for a garage.

If you have enough space in your garage, old office desks are incredibly cheap. The older, heavier, metal ones make great workbenches with lots of storage drawers. We've bought old government issue metal office desks for less than five dollars. We once bought a pallet with several desks on it for one dollar. These big, heavy desks are a liability to the auction companies.

Most people want newer, nicer, wooden desks, so the old metal ones are give away deals. You need a truck or trailer to get them home, they're awkward to move around, and they're very hard to get rid of if you decide you don't want them. We've had occasions where we ended up with parts of broken and mismatched desks. Big companies often have pieces left over from remodeling or re-configuring offices. We take the desks apart and keep the drawer units for storage. The rest of the junk goes to the dump. You can get a lot of substantial storage drawers with nice ball bearing sliders for very little money this way.

If you're tight on space for permanently installed workbenches, get a couple of folding tables. These composition board tables with the fake wood surfaces come in lengths ranging from 4 to 8 feet long. They aren't very expensive new and they're more affordable used. Since the tables fold, you can leave them out of the way until they're needed. If you want to protect the tabletops, get a roll of brown Kraft paper and cover the table. Throw the paper away when you're finished with the project. Another way to protect the tabletop is to tape a big piece of cardboard to it.

Another inexpensive workbench alternative is sawhorses and an old door. A pair of sturdy, metal, folding sawhorses makes a good base for an old hollow-core door. The door is a good size for lots of parts, it's light enough to move around, and it can be easily stored. If you don't have any old doors, unfinished new blank hollow-core doors aren't expensive. If space is really tight, you can get a narrow 24-inch door. When you're shopping for a door blank at a lumber store or home improvement center, ask if they have any seconds or damaged ones. You'll probably scratch and ding the door, so don't pay extra for a perfect one.

TOOLS

A basic set of mechanic's hand tools will handle the majority of the tasks you'll encounter when assembling a bolt-together street rod. The high-end professional tools like Snap-On and Mac are nice if you can afford them, but you can't go wrong with the affordable Sears Craftsman line of tools. If you don't already have a tool set, watch the ads for specials on tool sets. The tools are far less expensive when purchased in sets rather than one at a time.

Whenever you're buying a tool set, look carefully at what the set includes. Most tool sets list a large number of tools, but if you look closely, you'll see that there's usually a lot of Allen wrenches or hex keys. An example Craftsman set is marketed as a 241 piece mechanics' tool set, but 40 of those

pieces are inexpensive hex keys. Not that you won't need hex keys, you will, but they're much less expensive than wrenches and ratchets.

A tool set that includes both standard and metric tools is handy. These days you're likely to encounter both types of fasteners with relative frequency. You're much more likely to use 1/2-inch drive and 3/8-inch drive sockets than 1/4-inch sockets.

Power tools are nice, but not mandatory. If you have an air compressor, you might consider getting an air ratchet. When you're installing, checking for fit, removing, and then re-installing parts, an air ratchet saves a lot of wrist work. A quality drill motor is a necessary tool. The powerful battery operated ones are handy because you don't have to deal with the cord. The stronger cordless drills can be used to run up fasteners and then do the final tightening with a wrench.

A dead blow hammer is a useful tool for assembling a chassis. The soft-faced, shot-filled hammers deliver a good wallop without damaging the fastener. Various chassis components are tightly fitted. A dead blow hammer helps position those parts.

A full-size two-ton floor jack and

good, sturdy jack stands are important tools to have. The jack stands are necessary to support the chassis before the wheels and tires are mounted. The floor jack is needed to position heavy sub-assemblies like the rearend and the front suspension system. Spend a little more and get a quality floor jack. You don't want to risk personal injury or damage the car by using a cheap, third-world jack. Always support things with jack stands as soon as the item has been lifted or moved.

If you decide to rebuild an engine, you'll need a variety of specialized engine tools. Foremost is a good torque wrench. A torque wrench is also useful when tightening suspension components.

An engine stand is needed to rebuild an engine. The cost of quality engine stands has dropped considerably, so buy a premium one instead of some flimsy, low-dollar special. You definitely don't want an engine to fall on your feet.

An engine hoist is needed to install the engine and transmission. Many people rent an engine hoist, but it's not a bad idea to buy one. Warehouse clubs sell them at very attractive prices. Since you'll probably take the engine in and out of the chassis several times, owning a hoist is much more convenient than making sev-

This jumble of cars and parts was the author's workshop before he got organized. There was room for four cars, but you wouldn't know it because of all the clutter. The '40 Ford coupe was on a very sturdy roll-around work cart. The cart raised the body to a comfortable working level and made it easy to move.

Heavy-duty jack stands are a must for working on a car when the wheels are off. The stands should be padded to protect the vehicle. There are specially made pads for jack stands or you can tape clean shop rags to them. A quality floor jack is also a must have tool. There are pads for jacks or you can use an old wool buffing pad. (So-Cal Speed Shop)

eral trips to the rental store. You can also use an overhead chain hoist if the rafters of your garage are sufficiently reinforced. You don't know what a good scare is until you've had a big chain hoist and half of the garage roof crash down on your car while trying to pull an engine without reinforcing the rafters.

A creeper and a roll-around stool are nice to have. A creeper with little storage recesses for nuts, bolts, and tools is preferable to not being able to find things or constantly running over tools. Most roll-around stools have a tray underneath the seat.

WORK AREAS

Besides having lots of floor space, it's nice to have a large, uncluttered workbench. These areas should be well lighted and at a comfortable height. If you're building or installing some workbenches, consider making them a couple inches higher than standard kitchen counters. The added height is nice for working on automotive parts.

If workbench space is in short supply, consider getting a rolling workbench. Hardware stores and home improvement centers have lots of handy work centers in various sizes. These rolling workbenches usually have drawers, too. You can store tools or parts in the drawers so everything you need is close at hand.

It's recommended that you assemble your street rod before any parts are painted. That way you can make adjustments without worrying about chipping or scratching the paint. When it comes time to work with painted parts, you should have a variety of soft or protected work surfaces.

A couple things that work well are padded, moving blankets. You can buy them at warehouse stores. Old bed spreads or blankets also work well as large, protected work surfaces. Big pieces of cardboard make nice floor mats. We like to put them under areas of the car that we're working on. The cardboard is easier on your knees than the bare cement floor. If cardboard gets greasy, simply dispose of it. We like to have a couple foam garden kneepads around to protect our creaky knees from the hard cement floor.

Soft surfaces are also needed for some clamping activities. A sturdy vise is a helpful street rod building tool. There are special plastic, aluminum, or even copper vise jaws pads that can be used protect delicate or easily marred parts. There are also special jack pads made of similar material. If you have an old, wool polishing bonnet, they make good jack pads. A car wash mitt can also be used.

Save old bathroom towels or buy cheap ones at garage sales. Towels can be used to wrap and protect parts while you're working on them and when they're stored. If the towels are cheap enough, they're often less expensive than shop rags.

If wrecking yard parts are used on your project, try to clean them before you bring them home. The cleaner you keep your work area, the easier it will be to work on the car. Since most street rod parts are new, it's much cleaner than working on an existing car. Adding fluids is one of the last things you do before driving a street rod. It's worth a huge pile of quarters to steam clean a used engine at the local car wash. You'll most likely want to paint a used engine so it has to be clean for the paint to adhere well.

A nice work environment will make the whole street rod building experience much more enjoyable.

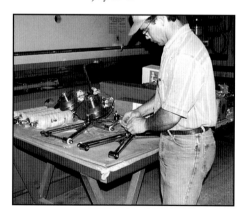

It almost seems like you can't have workbenches that are too big. This 4x8-foot bench is portable and covered with a thin foam pad. A clean, protected surface like this is great for assembling polished or freshly painted suspension components. (Hercules Motor Car Company)

RESOURCES

The street rod industry has grown rapidly in the last 10-15 years. Many major companies started out as someone building a few cars in their back yard. Other companies were offshoots of other manufacturing categories. Companies involved in stamping and precision machine work (like aerospace contractors) were natural crossovers for street rodding.

Most street rod companies are small compared to general manufacturing. That's a plus because you're much more apt to deal with principles of the company rather than some hourly wage drone. Street rodding companies are almost exclusively run by automotive enthusiasts. They understand your needs and speak the language because they've been there themselves.

The following list is by no means all-inclusive. It's a list of companies that make major components. Many of these companies also sell retail and mail-order. You can also find their products at local street rod shops. It's always nice to be able to put your hands on the product and inspect it up close, but if no shops are near you or if you want to benefit from the time savings of mail-order, it's nice to know that quality products are only a phone call and a credit card away.

Web addresses are given when applicable. If you have trouble reaching a company, check the latest issues of the major street rod publications for up-to-the-minute numbers in their ads. The way street rodding is growing, it's not uncommon for companies to move to larger facilities.

Affordable Street Rods
1220 Van Buren
Great Bend, KS 67530
316-792-2836
Fuse panels and complete wire kits

Air-Tique
209 Kimberly Dr.
Cleburne, TX 76031
871-641-6933
www.air-tique.com
Heating and air-conditioning

Alan Grove Components, Inc.
27070 Metcalf Rd.
Louisburg, KS 66053
913-837-4368
www.alangrovecomponents.com
Fabricated mounting brackets

Aldan Shock Absorber Co.
646 E. 219th St.
Carson, CA 90745
310-834-7478
www.aldanshocks.com
Coil over shock absorbers

American Collectors Car Insurance, Inc.
P.O. Box 8343
Cherry Hill, NJ 08002
800-360-2277
Agreed-value insurance coverage

American National Property & Casualty Co.
1949 E. Sunshine
Springfield, MO 65899
417-476-1599
www.anpac.com
Insurance coverage

American Racing
19067 S. Reyes Ave.
Rancho Dominguez, CA 90221
888-AR-WHEEL
www.americanracing.com
Custom wheels, specifically the Torq-Thrust 5-spoke

American Stamping
8719 Caroma
Olive Branch, MS 38654
601-895-5300
Reproduction '32 Ford frame rails

Antique & Collectible Autos
35 Dole St.
Buffalo, NY 14210
716-823-0007
www.acrods.com
'32 and '34 Ford street rod bodies and chassis

ARP Automotive Racing Products
531 Spectrum Circle
Oxnard, CA 93030
805-278-7223 or 800-826-3045 (tech)
www.arp-bolts.com
High-performance fasteners

Auto Loc
1281 N.E. 25th Ste. M
Hillsboro, OR 97124
800-873-4038
503-640-3091
www.autoloc.com
Kits for power door locks, power windows, and power trunks

Auto Meter Products Inc.
413 W. Elm St.
Sycamore, IL 60178
815-895-8141
www.autometer.com
Street rod tachometers, speedometers, and gauges

AVO USA Performance Shocks, Inc.
P.O. Box 1129
Palm City, FL 64991
561-221-0164
Coil-over shock absorbers

Backyard Buddy Corp.
1815 N. Main St.
P.O. Box 5104
Niles, OH 44446
800-837-9353
330-544-9372
www.backyard-buddy.com
Automotive lifts

Baer Racing
3108 W. Thomas Rd., No. 1201
Phoenix, AZ 85017
602-233-1411
brakes@baer.com
DOT braking technology for street rods

Ball's Rod and Kustom
10121 N. State Rd. 13
Syracuse, IN 46567
www.ballsrodandkustom.com
Electrical accessories for interior products

Barry Grant Inc.
1450 McDonald Rd.
Dahlonega, GA 30533
706-864-8544
www.barrygrant.com
BG Fuel Systems, Demon Carburetion, Nitrous Works

Bassani
2900 E. La Jolla
Anaheim, CA 92806
714-630-1821
Exhaust systems

BeBop's
392 County Rd. 609
Athens, TN 37303
877-577-8480
www.bebios-glassworks,com
Fiberglass bodies for '29 roadsters, '32 roadsters, '32 three-window coupes

Beck Racing Engines
21616 N. Central Ave., No. 1
Phoenix, AZ 85024
623-780-1001
www.beckracingengines.com
High-performance small- and big-block Chevrolet engines

Be Cool
310 Woodside Ave.
Essexville, MI 48732
517-895-9699
Radiators

Belmont's Rod & Custom
138 Bussey St.
Dedham, MA 02026
781-326-9599
Retail street rod parts, vintage speed equipment

Bill Mitchell Products
35 Tradezone Dr.
Ronkonkoma, NY 11720
516-737-0372
Street rod and racing engines

Billet Specialties
340 Shore Dr.
Burr Ridge, IL 60521
800-245-5382
www.billetspecialties.com
Billet wheels, steering wheels, accessories

Bill's Rod & Custom Inc.
523 W. Main St.
Springfield, OH 45504
937-322-5134
Street rod chassis

Bilstein of America
8845 Rehco Rd.
San Diego, CA 92121
619-453-7723
619-453-0770
www.bilstein.com
Street rod shock absorbers

Bitchin' Products
9392 Bond Ave.
El Cajon, CA 92021
619-443-7703
Steel parts for '28-'48 Fords including firewalls and floor pans

Blower Drive Service Co.
12140 E. Washington Blvd.
Whittier, CA 90606
562-693-4302
Blowers and fuel injection plumbing

B & M Automotive
9142 Independence Ave.
Chatsworth, CA 91311
818-882-6422
www.bmracing.com
Racing/performance parts, transmissions, superchargers

Bob Drake Reproductions
1819 N.W. Washington Blvd.
Grants Pass, OR 97526
800-221-3673
www.bobdrake.com
Street rod & original parts for '32 –'48 passenger cars

Borgeson Universal Co.
187 Commercial Blvd.
Torrington, CT 06790
860-482-8283
www.borgeson.com
Steering system components

Borla Performance
5901 Edison Dr.
Oxnard, CA 93033
805-986-8600
Stainless steel exhaust systems

Brassworks/Flow Kooler
289 Prado Rd.
San Luis Obispo, CA 93401
888-544-8841
www.flowkooler.com
Radiators and high-performance water pumps

Brizio Street Rods
505 Railroad Ave.
So. San Francisco, CA 94080
650-952-7637
www.roybriziohotrods.com
Custom street rod builder

Brookville Roadster
718 Albert Rd.
Brookville, OH 45309
937-833-4605
Exact-reproduction all-steel '28-'32 Ford Model A bodies, including stock, highboy, and pickup bodies

Budnik Wheels
7412 Prince Dr.
Huntington Beach, CA 92647
714-848-1996
Billet aluminum wheels and steering wheels

Butch's Rod Shop
330 Industry Dr.
Carlisle, OH 45005
513-746-7420
www.butchsrodshop.com
Do-it-yourself chassis and suspension components

California Car Cover Co.
9525 Desoto Ave.
Chatsworth, CA 91311
800-423-5525 or 818-998-2100
www.calcarcover.com
Car care and custom car covers

California Custom Roadsters Inc.
1211 N. Barsten Way
Anaheim, CA 92606
714-630-9085
'26-'27 Model T frames and Model A frames

California Rewire
11419 White Rock Rd.
Rancho Cordova, CA 95742
916-638-5424
www.calrewire.com
Fuse panels and wire kits

California Roadster Company
20460 Williams Ave.
Saratoga, CA 95070
408-872-0990
calroadster@compaq.net
'28-'32 street roadster bodies, parts, and accessories

California Street Rods
17112 Palmdale
Huntington Beach, CA 92647
714-847-4404
Chassis and street rod parts, custom built cars

Carrera Racing Shocks
5412 New Peachtree Rd.
Atlanta, GA 30341
770-451-8811
www.carrerashocks.com
Shocks, springs, and suspension components

Centech Wiring
P.O. Box 493
Frederick, PA 19435-0493
610-754-0720
www.centechwire.com
Electrical wiring products

Center Line Wheels
13521 Freeway Dr.
Santa Fe Springs, CA 92665
562-921-9637
www.centerlinewheels.com
Custom aluminum wheels

Chassis Engineering Inc.
P.O. Box 70
119 N. Second Street
West Branch, IA 52358
319-643-2645
www.chassisengineeringinc.com
Components for street rod chassis and suspensions

Chubby Chassis
17763 Valley Blvd.
Bloomington, CA 92316
909-874-8898
www.chubbychassis.com
Street rods and chassis

Chuck's Highboys
3099 Carter Circle
Kennesaw, GA 30144
770-427-5238
www.cobrarestorers.com
Nostalgia '32-'34 hot rods

Classic Instruments
P.O. Box 411
1299 M-75 South
Boyne City, MI 49712
800-575-0461
www.classicinstruments.net
Street rod gauges and gauge kits

Classic Tube
80 Rotech Dr.
Lancaster, NY 14086
800-882-3711
716-759-1800
www.classictube.com
Pre-bent, or custom-made lines for brake, fuel, transmission, vacuum, and other systems

Coker Tire
1317 Chestnut St.
Chattanooga, TN 37402
800-251-6336
www.coker.com
Reproduction tires for old cars

Collector Car Insurance
P.O. Box 414
Leo, IN 46765
219-627-3355
Insurance for street rods

Colorado Custom
2421 International Blvd.
Ft. Collins, CO 80524
970-224-5750
www.coloradocustom.com
Billet wheels

Concours West/CWI
306 Dwight Rd.
Castle Rock, WA 98611
360-274-3373
Custom independent rearends and Ford 9-inch units

Condon & Skelly
121 E. Kings Hwy, No. 203
Maple Shade, NJ 08052
800-257-9496
www.condonskelly.com
Street rod insurance

Cornhusker Rod & Custom Inc.
RR 1, Box 47
Alexandria, NE 68303
402-749-1932
www.cornhuskerandcustom.com
'28-'40 Ford chassis and turnkey cars

Crutchfield
1 Crutchfield Park
Charlottesville, VA 22911
800-955-9009
www.crutchfield.com
Car stereos

Currie Enterprises
1480 N. Tustin Ave.
Anaheim, CA 92807
714-528-6957
Custom 9-inch Ford rearends and related components

Custom Auto Radiator
495 Hyson Rd.
Jackson, NJ 08527
732-928-3700
Air conditioners and radiators

Custom Autosound
808 W. Vermont Ave.
Anaheim, CA 92805
800-889-TUNES
714-535-1091
www.custom-autosound.com
Audio products for street rods

Cutting Edge Street Rods
P.O. Box 45
Albany, PE
COB 1A0 Canada
902-437-6607
Resin-infused composite '32 and '34 Ford bodies

C.W. Moss
402 W. Chapman Ave.
Orange, CA 92866
714-639-3083
www.cwmoss.com
Street rod parts and accessories

Cyberdyne Instruments Inc.
205 Main St.
New Eagle, PA 15067
412-258-8440
Digital gauges

Dakota Digital Inc.
3421 W. Hovland Ave.
Sioux Falls, SD 57107
605-332-6513
www.dakotadigital.com
Digital gauges

Denny's Drive Shaft Service Inc.
1189 Military Rd.
Kenmore, NY 14217
716-875-6640
Custom-built drive shafts

Devilbiss/Binks
1724 Indian Wood Circle
Maumee, OH 43537
419-891-8100
www.devilbiss.com
Spray-paint equipment

Deuce Factory
424 W. Rowland Ave.
Santa Ana, CA 92707
714-546-5596
www.deucefactory.com
'28-'34 chassis and suspension parts

D.F. Metalworks
17872 Metzler Lane
Huntington Beach, CA 92647
714-841-6200
Body parts for street rods, custom grilles

Dick Spadaro Early Ford Reproductions
6599 Rte. 158
P.O. Box 617
Altamount, NY 12009
518-861-5367
'32-'48 Ford parts, hot rod chassis and suspension systems

Downs Manufacturing
715 N. Main St.
Lawton, MI 49065
616-624-4081
www.downsmfg.com
Fiberglass street rod bodies

Dr. K's Fuel Injection & Wiring
P.O. Box 4288
Gadsden, AL 35904
205-543-7165
Fuel injection wiring

DuPont
Barley Mill Plaza
P 10-2127
Wilmington, DE 19880
800-533-1313
Automotive finishes

Dutchman Motorsports Inc.
P.O. Box 20505
Portland, OR 97294
503-257-6604
www.dutchmanms.com
Performance axles, quick-change rearends

Early Wheel Co.
P.O. Box 1438
Santa Ynez, CA 923460
805-688-1187
www.earlywheel.com
Smooth and chrome wheels

The Eastwood Co.
580 Lancaster Ave.
P.O. Box 296
Malvern, PA 19355
610-640-1450
Automotive tools and restoration supplies

Edelbrock Corp.
2700 California St.
Torrance, CA 90503
310-781-2222
High performance engine components and custom wheels

Engineered Components Inc.
P.O. Box 841
Vernon, CT 06066
860-872-7046
www.ecihotrodbrakes.com
Disc brake conversions, brake system components

E-Z Wiring
212 N. Sixth St.
Flagler Beach, FL 32136
904-437-1077
Wiring panels and kits

Flaming River Industries Inc.
800 Poertner Dr.
Berea, OH 44017
800-648-8022 or 440-826-4488
www.flaming-river.com
Specialty steering system components

Flatlander's Hot Rods
1005 W. 45th St.
Norfolk, VA 23508
757-440-1932
'28-'48 Ford chassis & components, '32-'34 custom chassis

Flowmaster
100 Stony Point, No.125
Santa Rosa, CA 95401
800-544-4761
www.flowmastermufflers.com
Exhaust systems

Ford SVO Motorsports
44050 N. Groesbeck Hwy.
Clinton Township, MI 48036
810-468-1356
Ford engine performance products

Fuel Injection Specialties
4317 Centergate
San Antonio, TX 78217
210-654-0774
Complete TPI systems

Gardner-Westcott
10110 6 Mile Rd.
Northville, MI 48167
248-305-5100
www.gardner-westcott.com
Chrome-plated and stainless steel bolts, nuts, screws, and washers

Gennie Shifter
930 S. Broadmoor Ave.
West Covina, CA 91790
626-337-2536
Shifters, throttles, kick-down cables, and handbrakes

Gibbon Fiberglass Reproductions
132 Industrial Way
Darlington, SC 29532
843-395-6200
www.gibbonfiberglass.com
'32-'39 Ford car bodies, fenders, and parts

Glide Engineering
10662 Pullman Ct.
Rancho Cucamonga, CA 91730
909-944-9556
www.glideengineering.com
Seat frames for older cars and trucks

Goodguys Rods & Custom Association
P.O. Box 424
Alamo, CA 94507
925-838-9876
www.goodguysgoodtimes.com
Membership association for rod and custom owners

Grant Products
700 Allen Ave.
Glendale, CA 91201
818-247-2910
Custom steering wheels

Griffey Seats
4713 Zirkle Dr.
Knoxville, TN 37918
615-922-4601
Seating products for street rods

Griffin Racing Radiators
100 Hurricane Creek Rd.
Piedmont, SC 29673
864-845-5000
Custom radiators

Hagan Street Rod Necessities
2179 Joanne, No. 4
Carson City, NV 89701
775-885-1969
www.haganstreetrods.com
Three-piece hoods, headlamp kits, taillights

Hagerty Insurance
P.O. Box 87
Traverse City, MI 49685
616-947-6868
Street rod insurance

Halibrand
P.O. Box 100
Wellington, KS 67152
800-824-7947
www.halibrandengineering.com
Custom wheels and quick-change rear-axle assemblies

Harwood Industries Inc.
13240 Hwy. 110 S.
Tyler, TX 75705
903-561-6338
'32 roadster, sedan, and three-window coupe bodies, chassis, and accessories

Haywire Inc.
1415 Prairie View Rd.
Joplin, MO 64804
417-623-7239
www.haywireinc.com
Electrical systems

Heinzman Street Rod Shop
1305 N. C Rd.
Phillips, NE 68865
402-886-2275
Street rod parts, chassis, and frames and turnkey cars

Hercules Motor Car Company
2502 N. 70th St.
Tampa, FL 33619
813-621-2220
www.34woodie.com
'33-'34 Ford woodies (two- or four-door models), custom hoods, street rod chassis

HPC/High-Performance Coatings
14788 S. Heritage Crest Way
Bluffdale, UT 84065
800-456-4721 or 801-501-8315
www.hpcoatings.com
Coatings for headers and exhaust systems

Holley Performance Products
1801 Russellville Rd.
Bowling Green, KY 42101
270-782-2900
www.holley.com
High-performance automotive engine parts

Hooker Headers
1024 W. Brooks St.
Ontario, CA 91762
909-983-5871
Headers, mufflers, do-it-yourself components

Hot Rod Air Inc.
9330 Corporate Dr., No. 308
Selma, TX 78154
888-357-0040
Air conditioning systems

Hot Rods & Horsepower
11 Business Park Drive
Branford, CT 06405
203-481-1932
www.hotrodsandhorsepower.com
Repro steel '32 Ford three-window body (modified)

House of Kolor
210 Crosby St.
Picayune, MS 39466
601-798-4229
www.houseofkolor.com
Custom paint finishes

Howell Engine Developments
6201 Industry Way
Marine City, MI 48039
810-765-5100
Wiring harnesses and components for TPI or throttle-body systems

HTP America Inc.
3200 Nordic Rd.
Arlington Heights, IL 60005
800-USA-WELD
www.htpweld.com
MIG welders, TIG welders, and welding accessories

Hydraulic Interlock
P.O. Box 1757
Cape Coral, FL 33910
941-772-4490
Brake-lock vehicle-security system

Ididit Inc.
610 S. Maumee St.
Tecumseh, MI 49286
517-424-0577
www.ididitinc.com
Steering column specialists

Inland Empire Driveline Service
4035 E. Guasti Rd., No. 301
Ontario, CA 91761
800-800-0109
www.iedls.com
Drive shafts

Jasper Performance Products
815 Wernsing Rd.
Jasper, IN 47546
800-827-7455
www.jasperengines.com
Performance engines and transmissions

Juliano's Interior Products
321 Talcottville Rd.
Vernon, CT 06066
860-872-1932
www.julianos.com
Seatbelts, power windows

Keiper Recaro Seating, Inc.
905 W. Maple Rd., No. 100
Clawson, MI 48017
248-288-0130
Custom bucket seats

K & K Insurance Group Inc.
1712 Magnavox Way.
Ft. Wayne, IN 46801
219-459-5745
Insurance products

KoolMat
26258 Cranage Rd.
Olmsted Falls, OH 44138
440-427-1888
www.koolmat.com
High-temperature insulation

Kugel Komponents
451 Park Industrial Dr.
La Habra, CA 90631
562-691-7006
Chassis construction, independent suspensions, and street rod parts

Kwiklift Inc.
610 N. Walnut
Broken Arrow, OK 74012
918-258-8492
www.kwiklift.com
Portable, low-level, drive-on car lift

Lecarra Steering Wheels
711 Industrial Lane
Oneida, TN 37841
423-569-6670
Steering wheels and adapters

Lobeck's V-8 Shop
560 Golden Oak Pkwy.
Cleveland, OH 44146
440-439-8143
Complete chassis shop

Lokar Performance Products Inc.
10924 Murdock Dr.
Knoxville, TN 37932
865-966-2259
www.lokar.com
Components for street rods

Magnum Axle Co.
P.O. Box 2342
Oakhurst, CA 93644
559-877-4630
Frames, chassis components, and disc-brake kits

Main Street Rod Company
715 E. Main St.
Bellville, IL 62220
618-222-203
618-257-1418
www.mainstreetrodco.com
Roller packages for '23s, '26s, '31s, and '34s

Mark Williams Enterprises
765 S. Pierce Ave.
Louisville, CO 80027
303-665-6901
High-performance rearends and related components

Martz Chassis
P.O. Box 538
Bedford, PA 15522
814-623-9501
Suspension kits, complete rolling chassis, rearend narrowing

Master Power Brakes
110 Crosslake Park Rd.
Mooresville, NC 28117
704-664-8866
www.mpbrakes.com
Power boosters, power-disc brake kits

Minotti's Fiberglass
1981 J & C Blvd.
Naples, FL 33942
941-592-6010
Fiberglass bodies, chassis, and accessories

Mooneyes USA Inc.
10820 S. Norwalk Blvd.
Santa Fe Springs, CA 90670
562-944-6311
www.mooneyes.com
Moon discs, fuel tanks, custom accessories

Mullins Steering Gears and Hot Rod Parts
2876 Sweetwater Ave., No. 2
Lake Havasu City, AZ 86406
520-505-3032
www.mullinssteeringgears.com
Power and manual steering boxes and accessories

National Street Rod Association (NSRA)
4030 Park Ave.
Memphis, TN 36111
901-452-4030
Pre-'49 street rod association and magazine

O'Brien Truckers
29 A. Young Rd.
Charlington, MA 01507
508-248-1555
Cast-aluminum parts, including car-club plaques, nostalgic air cleaners

Old Air Products
4615 Martin Ave.
Ft. Worth, TX 76119
817-531-2665
www.oldairproducts.com
A/C and heating systems

Outlaw Performance
P.O. Box 550, Rte. 380
Avonmore, PA 15618
742-697-4876
outlawlc@bankswith.appollotrust.com
Fiberglass bodies

Pacific Western Design Inc. (Raingear Line)
P.O. Box 16465
Seattle, WA 98116
206-933-9555
www.pacificwesterndesign.com
Wiper systems for street rods and classic pickups

Painless Wiring
9505 Santa Paula Dr.
Ft. Worth, TX 76116
800-423-9696
www.painlessperformance.net
Chassis wiring harnesses, fuel injection harnesses

Performance Automotive Warehouse
21001 Nordhoff St.
Chatsworth, CA 91311
818-678-3000
Mail-order high-performance engine kits and parts

Pete & Jake's Hot Rod Parts
401 Legend Ln.
Peculiar, MO 64078
800-334-7240
www.peteandjakes.com
Suspension systems and brake packages

Poli-Form Industries
15 Grove St., No. 101
Watsonville, CA 95076
831-722-4418
poliform@cruzio.com
Fenders and components for '26-'37 Fords, '27 and '29 roadsters, and '34 coupes

Posies Inc.
219 N. Duke St.
Hummelstown, PA 17036
717-566-3340
www.posierodsandcustoms.com
Leaf springs and suspension kits

PPG Industries Inc.
19699 Progress Dr.
Strongsville, OH 44136
440-572-2800
Automotive paint finishes

Randy's Ring & Pinion
11630 Airport Rd., No. 300
Everett, WA 98204
425-347-1199
www.ring-pinion.com
Ring-and-pinion sets, locker rearends, installation kits, complete third members

Rat's Glass
R.R. 2 Box 844, Collies Cove Rd.
Friendsville, TN 37737-0117
423-995-2756
Fiberglass bodies

Ravon Street Rods
701 Daniel St.
Billings, MT 59101
406-245-9246
'32 Ford Bodies, '33-'34 Ford bodies and chassis

RB's Obsolete Automotive
7711 Lake Ballinger Way
Edmonds, WA 98026
Bolt-in chassis components and mail-order street rod parts and accessories

Redneck Corp.
R.R. 2, Box 174-1A
Fort Branch, IN 47648
812-753-3199
Reproduction Ford '33-'34 coupes and '33 two-door sedans

Richmond Gear
1208 Old Norris Rd.
Liberty, SC 29657
864-843-9231
High-performance ring-and-pinion kits; high-performance transmissions

The Roadster Shop
275 N. Grove Ave.
Elgin, IL 60120
800-332-1932
www.roadstershop.com
Frames and chassis for '28-'48 Fords

Rock Valley Antique Auto
P.O. Box 352
Stillman Valley, IL 61084
815-645-2271
www.rockvalleyantiqueautoparts.com
Stainless steel gas tanks, fuel pumps for injected cars

Rod Bods
1703 Greg St.
Sparks, NV 89431
775-358-4261
All-steel '32 Ford roadster body

Rodder's Journal
P.O. Box 1880
Huntington Beach, CA 92647
714-375-0460
Quarterly street rodding publication

Rodtronics Corp.
3500 Bloomington Ave. S.
Minneapolis, MN 55407
612-724-8955
Remote actuators, power-window kits

Ron Francis' Wire Works
167 Keystone Rd.
Chester, PA 19013
610-485-1937
610-485-1957
www.wire-works.com
Custom wiring kits, fuel injection, lights, and wiring accessories

Rootlieb Inc.
P.O. Box 1810
Turlock, CA 95381
209-632-2203
Street rod and stock hoods, running boards, and splash aprons for Fords

SAC Hot Rod Products
633 W. Katella Ave.
Orange, CA 92867
714-997-3433
www.sachtrod.com
Frames and chassis components for '28-'40 Fords

Sachse Rod Shop Inc.
3904 Miles Rd.
Sachse, TX 75048
800-495-3904 or 972-495-1557
Full service street rod construction

Scott's Hot Rods 'n Customs
1255 Callens Rd.
Ventura, CA 93003
805-658-7467
www.scottshotrodsncustoms.com
Street rod shop

Sid Chaver's Company
880 Aldo Ave.
Santa Clara, CA 95054
408-980-9081
www.sidchaverscompany.com
Collapsible soft tops for '28-'29 and '33-'34 Fords

Sneed, Robinson, Gerber Inc.
Sneed Bldg.
6645 Stage Road
Bartlett, TN 38134
901-372-4580
Special-interest vehicle insurance

So-Cal Speed Shop
1357 E. Grand Ave.
Pomona, CA 91766
909-469-6171
www.so-calspeedshop.com
Traditional hot rods, mail-order hot rod parts, accessories, suspension engineering

Spal Advanced Technologies
512 Tuttle St.
Des Moines, IA 50309-4618
800-345-0327
www.spal-usa.com
High-performance fans

Specialty Cars
17211 Roseton Ave.
Artesia, CA 90701
562-924-6904
Street rod frames

Specialty Power Windows
2087 Collier Rd.
Forsyth, GA 31029
478-994-9248
Electric windows and wiper kits

Speedway Motors
P.O. Box 81906
Lincoln, NE 68501
402-474-4411
www.speedwaymotors.com
High-performance specialty auto products, fiberglass bodies, and chassis kits

Springfield Street Rods
219 Buxton Ave.
Springfield, OH 45505
800-752-9763
www.springfieldstreetrods.com
Street rod components

Stainless Specialties
P.O. Box 781035
Sebastian, FL 32978
561-589-4190
www.stainless-specialties.com
Stainless steel exhaust components

Stainless Steel Brakes
11470 Main Rd.
Clarence, NY 14031
716-759-8666
www.ssbrakes.com
High performance brake components and brake kits

Steve's Auto Restorations Inc.
4440 SE 174th Ave.
Portland, OR 97236-1381
503-665-2222
www.stevesautorestorations.com
Turnkey street rods

Stewart-Warner Instrument Group
200 Howard Ave.
Des Plaines, IL 60018
708-803-0200
Speedometers, tachometers, gauges

Stockton Wheel
648 W. Fremont St.
Stockton, CA 95203
800-395-9433
www.stocktonwheel.com
Custom wheel fabrication and design

Street & Performance
Rte. 5, No. 1 Hot Rod Ln.
Mena, AR 71953
501-394-5711
www.tuneport.com
TPI wiring harnesses, fuel injection components

Super Bell Axle Co.
401 Legend Ln.
Peculiar, MO 64078
816-758-4504
www.superbellaxle.com
Dropped axles (tube and I-beam), spindles, brake kits

Superior Glass Works
P.O. Box 1140
Mulino, OR 92042
503-829-9634
www.superiorglassworks.com
Fiberglass reproduction bodies

Supertrapp
4540 W. 160th St.
Cleveland, OH 44135
888-249-2786
www.supertrapp.com
Performance exhaust system components

Tanks Inc.
P.O. Box 400
Clearwater, MN 55320
320-558-6882
Custom gas tanks for street rods

TEA's Design
2038 15th St. NW
Rochester, MN 55901
507-289-0494
Street rod seats

Total Cost Involved Engineering Inc.
1416 W. Brooks St.
Ontario, CA 91762
909-984-1773
www.totalcostinvolved.com
'28-'48 Ford frames and chassis; suspension components, brake kits

Total Performance Inc.
400 S. Orchard St., Rte. 5
Wallingford, CT 06492
203-265-7107
www.tperformance.com
Pro Street T and '23 T Roadster kits

Totally Stainless
1709 Old Harrisburg Rd.
Gettysburg, PA 17325
717-337-2151
Stainless steel bolts, nuts, screws, washers

TPI-Tech
8 Canterbury Ln.
Pawcatuck, CT 06379
860-599-0382
Wire harness kits, fuel-injection TPI, TBI and LT1

United Speedometer
2431 University Ave.
Riverside, CA 92507
909-384-0292
Instruments and gauge restoration/repair

U.S. Radiator
6921 S. Avalon Ave.
Los Angeles, CA 90003
323-778-5390
Custom radiators

VDO Performance Instruments
188 Brooke Rd.
Winchester, VA 22603
540-678-2933
www.vdona.com
Instrumentation and sensors for automotive aftermarket

Vintage Air
10305 I.H. 35 N.
San Antonio, TX 78233
800-725-3203
www.vintageair.com
Performance air conditioning for street rods

Walker Radiator Works
694 Marshall Ave.
Memphis, TN 38103
901-527-4605
Radiators, fans and accessories

Weedetr Street Rod Components
1355 Vista Way
Red Bluff, CA 96080
808-772-8187
530-527-2040
Frames and chassis

Weld Racing
933 Mulberry
Kansas City, MO 64101
800-488-9353
www.weldracing.com
Billet aluminum wheels

Wescott's Auto Restyling
19701 S.E. Hwy. 212
Boring, OR 97009
503-658-3183
www.wescottsauto.com
Fiberglass bodies

Wheel Vintiques
5468 E. Lamona Ave.
Fresno, CA 93727
559-251-6957
Hot rod Rally wheels

Wilwood Engineering
4700 Calle Bolero
Camarillo, CA 93012
805-388-1188
www.wilwood,com
Disc brake kits for street rods

Wireforce
181 St. Andrews St. E.
Fergus, Ontario
Canada N1M 1P9
800-865-7366
Wiring kits and panels

Zig's Street Rod Center
12700 W.E. Canyon Rd.
Beaverton, OR 97005
503-277-2232
www.zigsstreetrods.com
Products for building street rods

Zipper Motors
2146 Hwy. 6 and 50
Grand Junction, CO 81501
970-243-6558
'32 Ford roadster and Vicky phaeton bodies, complete chassis

Zoop's Products
931 E. Lincoln St.
Banning, CA 92220
909-922-2396
www.zoops.com
Billet aluminum products for street rods, custom brackets